ARTHUR GREEN

Radical Judaism

Rethinking God and Tradition

YALE UNIVERSITY PRESS · NEW HAVEN AND LONDON

Published with assistance from the Lewis Stern
Memorial Fund and from the Franz Rosenzweig
Lectures in Jewish Theology and History Fund in the
Program in Judaic Studies at Yale University.

Set in Janson Oldstyle by Keystone Typesetting, Inc.
Printed in the United States of America.

Library of Congress Cataloging-in-Publication Data
Green, Arthur, 1941–
Radical Judaism : rethinking God and tradition /
Arthur Green.
p. cm. — (Franz Rosenzweig lecture series)
Includes bibliographical references and index.
ISBN 978-0-300-15232-6 (pbk. : alk. paper)
1. God (Judaism) 2. Spiritual life — Judaism.
3. Judaism — Doctrines. I. Title.
BM610.G74 2010
296.3'11 — dc22   2009033195

A catalogue record for this book is available from the
British Library.

This paper meets the requirements of ANSI/NISO
Z39.48-1992 (Permanence of Paper).

10   9   8   7   6   5   4   3   2   1

For Kathy,
beyond Kabbalah

CONTENTS

PREFACE

This book is an expansion of the Franz Rosenzweig Lectures at Yale University, delivered in the fall of 2006. Funding for these lectures was provided from the estate of the late Arthur Cohen, himself a significant figure in American Jewish religious thought. I am grateful to the Yale faculty in Judaic studies, especially Paula Hyman and Ivan Marcus, for their invitation, hospitality, and encouragement.

Because the lectureship was named for Rosenzweig, I felt it appropriate to reflect on the themes of God, Torah, and Israel, complementing my earlier discussions, in *Seek My Face, Speak My Name: A Contemporary Jewish Theology* (Northvale, NJ: Jason Aronson, 1992), of Creation, Revelation, and Redemption, thus retracing the well-known Rosenzweigian Star.

The book before you represents some four years as my major intellectual project. In a sense it concludes a theological trilogy that began with *Seek My Face* and continued in *EHYEH: A Kabbalah for Tomorrow* (2006). I undertook this project while working as dean, and more recently as rector, of the Hebrew College Rabbinical School, which I helped to establish in 2003. I am grateful to my colleagues and students for both inspiration and questioning, but also for allowing me time to work on this book.

My acceptance of the Yale invitation gave me a chance to respond to a challenge by my old friend Arnold Eisen. He said to me, during one of our walks around Jerusalem: "You write serious theology in books addressed to seekers. When are you going to write theology for theologians?" I cannot say this book is entirely that, but I did try to include enough reflection on my premises and my use of sources to satisfy some of his demand. Because of that, I had dedicated the lectures to Eisen. I continue to have him in mind in the book, though I know he will not mind my dedicating it to my wife, who has been my first reader — and so much more — all along.

Upon completion of a nearly final draft, I gave the manuscript to three friends for their comments. I am grateful to Nancy Flam, Barry Holtz, and Elie Lehmann for reading and responding. More recently, Rabbi Levi Weiman-Kelman added a few comments, for which I am especially thankful. My blessings to them all.

INTRODUCTION

Who Is Writing This Book?

The author of this book is a Jewish seeker. I have been reading, studying, writing, and teaching theology to Jews — including many present and future rabbis — for nearly half a century. Yet I still think of myself primarily as a seeker. That means living in pursuit of an ever-present yet ever-elusive God, the One of Whom Scripture says: "Seek His face, always" (Ps. 105:4).[1] There is no end to such seeking. But it also means questing after truth, or at least *my* truth, one that wells up from my own life experience and feels authentic to who I am, as person and as Jew. Personal and intellectual honesty are essential to my life as a seeker; I try not to permit them to be overwhelmed by traditional claims or by emotional need. In this I am a longtime disciple of Rabbi Bunem of Przysucha who taught: " 'Do not deceive anybody (Lev. 25:17)' — not even yourself!"

These two realities, being a God seeker and a truth seeker, might seem to go hand in hand. Supposedly God *is* truth, after all. But in my case the simultaneous quest for both God and truth presents a terrible yet wonderful conflict. It is this conflict, and my ongoing attempt to resolve it, that the book you have just opened is all about.

I have understood since childhood that I am a deeply religious person, one easily moved by the power of sacred language, rites, and symbols. Through them I am sometimes able to enter into states of inner openness to a nameless and transcendent presence, that which I choose to call "God." Raised in a Jewish atheist household, I was powerfully attracted to the synagogue by the time I was seven or eight years old. The grandeur and mystery of its liturgy, the drama of its sacred calendar, and the infinite beauty of the Hebrew language and its classical literature all drew me in and have never ceased to fascinate me.

At the same time, I have long known that I am not a "believer" in the conventional Jewish or Western sense. I simply do not encounter God as "He" is usually described in the Western religious context, a Supreme Being or Creator who exists outside or beyond the universe, who created this world as an act of personal will, and who guides and protects it. Indeed, I do not know that such an "outside" or "beyond" exists. Challenges to conventional theological views, as well as to all the apologetic reformulations that seek to save them, came at me rather hard at the end of adolescence. I had chosen the religious life on my own, becoming quite fully (and somewhat compulsively) observant as an adolescent. But the regimen of Orthodox practice I had adopted, at the cost of terrible family battles, came crashing down during my college years, when I accepted that its theological underpinnings had been rooted in fantasy and denial of reality.

The challenges came from two directions: theodicy and critical history. The former included both personal loss (my mother died when I was eleven, and I had spent much of adolescence mourning her and struggling with that loss) and the fact of being a Jew in the immediate post-Holocaust generation. I remember the day my beloved East European grandfather found out just what had happened to the Jews of his town, as I recall my mother and grandmother going through newspaper lists of "relatives sought" in the early postwar years. These experiences, both personal and collective, made it clear to me that I could affirm neither particular providence nor a God who governed history. The God of childhood dreams, the One who could "make it all better" and show that life was indeed fair after all, was gone. My initiation into adulthood meant full acceptance of the arbitrariness of fate, including the finality of death.

At about the same time, I was exposed to Jewish scholarship, including the critical reading of the Hebrew Bible and its history. This exciting intellectual enterprise, which gripped my imagination, also undermined the residue of faith I had in Scripture as revealed. The text was edited, composed of many sources. Each of these represented a particular human community or interest group. What, then, was left of revelation? Where was the authority of Scripture, if the text was *merely* human? I struggled with what it could mean to claim that God had "given us His Torah" when the Torah text itself seemed to "evaporate" into so many documents. Without that, I had no basis for believing in a God who had commanded specific forms of religious behavior. (This seemed to be the essential "payoff" question in Judaism.) So the pillars of naive faith had given way, and its edifice lay in ruins. I had no answers to the great questions around which my religious life had been constructed.

I was no longer a believer, in the usual sense of that term, but I learned rather quickly that I was still a religious person, struggling with issues of faith. I still sought after God, perhaps even more so once I had given up on my naïve understandings of reality. That was the true beginning of my quest, one in which the only questions that mattered were the unanswerable ones. I absorbed much of Nietzsche, Kafka, and Camus in those years of questioning. From Nietzsche came the moment of joy at the death of my childhood God and the liberation from all that authority. But this gave way rather quickly to the bleak and empty universe Kafka so poignantly described, a joyless world from which God was absent and there was no air left to breathe, no room left to live, to love, or to create. From Camus and Nikos Kazantzakis came the noble call to make meaning on my own, to defy meaninglessness with creativity and moral action. But the more I sought to *create* a framework of meaning, picking up the shattered tablets of my onetime Jewish life, the more I came to realize that I was in fact only *rediscovering* patterns that were there to be seen, and had indeed been seen and articulated by countless generations before me.

It was in the course of this re-creation that I had to come back to the question of God. Who or what was the God I sought — and still seek today, half a century later! — once I had accepted that I was such a "nonbeliever" in the God of my childhood? The question seemed to be whether we post-naïve seekers dare to use the word "God" any more, and what we might — or might not — mean by it, while remaining personally and intellectually honest.

To explain this, I have to go back to the phrase "I was still a religious person." What can it mean to "be religious," in a Jewish (and not Buddhist) context if one does not "believe in God," at least as defined by the above parameters? It means that I still consider the sacred to be the most important and meaningful dimension of human life. "The sacred" refers to an inward, mysterious sense of awesome presence, a reality deeper than the kind we ordinarily experience. Life bears within it the possibility of inner transcendence; the moments when we glimpse it are so rare and powerful that they call upon us to transform the rest of our lives in their wake. These moments can come without warning, though they may be evoked by great beauty, by joy, by terror, or by anything else that causes us to stop and interrupt our ordinary all-encompassing and yet essentially superficial perception of reality. When that *mask of ordinariness* falls away, our consciousness is left with a moment of nakedness, a confrontation with a reality that we do not know how to put into language. The astonishment of such moments, that which my most revered teacher termed "radical amazement," is the starting point of my religious life.[2] I believe, in other words, in the possibility and irreducible reality of religious experience. Such experience stands behind theology; it is the most basic datum with which the would-be theologian has to work. The awareness that derives from that range of human experiences, distilled by reflection, is the basis of religious thought, and therefore of everything I will have to say in the pages before you.

What is the nature of this experience? It is as varied as the countless individual human beings in the world, and potentially as multifarious as the moments in each of those human lives. In the midst of life, our ordinariness is interrupted. This may take place as we touch one of the edges of life, in a great confrontation with the new life of a child, or of an approaching death. We may see it in wonders of nature, sunrises and sunsets, mountains and oceans. It may happen to us in the course of loving and deeply entering into union with another, or in profound aloneness. Sometimes, however, such a moment of holy and awesome presence comes upon us without any apparent provocation at all. It may come as a deep inner stillness, quieting all the background noise that usually fills our inner chambers, or it may be quite the opposite, a loud rush and excitement that fills us to overflowing. It may seem to come from within or without, or perhaps both at once. The realization of such moments fills us with a sense of magnificence, of smallness, and of belonging, all at once. Our hearts well up with love for the world around us and awe at its grandeur. The experience is usually one that renders us speechless. But then we feel lucky and blessed if we have enough ties to a tradition that gives us language, that enables us to say, "The whole earth is filled with God's glory!"

For me God is not an intellectual proposition but rather the ground of life itself. It is the name I give to the reality I encounter in the kind of moment I have been describing, one that feels more authentic and deeply perceptive of truth than any other. I believe with complete faith that every human being is capable of such experience, and that these moments place us in contact with the elusive inner essence of being that I call "God." It is out of such moments that religion is born, our human response to the dizzying depths of an encounter we cannot — and yet so need to — name. I returned to tradition, the one of my ancestors and my early attempts at faith, because it gave me a language with which to name that inner "place." I find myself less convinced by the dogmatic truth claims of tradition than powerfully attracted to the richness of its language, both in word and in symbolic gesture. Through the profound echo chamber of countless generations, tradition offers a way to respond, to channel the love and awe that rise up within us at such times, and to give a name to the holy mystery by which our lives are bounded.

I was about twenty years old when I began studying the Zohar (the thirteenth-century classic of medieval Kabbalah) and the teachings of the early Hasidic masters (of eighteenth-century Eastern Europe). This encounter with the mystical tradition saved Judaism for me. Without it I would have wandered away. These works, almost all composed in homiletical form, are the living antithesis to systematic theology. Often they were first offered as oral teachings, appropriate to a certain sacred or personal moment. Only later were they written down, in somewhat disembodied form. But they are endlessly rich in *insights*, insights into the soul, the human condition, and sometimes even the cosmic order. They are marked by the transforming awareness of a mysterious divine presence, to be found everywhere and in each moment, once we open our eyes to it. The combination of deep conviction and playful religious creativity in those sources immediately touched my soul, and continues to do so nearly a half-century later. The essential insights of Hasidism—that God is to be sought and found everywhere and in each moment, that our response to this deeper truth is both a daily practice and a lifelong adventure, and that our ongoing discovery of God can uplift and transform both soul and world—soon became *my* truths. The best semisystematic work where I found them presented in those early years was a little treatise called *Fundamentals of Hasidism* by Hillel Zeitlin, one of the two key neo-Hasidic thinkers of interwar Europe (along with Martin Buber), and famous martyr of the Warsaw ghetto.[3] When I read those pages— Zeitlin's discussions entitled "Being and Nothingness," "The Self-Contraction of God," and "Uplifting Sparks"—I remember somehow knowing that I had found my own religious language, one that spoke deeply to my soul, while challenging rather than offending my mind. It has served me well across the decades, and I hope that I have come to serve it faithfully as well. One of my goals here is to share some of that language—and my enthusiasm for it—with you.

The most important religious questions, I understood from the beginning, are universal: the quest for meaning, the purpose of human existence, the true nature of both world and self. I think about these overwhelmingly universal matters from within the context of a very particular religious language. I am not only a Jewish theologian, working within a religious language and historical context familiar to no more than the tiniest fraction of humanity. As one who draws deeply upon the language and symbolism of the Jewish mystical tradition, I represent a minority within this minority. I am a neo-Hasidic Jew, one influenced by the lives and teachings of the early Hasidic masters, but choosing not to live within the strict parameters of religious praxis that characterize Hasidism, and not sharing the later Hasidic disdain for secular education or for the modern world as a whole. It has long been clear to me that the insights into reality to be found in the texts, lives, and stories of the Jewish mystical and Hasidic tradition need to be shared more broadly, something I have tried to do over a lifetime of writing and teaching. I also have a sense that this spiritual legacy should not belong to Jews alone. Its insights into the great universal questions, though expressed in uniquely Jewish language, have importance for Jews and non-Jews alike, for all who take religious questions seriously and who understand the critical hour in which we live.

I also think of myself as a *religious humanist.* Humanism means an understanding that our fate, along with that of the entire planet, depends on human action. There is no one to hold back our hand, to keep us from destroying this garden in which we have been placed. We are totally responsible. *Religious* humanism means that we will fulfill that awesome role only by realizing that we are part of a reality infinitely more ancient, more profound, and more unified than any of us can express or know. Much of this book is an unpacking of the ways in which I see mysticism and humanism, two seemingly very distinct approaches to life, complementing one another.

The book is clearly and unabashedly Jewish in its language. Its examples are brought mainly from the tradition I know best and from my own life of religious experience. But its address is to a new and broad religious community, one that transcends conventional borders in order to deal with questions too big to be confined. My job is to translate the specifics in a way that carries them beyond the particular Jewish context and renders them accessible to everyone. If I have succeeded, the book will be "heard" as a clarion call, coming from an ancient tradition, for a transformation of human consciousness uniquely befitting this critical hour in human history, a new and universal religious awareness that will serve as an enabling vehicle for other changes that will soon be required of us.

I have lived much of my life at the juncture of historical scholarship and religious creativity. Trained as a historian of premodern Jewish thought, I am still committed to scholarly understanding, as some sections of this book will attest. But I have become more concerned with what Jews might believe in the uncertain future and what we as an ancient civilization might have to say to humanity at the present moment. This takes on a special urgency in the times in which we live. The most essential truth I glean from Hasidic teachings, the unity and holiness of all life, even of all existence, is one the world most urgently needs to hear. Having reached that point in my own life where you notice "the day is short," it is time for me to give a full account of what I have learned along this journey and pass it on to another generation. "The day is short," however, applies not only to the course of my own life. I believe that we stand at a great moment of transition in human and planetary history. Unless we take drastic steps to change our way of living, our patterns of consumption, and our most essential understanding of our relationship to the world in which we exist, we are at great risk of destroying our earthly home and rendering it a wasteland. Our future, and that of our planet, is in our hands. In this moment I believe that a universalized reading of the Hasidic legacy has much to offer.

While I do not await a God who will intervene in history to save the planet from us, God may be present in another way as we face the crucial challenge of our age. Religion, a more powerful human force in our day than anyone would have imagined, will have a major role to play in this needed transformation. If something we call God dwells within our sacred traditions (Ps. 22:4), we people of faith may indeed find a way to bring forth a ray of what we might call divine salvation. We need to reshape our religious languages in such a way that they will inspire the great collective act of *teshuvah*, "return" or "repentance," required of us at this moment. We need to repent of our cavalier treatment of the biosphere in which we live, of our indifferent overconsumption and waste of resources, of our virtual disdain for nonhuman forms of life. We need to repent of the separation we have created between the sacred and the mundane, between the godly and the natural. Without such *teshuvah* humanity will not survive. Without marshaling the power of the religious and mythic imagination, we will not be able to make the turn we must in order to exist. Read this book as a call to that collective and universal human effort.

Toward a Postmodern Judaism

Chapter 1 of the book centers on a discussion of religion and its relationship to evolution, beginning with the biological evolution of species and leading into an evolutionary approach to the history of religion itself. The battle against evolution in the United States, from the Scopes trial to ongoing media fascination with political candidates' views of the subject, represents the last great gasp of traditional religion's struggle against the inevitable triumph of modernity. While the modern consciousness was in the making a good century before Darwin, no one defines more than he does the impossibility of going backward and wishing out of existence the great gulf that modernity has opened up between the pursuit of truth and a literalist faith in biblically based religion. It is because of Darwin — and "Darwin" here means not only his evolutionary biology but also the accompanying evidence of geology, astrophysics, and a host of other scientific data regarding the origins of our planet and its life system — that theology has been transformed. Religion's response to Darwin has extended over a century. But, as recent headlines tell us, the conversation is not quite over.

The "new atheists" of the past decade have come largely from the scientific community, convinced post-Darwinians who are shocked at the resurgence of religion in our society. They have emerged from scientific laboratory and university classroom to take on the public fight against religious, mostly Christian, fundamentalism, often feeling that they need to save the entire modern enterprise from medieval Philistines who would bring it crashing down. Unfortunately some of these writers have little sophistication in approaching religion, tending to view it simplistically and paint it all with a single brush. "Religion," to them, seems to allow for nothing other than literal belief in nonsensical biblical tales and various accruing superstitions. This caricature obviates the need for serious dialogue and the encounter thus devolves into mutual distrust and recrimination, great fodder for the media but quite useless for the future of civilization.

In fact much of theological conversation in modern times has focused on the *idea* of God rather than on an actual Being who precedes this universe and is responsible for its existence. Philosophically, of course, it is more Immanuel Kant than Charles Darwin who is responsible for this change. But the inevitability of this move is most loudly proclaimed by the fact that we talk about the biohistory of our planet and its species without recourse to divine intervention. If God is not present in "Creation," as the medievals already understood, neither providence nor the possibility of miracles remains. With that, there is little more to talk about than the human idea of God and the various psychological and social benefits — or perhaps detriments — that such belief entails. The best representatives of modernity in the Jewish theological conversation, Hermann Cohen in the German neo-Kantian context and Mordecai M. Kaplan against the background of American pragmatism, both operated within these bounds.

The most impassioned and inspiring Jewish religious voices in the twentieth century were those shaped by religious existentialism and phenomenology, attempts to set aside or "bracket" the seemingly insurmountable modern objections to the claims of faith and to rebuild Judaism around an intimate personal relationship with God, a renewed study of the premodern Jewish sources, and the need for religious community. In varying ways, Franz Rosenzweig, Martin Buber, J. B. Soleveitchik, and A. J. Heschel all fall into this category. They opened up for moderns the possibility of a Jewish faith marked by emotional resonance and profundity. But like their existentialist counterparts in Christendom, these thinkers were all longer in passion than in defining precisely what they meant by "God," invoking the old Pascalian bon mot decrying definition in matters of faith. None of them was quite able or willing to tell his readers just what the God of love, devotion, and demand might have to do with the history of our physical universe, the evolution of life, and the emergence of humanity from among the primates. None of these sophisticated and university-educated thinkers was willing to enter the lists against the Darwinian narrative (as did the late Lubavitcher rebbe, by contrast), but neither were they willing to make it their own or imagine a Judaism that fully embraced it. The same was mostly the case with regard to biblical and Near Eastern scholarship and the obvious challenges they offered to Judaism. Existential religion chose to operate on a plane of reality different from that of the scientific worldview and thus to have little intersection with it.

The challenge to modernity that arose in the second half of the twentieth century had much to do with the aftermath of World War II and the onset of the nuclear age, the realization that the scientifically dominated worldview, hallmark of the modern era, had brought us not to peace and understanding but rather to potential and real viciousness and destruction on a previously unimagined scale. Beginning in the 1960s, many of the best minds of the West began to look outside the modern, progressivist, scientific canon and turned instead to areas of human knowledge that had been overthrown or ignored in the rush toward modernity. Some in fact turned to religious existentialism, which had its greatest influence in the early postwar era. Many others, however, sought out more obscure sources of truth. The hope was that somewhere in the recesses of past human creativity we would find the wisdom that might help us change our way of life, slow the maddening pace of contemporary existence, and desist from the violent behaviors that social Darwinism seemed to proclaim an inevitable part of our biological legacy. That truth might be found by sitting with a Zen master, by breathing with the Yogis, by smoking a Native American peace pipe, or by climbing the Himalayas (both real and metaphorical) to reach some obscure Tibetan monastery. As we watched the great crisis of our era shift from the threat of imminent nuclear self-destruction to that of environmental degradation and the overconsumption of resources, the urgency of that quest only grew greater. Even Kabbalah, perhaps the best-known of Western esoteric traditions, has come to be considered a possible source of such alternative insight as to how to live in this new era.

This perceived weakening of modernity's hold on intelligent conversation pulled in several directions at once. Surely it reinvigorated the surviving circles of premodernists, those who had all along lived on the sidelines of the intellectual mainstream and continued in their classical premodern constructions of faith, based either on scriptural literalism (Protestant evangelicals and most Muslims) or on theological premises that dated from centuries before modernity (Catholics, Orthodox Jews, and Muslim intellectuals). These bastions of alternative visions of reality have all demonstrated surprising strength in recent decades, both in holding on to their own respective flocks and in attracting significantly numerous converts. To one degree or another, all of them have stood as challengers of modernity, insisting on holding on to truth claims (usually regarding both the twin pillars of Creation and revelation) that modern scientific scholarship denies. Traditionalist Jewish and Catholic intellectuals, following long internal traditions, found more room for accommodation with science but avoided dealing with some of the toughest issues. Muslims, who felt that modernity had been imposed on them from without by dint of imperialist conquest, were the most resentful. Only a few Muslim intellectuals were able to defend the old broad-minded traditions of Islam's hosting and embracing scientific truth.

During the same era, however, a very different turn toward religion as the source of an alternative vision has been taking place. Here the emphasis is on *consciousness* rather than on Scripture or doctrine as the source of truth. Beginning with the psychedelic revolution of the 1960s (quickly corrupted, to be sure, but also much too readily dismissed by both government and media), there arose an interest in altered states of mind, deeper realms of consciousness, and a sense that our notions of "truth," based on sense perception and logical deduction, might be the limited vision of a narrow range of mental activity, challenged by the vast experience of prophets, mystics, and meditators through the ages. It may be said that this approach to religion took the existentialists' awareness of inner reality as its point of departure, but sought to anchor it in a nuanced understanding of consciousness that was open to elements of both mysticism and scientific analysis. This new receptiveness generally embraced Eastern rather than Western teachings, primarily because they were offered more in the spirit of experiential learning and without insistence on either dogma or ritual. (Eastern religions in their native habitat are of course replete with both of these, but those who imported them to the

West were able to repackage the essential insights, shorn of their traditional baggage.) This branch of the postmodern turn toward religion generally, though not always, eschewed orthodoxies and exclusivist claims, looking rather toward cross-traditional insights and teachings. Whether dressed in the trappings of Buddhism, Vedanta, Sufism, or Kabbalah, it tended to wear them lightly. Its essential faith claim is that there is a truth greater than that offered by the scientific worldview, one lying beneath the surface of reality and accessible by means of meditation, silence, chant, or other forms of disciplined religious praxis. The verbal articulation of such inner realities is often difficult; this too the "new mystics" have inherited from the existentialists. Here the relationship between the rational-scientific perception of reality and this religious (more often called "spiritual") claim is placed less in confrontational terms than is the case with Western-based fundamentalism. Scientific truth is not "wrong"; it is simply not the entire picture.

This book draws on both of these approaches to religion and its role in proclaiming a truth or reality that is an alternative to that of our modern scientific worldview. The reader will immediately see that I take both Scripture and tradition quite seriously, though I am far from literalism or fundamentalism. I am also much influenced by the rediscovery of mystical consciousness that has taken place in our time. Though my theology and the roots of my imagination are deeply and particularly Jewish, I write with a broad awareness of contemporary, including Eastern, religious thought. In proposing a Jewish theology for the twenty-first century (or the approaching fifty-ninth, if you prefer), I proceed from an understanding that the twentieth century's battles are very much over and that an essential re-framing of our response to the great religious questions is needed. I hope the reader will find some pieces of it in these pages.

The title of the book shows my roots in the Radical Theology movement of the late 1960s. I have recalled elsewhere a conversation I had with my mentor Abraham Joshua Heschel in which I asked him what he thought about Radical Theology, a movement that spoke of the "death of God," which Heschel had termed blasphemy.[4] But this very "death of God," a realization that conventional Western religious language had reached a point of exhaustion, was also pushing away much theological debris, making room for precisely the sort of "depth theology" that Heschel himself had advocated. "Radical theology is very important," he answered, "but it has to begin with the teachings of the later Hasidic masters."[5] Some forty years later (a number of some significance among Jewish journeyers!), I hope this book is that theology.

The "radicalism" of this work may not be what some readers would expect. I am primarily a thinker and teacher, not an activist. Although I share strong liberal or progressivist views on most political and social issues, this book is about a different sort of radicalism, one that takes us back to our deepest spiritual roots and challenges us to rethink our lives from that perspective. It has implications in the social sphere, to be sure, but its core lies in the realm of a contemporary mystical understanding of who we are, how we got here, and where we are going. In Jewish terms, it is a call to return to our Source, the one that underlies and precedes all our so-venerated "sources."

A few words about some of the readers I have in mind would probably be appropriate here. In earlier times, theology was written only for those who lived within a particular religious community and shared the symbols and liturgical language of that faith. Its function was largely to explicate those symbols and to give an intelligible account of how they bore that community's message. But given the wider concerns and the urgency of the hour, I have set myself a different goal. I am writing a theological work for a broad and as yet undefined audience. The fact that I am writing in English rather than Hebrew is significant to me. It means that my community of readers should include both Jews and non-Jews. I especially welcome readers of Christian or Islamic heritage. Despite the differences in religious language, they will find many key issues, and much of my own struggle with them, quite familiar. This audience will also, I hope, embrace readers who have been exposed to the religious languages of the East, including some of the many who are making a journey "homeward" after encountering meditation and spirituality first in an Eastern setting. I think they will find the language spoken here to represent a Judaism closer to those teachings than they might have expected.

As a teacher, I also think of the broadest circle of "my students" as readers of this book. These include rabbis of all denominations and none, as well as many other Jewish seekers. Some of them will undoubtedly feel pushed beyond their usual comfort zones in confronting the more radical ideas found here, whether with regard to God, nature, and evolution, or those in the later sections dealing with *halakhah* and Jewish practice or the Jewish people, the state of Israel, and the Jewish diaspora. I speak more frankly and less defensively here than is usual in Jewish circles, and I anticipate some protest.

The object is not just to explicate Judaism, to tell you what our tradition has to say about the world, and why it all makes sense. There are plenty of books, including some good ones, seeking to do that. I want to reflect, as a Jew, on the big and universal issues: what we might mean today by saying "God"; the purpose of human existence, how we got here, where we are going, and what we can do to save this beloved planet. I can do so only by speaking my own religious language. But the objective is never just to explain or defend that language; rather, it is to use it as a pathway to universal insights that lie within it. At times this process will demand your patience and a bit of perseverance, especially as I lead you into the labyrinth of Kabbalistic symbolism. Please stay with me; I promise you will be well rewarded. The book is supplied with a glossary of Hebrew terms that may render the journey a bit easier.

Y-H-W-H: GOD AND BEING

In the Beginning

I open with a theological assertion. As a religious person I believe that the evolution of species is the greatest sacred drama of all time. It is a tale—perhaps even *the* tale—in which the divine waits to be discovered. It dwarfs all the other narratives, memories, and images that so preoccupy the mind of religious traditions, including our own. We Jews, Christians, and Muslims are all overinvolved with proclaiming—or questioning—the truth of our own particular stories. Did Moses really receive the Torah from God at Mount Sinai? Did Jesus truly rise from the tomb? Was Muhammad indeed God's chosen messenger? We refine our debates about these forever, each group certain that its own narrative is at the center of universal history. In the modern world, where all these tales are challenged, we work out sophisticated and nonliteralist ways of proclaiming our faith in them. But there is a *bigger* story, infinitely bigger, and one that we all share. How did we get here, we humans, and where are we going? For more than a century and a half, educated Westerners have understood that this is the tale of evolution. But we religious folk, the great tale-tellers of our respective traditions, have been guarded and cool toward this story and have hesitated to make it our own. The time has come to embrace it and to uncover its sacred dimensions.

I believe that "Creation," or perhaps more neutrally stated, "origins," a topic almost entirely neglected in both Jewish and liberal Christian theology of the past century, must return as a central preoccupation in our own day. This indeed has much to do with the ecological agenda and the key role that religion needs to play in changing our attitudes toward the world within which we humans live.[1] But it also emerges from our society's growing acceptance of scientific explanations—those of the nuclear physicist, the geologist, the evolutionary biologist, and others—for the origins of the world we have inherited. The finality of this acceptance, which I share, seemingly means the end of a long struggle between so-called scientific and religious worldviews. This leaves those of us who speak the language of faith in a peculiar situation. Is there then no connection between the God we know and encounter daily within all existence and the emergence and history of our universe? Does the presence of eternity we feel (whether we call ourselves "believers" or not) when we stand atop great mountains or at the ocean water's edge exist only within our minds? Is our faith nothing more than one of those big mollusk shells we used to put up against our ears, convinced we could hear in them the ocean's roar? Is our certainty of divine presence, so palpable to the religious soul, *merely* a poetic affirmation, corresponding to nothing in the reality described by science? We accept the scientific account of how we got here, or at least understand that the conversation about that process and its stages lies within the domain of science. Yet we cannot absent God from it entirely. Even if we have left behind the God of childhood, the One who assures and guarantees "fairness" in life, the presence of divinity within nature remains essential to our perception of reality. A God who has no place in the process of "how we got here" is a God who begins in the human mind, a mere *idea* of God, a post-Kantian construct created to guarantee morality, to assure us of the potential for human goodness, or for some other noble purpose. But that is not God. The One of which I speak here indeed goes back to origins and stands prior to them, though perhaps not in a clearly temporal sense.[2] A God who underlies all being, who *is* and dwells within (rather than "who controls" or "oversees") the evolutionary process is the One about which—or about "Whom"—we tell the great sacred tale, the story of existence.

I thus insist on the centrality of "Creation," but I do so from the position of one who is not quite a theist, as understood in the classical Western sense. I do not affirm a Being or a Mind that exists separate from the universe and acts upon it intelligently and willfully. This puts me quite far from the contemporary "creationists" or from what is usually understood as "intelligent design" (but see more on this below). My theological position is that of a *mystical panentheist*, one who believes that God is present throughout all of existence, that Being or Y-H-W-H underlies and unifies all that is.[3] At the same time (and this is panentheism as distinct from pantheism), this whole is mysteriously and infinitely greater than the sum of its parts, and cannot be fully known or reduced to its constituent beings.[4] "Transcendence" in the context of such a faith does not refer to a God "out there" or "over there" somewhere beyond the universe, since I do not know the existence of such a "there." Transcendence means rather that God — or Being — is so fully present in the here and now of each moment that we could not possibly grasp the depth of that presence. Transcendence thus dwells *within* immanence. There is no ultimate duality here, no "God and world," no "God, world, and self," only one Being and its many faces. Those who seek consciousness of it come to know that it is indeed *eyn sof*, without end. There is no end to its unimaginable depth, but so too there is no border, no limit, separating that unfathomable One from anything that is. Infinite Being in every instant flows through all finite beings. "Know this day and set it upon your heart that Y-H-W-H is *elohim*" (Deut. 4:39) — that God within you *is* the transcendent.[5] And the verse concludes: "There is nothing else."

By *mystical* panentheism I mean that this underlying oneness of being is accessible to human experience and reveals itself to humans — indeed, it reveals itself everywhere, always — as the deeper levels of the human mind become open to it. Access to it requires a lifting of veils, a shifting of attention to those inner realms of human consciousness where mystics, and not a few poets, have always chosen to abide. The "radical otherness" of God, so insisted upon by Western theology, is not an ontological otherness but an otherness of perspective. To open one's eyes to God is to see Being — the only Being there is — in a radically different way. Such a unitive view of reality is *entirely other* (*ganz andere*, in theological German) from the way we usually see things, yet it is the same reality that is being viewed. I am also one who knows that religious truth belongs to the language of poetry, not discursive prose. I recognize fully and without regret that theology is an art, not a science. We people of faith have nothing we can prove; attempts to do so only diminish what we have to offer. We can only testify, never prove. Our strength lies in grandeur of vision, in an ability to transport the conversation about existence and origins to a deeper plane of thinking. My faith, but also my human experience, tells me that this shift profoundly enhances our understanding of our own lives and of the world in which we live. Opening our minds, and ultimately the mind of our society, to the truth accessible from that inner "place" constitutes our best hope for inspiring change in the way we live on this earth. There is nothing *mere* about poetic vision.

This point in the discussion calls for a greater clarification of the terms "One," "Being," and "God," which I now appear to be using quite interchangeably. Am I speaking of a "what" or a "who," the reader has a right to ask. Let me answer clearly. When I refer to "God," I mean the inner force of existence itself, that of which one might say: "Being *is*." I refer to it as the "One" because it is the single unifying substratum of all that is. To speak of Being as a religious person, however, is to speak of it not detachedly, in scientific "objectivity," but rather with full engagement of the self, in *love* and *awe*.[6] These two great emotions together characterize the religious mind and, when carried to their fullest, make for our sense of the holy. A religious person is one who perceives or experiences holiness in the encounter with existence; the forms of religious life are intended to evoke this sense of the holy. In a mental state that cannot be fully described in words, such a person *hears* Being say: "I am." All of our personifications of the One are in response to that inner "hearing."

In biblical language, the "I am" of Sinai is already there behind the first "Let there be" of Genesis.[7] Creation *is* revelation, as the Kabbalists understood so well. To say it in more neutral terms, we religious types personify Being because we see ourselves as living in relationship to the underlying One. I seek to *respond* to the "I am" that I have been privileged to hear, to place myself at its service in carrying forth this great mission of the evolving life process. To do so, I choose to personify, to call Being by this ancient name "God."[8] In doing this, I am proclaiming my love and devotion to Being, my readiness to live a life of seeking and responding to its truth. But implied here is also a faith that in some mysterious way Being *loves me*, that it rejoices for a fleeting instant in dwelling within me, delighting in this unique form that constitutes my existence, as it delights in each of its endlessly diverse manifestations.

Creation: Reframing the Tale

With regard to "Creation," I understand the task of the theologian to be one of *reframing*, accepting the accounts of origins and natural history offered by the scientific consensus, but helping us to view them in a different way, one that may guide us toward a more profound appreciation of that same reality. The tale of life's origins and development, including its essential building block of natural selection, is well known to us as moderns. But what would it mean to recount that tale with our eyes truly open?

We would understand the entire course of evolution, from the simplest life forms millions of years ago, to the great complexity of the human brain (still now only barely understood), and proceeding onward into the unknown future, to be a *meaningful* process. There is a One that is ever revealing itself to us within and behind the great diversity of life. That One is Being itself, the constant in the endlessly changing evolutionary parade. Viewed from our end of the process, the search that leads to discovery of that One is our human quest for meaning. But turned around, seen from the perspective of the constantly evolving life energy, evolution can be seen as an ongoing process of revelation or self-manifestation. We discover; it reveals. It reveals; we discover. As the human mind advances (from our point of view), understanding more of the structure, process, and history of the ever-evolving One, we are being *given* (from its point of view) ever-greater insight into who we are and how we got here.

This ongoing self-disclosure is the result of a deep and mysterious inner drive, the force of Being directed from within, however imperfectly and stumblingly, to manifest itself ever more fully, in ever more diverse, complex, and interesting ways. That has caused it to bring about, in the long and slow course of its evolution, the emergence of a mind that can reflect upon the process, articulate it, and strive toward the life of complete awareness that will fulfill its purpose. Here on this smallish planet in the middle of an otherwise undistinguished galaxy, something so astonishing has taken place that it indeed demands to be called by the biblical term "miracle," rather than by the Greco-Latin "nature," even though the two are pointing to the exact same set of facts. The descendants of one-celled creatures grew and developed, emerged onto dry land, learned survival skills, developed language and thought, until a subset of them could reflect on the nature of this entire process and seek to derive meaning from it.

The coming to be of "higher" or more complex forms of life, and eventually of humanity, is not brought about by the specific and conscious planning of what is sometimes called "intelligent design." But neither is it random and therefore inherently without meaning. It is rather the result of an inbuilt movement within the whole of being, the underlying *dynamis* of existence striving to be manifest ever more fully in minds that it brings forth and inhabits, through the emergence of increasingly complex and reflective selves. I think of that underlying One in immanent terms, a Being or life force that dwells within the universe and all its forms, rather than a Creator from beyond who forms a world that is "other" and separate from its own Self. This One — the only One that truly is — lies within and behind all the diverse forms of being that have existed since the beginning of time; it is the single Being (as the Hebrew name Y-H-W-H indicates)[9] clothed in each individual being and encompassing them all.[10]

If we could learn to view our biohistory this way, the incredible grandeur of the evolutionary journey would immediately unfold before us. We Jews revere the memory of one Nahshon ben Aminadav, the first person to step into the Sea of Reeds after Israel left Egypt. The sea did not split, the story goes, until he was up to his neck in water. What courage! But what about the courage of the first creature *ever* to emerge from sea onto dry land? Do we appreciate the magnificence of *that* moment? Or the first to fly, to take wing into the air? Or the moment (of course each of these is a long, slow process rather than a "moment," but the drama is no less great) when animals were divided from plants, when one sort of being was able take nourishment directly from the soil while another was able to exist without this form of nourishment, developing the mechanism to "feed" on plant, and then animal, life. How is it possible, with all of them descending from the same single-celled creatures?

The incredibly complex *interplay* of forces and the thick web of mutual dependency among beings are no less amazing than the distance traversed in this long evolutionary journey. The interrelationships between soil, plants, and insects, or those between climate, foliage, and animal life, all leave us breathless as we begin to contemplate them. It is these very intricacies and complexities that have led the religious fundamentalists to hold fast to the claim that there must be a greater intelligence behind it all, that such complexity can only reflect the planning of a supernatural Mind. But they miss the point of the religious moment here. Our task as religious persons is not to offer counterscientific *explanations* for the origin of life. Our task is to *notice*, to pay attention to, the incredible wonder of it all, and to find God in that moment of paying attention.

There is indeed something "supernatural" about existence, something entirely out of the ordinary, beyond any easy expectation. But I understand the "supernatural" to reside wholly *within* the "natural."[11] The difference between them is one of perception, the degree to which our "inner eye" is open. The whole journey is a supernatural one, not because some outside Being made it happen but because Being itself, residing in those simplest and most ancient of life-forms, pushing ever forward, step after simple step, to reach where we are today, continues to elude our complete understanding. The emergence of both bees and blossoms, and the relationship between them, took place over millions of years, step by evolutionary step. How could that have happened? There is an endless ingenuity to this self-manifesting Being, an endless stream of creativity of which we are only the tiniest part. If we do not destroy or do too much irreversible damage to our planet, it will continue to bring forth ever more diverse and creative manifestations long after we are gone.

The poetic reframing of our contemporary tale of origins that I am proposing here might be better understood by reference to a prior example, one with which we happen to have an intimate bond. I refer to the opening chapter of the Hebrew Bible. The authors of Genesis 1 effected a remarkable transformation of the creation myth that existed in their day. The common theology of the ancient Near East, reflected in both Canaanite and Mesopotamian sources, featured the rising up of the primal forces of chaos, represented by Yam and Tiamat, gods of the sea, against the order being imposed by the younger but more powerful sky gods. The defeat of that primordial rebellion was the background of Creation; earth was established upon the carcasses of the vanquished. That tale of uprising and its bloody end, now largely forgotten, was well known to the biblical writers and their audiences.[12] It is reflected in various passages in the prophets, Psalms, and Job, and is subtly hinted at even within the Genesis narrative. But those who wrote Genesis 1 reframed the story completely. Everything was created in harmony, willfully, by a single God who kept saying: "Good! Good!" in response to His creations, giving His blessing to each.

That reshaped tale helped to form and sustain Western civilization for several thousand years. The faith that God loves and affirms Creation provides the moral undergirding for all of Western religion, manifest differently in each of the three dominant faiths. Some believed it naively and literally; others interpreted it and tried to reconcile it with various other ways of thinking. I am suggesting that we need to undertake a similar effort of transformation for our current "Creation" story. Our civilization has been transformed in the past century and a half in no small part by our acceptance of a new series of tales of origin, an account that begins with the Big Bang (which itself may turn out to be myth) and proceeds through the long saga of the origins of our solar system, the geohistory of our planet, the emergence of life, and biological evolution. Nuclear physicists and cosmologists have become the new Kabbalists of our age, speculating in ever more refined ways on the first few seconds of existence much as our mystical sages meditated on the highest triad of the ten divine emanations. The picture that science offers is one of unimaginably violent explosion, of particles hurtling through indescribably vast reaches of space, and only then of the emergence of an order — solar systems, gravity, orbits, air, and water — that makes for the possibility of life's existence.[13] As living things emerge and develop we are again presented with a tale of violent and bloody struggle, that of each species and creature to eat and not be eaten, to strive for its moment at the top of the evolutionary mound of corpses. This story too, I am suggesting, is in need of reformulation by a new and powerful harmonistic vision, one that will allow even the weakest and most threatened of creatures a legitimate place in this world and will call upon us not to wipe it out by careless whim. This is the role of today's religion.

How would such a reframed tale read? It would be a narrative of the great reaching out by the inner One that inhabits each of us and binds us all together, a constant stretching forth of Y-H-W-H ("Being") in the endless adventure of becoming HWYH (Hebrew for "being" or "existence"), or of the One garbing itself in the multicolored garment of diversity and multiplicity. Every creature and each cell within it would be viewed as part of this tale, a mini-adventure within the infinitely complex narrative web that embraces us all. The meaning of this great journey would remain quite mysterious, but with a glimmer of hope that somewhere in the distant future "we" might figure it all out. The evolutionary movement forward would be seen as a striving toward complexity, toward ever-thicker and ever-richer patterns of self-manifestation.

Does this One *know* where it is going? Here I come trickily close to, yet remain distinct from, the advocates of intelligent design as they are usually understood. On the one hand, I do not attribute human-like consciousness to the One. There is no "plan" of Creation, no sense that humans are the apex or final goal of the process. I do not believe that the complexity or intricacy of the natural order is evidence of such design. As I said, we religious folk have no evidence, only testimony. Any attempt to claim otherwise only confuses the picture. On the other hand, however, it is fair to say that all mind and all consciousness ever to exist are part of the One. Mystics have always understood that this One transcends time, as the name Y-H-W-H itself indicates. All minds are thus one with Mind, as all beings are contained within Being. In this sense we can say that the fullness of Being's self-manifestation, including our understanding of it, is there from the start, not in the sense of active or intentional foreknowledge, but as potential that is ever unfolding. The One "knows" all because the One *is* all, all that ever was, is, and will be, in an undivided Self.

The reader who is aware of Jewish mystical language will understand that I am rereading contemporary evolutionary theory in the light of Kabbalistic thought. Kabbalah understands all of existence as eternally pouring forth from *hokhmah*, primordial Wisdom or Mind. *Hokhmah* is the primal point of existence, symbolized by the Hebrew letter *yod*, which is itself hardly more than a dot. This point, infinitesimally small, is the proverbial "little that contains a lot." Within it lies the entire unfolding of existence, every stage in the evolutionary journey, every plant and animal as it will live, reproduce (or not), and die, all of humanity and all that lies beyond us in the distant future. All this exists in a literal sense of *potential* (meaning that its potency, its power, is all fully present) in that primal point. In our contemporary language, that point is the instant of the Big Bang, the moment that contains the energy of existence in all its intensity. From there it flows forward into existence, garbing or "actualizing" itself at each stage in endless forms of existence.

To say this in another way, also derived from Kabbalistic language, I am depicting the entire course of evolution as the infinitely varied self-garbing of an endless energy flow. All being exists in an eternal dialectic of *hitpashtut*, the emanatory flowing forth of that single energy, and *hitlabbeshut*, the garbing of that energy in distinctive forms. But now we add an important post-Darwinian caveat to that mystical view of existence. The only means this One has in this process of self-manifestation are those of natural selection and its resulting patterns of change and growth. It *is* nature (yes, "nature" could be another name for that which I have called "God," "the One," and "Being"). Hence the length and slowness of the journey. But precisely in this lies the utterly marvelous nature of what has come forth, step after single step. To see that process with the eye of wonder is the starting point of religious awareness.

As more highly developed forms of animal life emerge, the forward movement of natural selection takes place partly in the form of aggression and competition, each creature and species grasping at its chance to survive and prosper. The competition for food and other resources, the devices created by males and females of various species to attract mates and reproduce, the struggle to find and eat one's prey rather than be consumed by one's predators, are all essential parts of the story — indeed, *our* story. This is an aspect of our biological legacy that we need to own and confront. We cannot understand our own human nature without taking into account the fierce struggle we underwent to arrive, and to achieve the dominance we have over this planet, for better and worse. But that same mysterious inner process also brings about more cooperative forms of societal organization, in which such creatures as ants, bees, and humans learn to work together toward fulfilling their species' goals. All of this is part of our biological legacy. Indeed, it is in grasping how these two trends, the competitive and the collaborative, combine and interact that we come to understand how our species survives. This should be a source of significant insight into the human condition. Once we achieve this understanding, we can make the value decisions as to which aspects of that biological heritage we want to take the lead as we proceed with our lives, both as individuals and as a species.

But it would also be disingenuous of me as a human to say that the emergence of human consciousness, even the ability to be thinking and writing about these very matters, is nothing more than a small series of steps in the unfolding linear process wrought by natural selection. That is indeed *how* we came about. But there is a different *meaning* to human existence that cannot be denied. The self-reflective consciousness of humans, combined with our ability to take a long biohistorical view of the whole unfolding that lies behind (and ahead of) us, makes a difference. All creatures are doing the "work of God" by existing, feeding, reproducing, and moving the evolutionary process forward. But we humans, especially today, are called upon to do that work in a different way. We have emerged as partners of the One in the survival and maintenance of this planet and all the precious attainments that have evolved here. Without our help, it will not continue to thrive. Being has thus turned a corner, or come back in a self-reflexive circle, as it manifests itself in the human mind.

The Call to Adam

In the long march toward increased complexity and ability of species, the emergence of the human brain is an important and transformative moment. We humans represent a significant step forward in the evolutionary path toward the self-articulation and self-fulfillment of that One. If the purpose of the journey is one of manifestation or becoming known, the development of our powers of reflective consciousness are surely key. But I do not view us humans — surely not as we are now — as the end or purpose of evolution. We, like all other species, are a step along the way. If existence survives on this planet, Mind will one day be manifest to a degree far beyond our present ability to comprehend or predict. On *that* day, says Scripture, "Earth will be filled with knowledge of Y-H-W-H as water fills the sea" (Is. 11:9) — just that wholly and naturally.

Because we humans represent a new and important step in this journey, the One manifest within us calls out to us in a particular human way. It addresses each of us with something more than the cry "Survive!" that is its instinct-borne call to every creature. We children of Adam (that's how you say "humans" in Hebrew, and note that here the language itself leads me to migrate farther into the realm of myth) are addressed with the word the God of Genesis used to call out to the first human: *"Ayekah?"* — "Where are you?"[14] The indwelling One asks this of every person, of every human embodiment of its own single Self. This question means "Where are you in helping Me to carry this project forward?" Are you extending My work of self-manifestation, participating as you should in the ongoing evolutionary process, the eternal reaching toward knowing and fulfilling the One that is all of life's goal? That is why you are here, tumbling and stumbling forward from one generation to the next! *What are you doing about it?*

"Where are you?" calls out to us in three distinctly human dimensions. The first of these is mental or intellectual: "Are you stretching your mind to move forward, to carry on the evolutionary process in the realm of understanding, as we think in ever more sophisticated and refined ways about the nature of existence and its unity?" Evolution does not end with the emergence of humanity. The process continues unabated, reflected in the growth of societies and civilizations over the millennia. The imperative to stretch the mind includes scientific thought, the ongoing attempt to understand and unpack the mysteries of our universe. But it also embraces the humanities and the arts, the expanding of human consciousness in more subtle ways. Some of the highest manifestation of this ongoing evolutionary process are to be found in our ideas and images of God, as we move from primitive tribal gods and local nature deities through classical polytheism (the pantheon of gods), on to primitive monolatry (there is but one god worthy of worship), into true universal monotheism, and then toward greater abstraction and depth of thought. All of these are stages on the road toward that total comprehension of Being in its oneness that lies somewhere in our future. We will trace some of this process, as seen through a Jewish lens, in the following pages. In our own day this quest takes place both in the scientific community, in the search for a contemporary understanding of the life-force or a unified field theory, and in the growing interest in monistic philosophies, including those rooted in Vedanta or Buddhism, that have begun to take root in the postmodern West. "Where are you?" Are you stretching your mind to its fullest to know the One?

The second way in which this "Where are you?" calls out to us involves a stretching of the human heart to become more open, more aware. If you believe as I do that the presence of God is everywhere, our chief task is that of becoming aware. But that job is not only an intellectual one; it involves heart as well as mind. God is everywhere, but we build walls around ourselves, emotional walls, barricades of defensiveness, because we are too threatened by the oneness of Being to let ourselves be open to it. "Where are you?" demands of us a greater openness to our own vulnerability and dependence on forces beyond ourselves than our frail ego is willing to accept. The walls behind which we barricade ourselves are the illusions of our strength and individual immortality, the sense that there is nothing more important than our own egos and the superficial pursuits toward which most of our lives have somehow become devoted. Liberation into the life of the spirit means doing the hard work of breaking through those self-created protections and coming face to face with the ultimate frailty of our lives and the great religious question that hovers over us. Only as we face this challenge do we begin to let go of that which separates us from the totality of Being or the all-embracing presence of the One. The spiritual work that each of us has to do consists primarily of letting go, allowing that presence to enter our consciousness and transform us. In the course of this process we enable ourselves to become *givers* or fonts of blessing in the grand economy of existence, rather than *consumers* who simply take all for ourselves without giving back to life.[15] "Where are you?" Are you stretching your heart to open as widely as it can?

The third area in which "Where are you?" calls upon us is that of the human deed. It is not enough to reach forth with mind and heart; these alone will not transform the world. *Every* human being is the image of God. Every creature and every life form is a garbing of divine presence. The way in which we treat them and relate to them is the ultimate testing ground of our own religious consciousness. The One seeks to be known and loved in each of its endless unique manifestations. The purpose of our growing awareness is to reach out and appreciate all things for what they really are. This is especially true with regard to our fellow humans. That every human being is the image of God is Judaism's most basic moral truth. We need to help all humans to discover this dimension of their own existence in whatever terms they may choose to articulate it. We recognize that this truth may be depicted differently in the varied religious and secular languages of human culture. We do not require others to accept the language of Judaism, but we do see justice, decency, and civility to one another as universal human imperatives that stem directly from the reality that we call *tselem elohim*, the image of God. A person cannot be expected to discover the image of God within himself or herself as long as he or she is hungry, or as long as he or she is homeless or degraded by poverty, addictions, or the seemingly overwhelming burdens of everyday life. Our task has to be to lessen and lighten those burdens as ways of helping all to see the radiant presence that surrounds us and fills us in each moment. In the realm of "heart" it was illusory walls we had to remove in order to see that light. But in the realm of "deed" the forces that block out the light are quite concrete — social, political, or economic barriers — and they too have to become the object of our attention as people and communities of faith. "Where are you?" Are you engaged in the work given to you by the call of God?

All of these aspects of the call are the stuff of Jewish moral theology. In a sense I am commenting here on the opening teaching of the Talmud, the great treasury of rabbinic law and wisdom. Although the Talmud seems to begin with discussion of prayer and its proper hour, buried within it lies a little treatise called *Avot* (Principles), an eternal favorite of Jewish moral teachers. This tractate was meant to serve as an introduction to the Talmud (or perhaps as a concluding summation). Hence it begins with a superscription, telling us whence authority for the Law is derived: "Moses received Torah from Sinai and gave it to Joshua, who gave it to the judges, who gave it to the prophets, who gave it to the elders," and so forth. But then the first teaching is stated: "*The world stands upon three things: on Torah* (teaching, wisdom, the cultivation of awareness), *on Worship* (the struggle to open the heart), *and on Deeds of Kindness* (the active transformation of the world; the bringing about of 'God's kingdom')."

Because I take this call seriously, when I read the old rabbinic dicta[16] that say "God looked at the righteous" or "Israel arose in God's mind" and ""For their sake God created the world," I surprisingly find myself to be among the affirmers. Of course I don't read these words literally, thinking of a Roman emperor or a Near Eastern potentate who calls in his advisers and asks, "Should I create humans?" But I do agree that there is a purpose to human existence, and that is what these statements really mean. Reading these ancient words for our day we also understand that "Israel" as generally understood is far too narrow and chauvinistic a term in this context and that even "the righteous" sounds rather smug and elitist. I by no means think that God created the world for the sake of the Jews or the pious Jews or anything like that. I need to universalize the "Israel" of this sentence (and so many others!) to include all those who struggle with God, referring back to the original etymology of that name.[17] "The righteous" here has to include all those who do the work of stretching toward the One, by whatever means and methods they employ. I affirm this universalizing of the rabbis' teaching to be in accord with the often ignored truth that lies at Judaism's core, rooted in the assertion that all humans are descended from the same parents, those of whom God says: "Let us make humans in our image."[18] The reality of that One is manifest across the great and diverse spectrum of our shared humanity.

In asserting that humans are "called" in a distinctive way by the One that dwells within us, I also realize that I am making a claim for our species that sounds as though we are the apex or final goal of this ongoing self-disclosing process that takes place within all creatures. Far from it! I do believe that there is an inbuilt drive toward greater complexity and higher forms of consciousness, in which the emergence of the human brain is a most significant step.[19] But again I want to acknowledge that the ultimate stages of this process lie far, far beyond us, as far beyond our awareness and sensitivities as our mind is from those forms of life we consider much simpler and more "primitive." Living as we do at the dawn of a new age, one in which the human mind will be augmented and challenged by our *golem* of "artificial intelligence," we can hardly imagine the new heights and depths that understandings of reality will attain, even in a relatively short expanse of time. As we unravel the genome and the mysteries of DNA, the truth that each of us bears within us the memory of all earlier generations—indeed, of the whole evolutionary process—becomes ever clearer. What will it take to convert that understanding into *conscious* memory, and how greatly will that add to our appreciation of who we are and the journey on which we have come?

Within the few millennia that we call human history, the tiny tip of evolution's timeline that we can reconstruct from the remains of human civilization, the evolutionary process continues unabated, manifest in the evolving human brain but also in the societies and civilizations that result from it. Within this ongoing process, a special place belongs to the evolution of religion, as ideas, images, and conceptions of the gods, God, the life-force, or the essence of Being grow and change with the times. This evolutionary approach to the history of religion forms the background for the next section of this book, my treatment of our Jewish and Western views of God, which I seek to address in the combined roles of scholar and seeker. I do this out of conviction that the evolution of species and the evolution of religious ideas, or of our understanding of reality, are continuous parts of a single evolutionary process. I ultimately suggest that the emergence of an explicitly pantheistic or panentheistic theology in our day is a natural result of this complex evolution, some key steps of which I hope to trace in the following pages. The journey from the tribal warrior god and the projected superhero to the unitive face of Being is indeed a long one, and one in which prior steps are never quite entirely left behind. Because of this, any current discussion of God, particularly in the context of a tradition as ancient as Judaism, is freighted with images, liturgical memories, and literary tropes from each stage along the way.

I have been making a transition here from God to "God" in a multilayered way. I began by talking about reality as I understand it, about the existence of a unifying single Being, a constant within all change, that which undergoes the astro-, geo-, and biohistory of our universe and planet. I then immediately complicated matters by referring to that constant as "God," an English term derived from ancient Teutonic mythology but for many centuries also used to designate other deities as well, including the One who is the chief subject of the

Hebrew Bible, and thus of Jewish and Christian faith. I use this term even though I mean it in a way that is quite different from that meant by most Jews and Christians, since I say quite openly that I choose it *in order to* personify this underlying singularity of being. As "the One" becomes personal, "Being" (HWYH in Hebrew) becomes "God" (Y-H-W-H). That which I designate as "the One" remains beyond naming; it is none other than transcendent mystery. My act of naming, my insistence on speaking of (and to) the core of scientific reality in a religious manner is intended as an act of mythopoetic transformation, a remythologization of the cosmos for our postmodern age. In order to understand the context in which I am doing this, we need to know a good deal more about the Western use of the word "God" and its history.

two

EVOLUTION CONTINUES: A JEWISH HISTORY OF "GOD"

Ancient Legacy Preserved and Transformed

Our Western religious history begins in the ancient Near East, among peoples who worshipped sky gods, deities who dwelt first within and later beyond the heavens and who were manifest in lofty mountains and mighty storms. Our ancestors celebrated the ancient memory of these gods, including their defeat of the netherworld gods, dwellers in the darkness and the deep. The reframing of the Creation story was part of a much larger evolution toward what was to become Israelite monotheism as it emerged in the later prophetic period. But the pre-Israelite polytheistic legacy, hidden as it was behind the harmonizing face of Genesis, could not be entirely set aside. Transformations of culture are never sudden or complete; aspects of old beliefs and fears are retained as the "shadow" side of seemingly new and different ways of thinking. I want to point out certain elements of that ancient Near Eastern legacy that have abided with us over the several millennia since what was once considered the "monotheistic revolution," probably better to be understood as the slow, long-term, and by no means consistent "monotheistic evolution."

First among these elements is the vertical metaphor: the sense that God stands (or sits, in fact) *above* us. The old sky gods did not disappear but conceptually morphed into the God of Hebrew Scripture. In the biblical period God was seen to dwell in a palace located on the far side of the upper waters that lay beyond the sky. "The heavens are the heavens of Y-H-W-H; the earth has He given to the children of Adam" (Ps. 115:16), wrote the Psalmist. Christianity inherited this belief from the Scripture it called the Old Testament; the risen Christ was depicted as dwelling "in heaven," at the right hand of the Father. Christian art depicted this two-tiered universe in infinitely more graphic detail than had previously been imagined. The rabbis and the earliest Jewish mystics, restricted to verbal descriptions, spoke also of God residing in the "seventh heaven," and of arduous heavenly journeys to reach the divine throne room. The early visionary or Merkavah tradition may be characterized as one of extreme, sometimes perhaps even self-mocking, verticality. Rabbinic teachings closely related to the Merkavah sources depicted Moses, as well as his latter-day successor Rabbi Akiva, rising through the clouds and holding onto God's Throne of Glory so as not to be pushed back to earth by those fire-breathing angels who opposed human ascent to a realm beyond our natural place.[1]

Far as we think we have traveled from those ancient beliefs, a certain attachment to the vertical metaphor in theology has never quite left us. As children we still think of God being "up there," of heaven as somewhere beyond the sky. Even if we as adults see ourselves as having outgrown such childish conceptions, verticality is hard to shake. We will still turn our thought to heaven or think of ourselves as seeking to reach a "higher spiritual level." In more casual moments, we might talk about "getting high" by exulting in God. Even the "superior" morality of the post-Kantian God rests on this ancient model of thought; it is, after all, a more "elevated" way of living. All of these are part of the legacy of the vertical metaphor. Of course, that metaphor is reinforced throughout the pages of Scripture, and anyone raised in Judeo-Christian-Islamic culture has great difficulty escaping it.

In fact there has been some competition over the course of two thousand five hundred years between this vertical language for understanding the divine-human relationship and another root metaphor, that which sees God to be found *within* reality and especially within the human heart, rather than above us in the heavens. The earliest direct statement of this competition is found in the Torah itself, when Moses, in his final speeches to the Israelites, proclaims: "The word I command you this day is not too wondrous for you and is not far off. It is not in heaven, as though to say 'Who will go up to the heavens to fetch it and bring it to us.' Nor is it over the sea. . . . But it is very close to you, within your own mouths and hearts to be fulfilled" (Deut.

30:11–13). I imagine this text as a counterpoint to the Torah's own great story of Moses going up the mountain and receiving the word from God in heaven. This seems to be another voice speaking from within the text, or at least one offering a different level of understanding. Here we are being told not to take that tale too literally, to understand Sinai rather as *a vertical metaphor for an internal event.* The true Torah already dwells within you.

The first truly important postbiblical Jewish religious thinker, Philo of Alexandria (c. 20 BCE–50 CE), was a great champion of the internalization of Scripture as he created a Judaism transposed into a Platonic setting.[2] Philo was the first of many who saw the detailed descriptions of the tabernacle in the book of Exodus as metaphorically referring to an inner sanctum, to a "place" for God that we fashion within the human heart.[3] "Let them make me a sanctuary," as later interpreters read the verse, "and I will dwell *within* them" (Ex. 25:8). So too, "They shall know that I am Y-H-W-H their God who brought them forth from the Land of Egypt to dwell within them [originally "in their midst"]; I am Y-H-W-H their God" (Ex. 29:46).

In Christianity, the presence of God within the self, as indeed the whole immanent pole within theology, came to be defined by Christology. As God chose to become manifest within the person Jesus, so is it Christ, the this-worldly embodiment of God (indeed, the new "Tabernacle" or "Temple"), who becomes manifest within the hearts of the faithful. The indwelling God, for the Christian, is usually experienced as "Christ within the heart." In the Qur'an and classical Islam, perhaps in reaction to what its founder perceived as the "excesses" of Christianity in this matter, there is rather little room for expressions of immanence. It was only as Islam absorbed Neoplatonism that a language was found for this understanding of the God who dwells within. Later the Sufis and their poets became perhaps the most outspoken Western witnesses to the presence of God within the heart and the journey to God as an internal one, undertaken by the seeking soul.

My own favorite setting for the face-off between the vertical and internal root metaphors within Judaism is a certain page of the Babylonian Talmud. The second chapter of the Tractate Ḥagigah (14b) tells the famous story of Rabbi Akiva and his friends, the four who entered the *pardes*, or "orchard" of mystical experience. To understand the nature of this experience we turn to RaShI, the eleventh-century French commentator who is usually our best guide to what the Talmud text means. On "four entered the orchard" RaShI says: "They ascended to the sky by use of a [divine] name." For RaShI the vertical picture of the universe is alive and well, taken quite literally in a somewhat magical context. There are powerful divine names that, when recited with proper intention and within appropriate bounds, can transport one up to heaven. But if we are unhappy with RaShI's reading,[4] we turn to another corner of the Talmudic page, where his contemporary, Rabbi Hananel of Kairouan in North Africa, tells us that there really was no heavenly journey at all. The event is an internal one, he says, "an understanding of the heart."[5]

Another aspect of the ancient Near Eastern legacy that abides with us has to do with the incomplete vanquishing of the primordial forces of chaos. God is indeed all-powerful and the single Author of Creation, according to the teaching of Scripture. Yet the world remains imperfect. Reality as we encounter it, filled with seeming arbitrariness and random suffering, cannot possibly represent life as a perfect God intended it. Western religions have invested great intellectual efforts in solving this problem of theodicy (*tsaddik ve-ra' lo* in Hebrew, "the righteous one whose lot is bad"), not a few of them directed toward either blaming the victims, as do Job's "comforters," or promising vindication in the World to Come. Christianity, it may be said, conquered Rome by conquering death with its promise of life eternal. Rabbinic teaching too, while avoiding the most extreme otherworldly focus of much Christian rhetoric, used the afterlife as its chief solution to the woes of theodicy. But some of the most profound and deeply felt responses to human suffering, perhaps feeling the inadequacy of this answer, turn back to the images of premundane forces that elude the control of God. Gnosticism, on the edge of early Christianity, and Kabbalah, arising in the heart of medieval Judaism, both have recourse to this myth of an incomplete conquest of the chaos that underlies creation. The opposing forces were not destroyed, only set aside by the imposition of creation's order. They retain their character as "forces of darkness," rejecting the goodness of God, producing demons that both tempt and punish humans, and representing an alternative, "evil" and yet sometimes surprisingly profound and attractive, vision of existence.[6] Monotheism in a moralizing context can thus never quite escape its own dualistic shadow. Insofar as the enemy of God and rectitude is real and powerful, it will be expressed by some demonic manifestation that is more or less a version of the ancient tale of God's inability or unwillingness to fully vanquish the forces of chaos or darkness.[7] The emerging monotheistic orthodoxies of both Judaism and Christianity both struggled mightily with this dualistic urge. The church rejected Gnosticism in its early centuries, but the presence of "the devil" in the imagination of so many Christians over the centuries shows that its influence never receded entirely. In Judaism it was the Kabbalists who opted for a limited dualism, seeing the demonic's origin within the inner divine process. While that view was dismissed in much of modern Judaism, it is now enjoying a certain comeback, along with much else in the mystical tradition.

The *complexity* of the divine personality as reflected in our sources also belongs to the legacy of the biblical struggle to both combat and subsume the polytheistic universe that preceded it. In a world of many gods, specialization of function can be rather clearly delineated and the conduct of a particular deity can be more or less predicted. It is no surprise that the god of war will act in an aggressive and warlike manner, that love gods seductively supply us with potions that lead us into love, or that gods and goddesses of the crops overflow with bounty. Rain gods have to be appeased in their proper season, and gods of fertility must be given their due, both in sacrificial offerings and in sexual rites, so that both human and animal wombs might be opened. You may have your tribal gods and I mine, but travelers venturing beyond their own people's territory are well advised to make some offering to the power ruling the land or city they are about to enter. Monotheism means that all these deities, along with their many functions and personae, are absorbed into a single Being, one God who has to represent them all. Y-H-W-H comes to be seen as the God who rules Assyria and Babylonia as well as Israel. He is the One who brings the rain and blesses the flocks; He is at once master of birth and death, of war and peace, of compassion and punishment, affliction and healing. How can one God manage so many emotions and act in so many different ways? God is a King with ten garments, according to an early Hebrew poem embedded in the New Year liturgy. "Which one shall I wear today?" he is constantly asking Himself. Will it be the white of forgiveness or the bloodred of vengeance? Shall I put on my *kova' yeshu'ah*, the "helmet of salvation?" Should I seat Myself on the judgment seat or the mercy seat? The conflicts between the gods of old have become the internal conflicts of the single deity, forcing a complexity in the divine personality not required by the earlier formulations.[8]

This new situation created by monotheism is given subtle but dramatic expression in the generic Hebrew term for "god," *elohim*. As anyone who knows even a bit of Hebrew will recognize, *elohim* is a plural form; its primary meaning is "gods." There is a singular, *eloha*, but this form is almost never used in the Bible. When speaking about non-Israelite (or "false") deities, *elohim* is treated as a full plural, requiring the use of plural verbs and adjectives, as in *elohim aherim* (Ex. 20:3), "other gods." But when applied to the God of Israel, *elohim* is treated as though singular, as in *bereshit bara'* (and not *bare'u*) *elohim*, "In the beginning God created." *Elohim* here is a collective form (not entirely unlike the Greek *pan-theon*, by the way), meaning that all the multiple and diverse powers of godhood are now concentrated within this single personality. The process of monotheistic transformation — with all its difficulty — is borne in the very language.

What we are seeing here, the cultural historian might claim, is a totemic representation of the increasing complexity of human personality. People who live complex and often conflicted lives need to imagine a deity who somehow reflects them, who bears within Himself the painful choices faced by humans on a daily basis. The rabbis tended to schematize the divine personality into a twofold model: the "Aspect of Mercy" and the "Aspect of Justice" together made up the divine self, and God, in response to the actions of humanity, was constantly wavering between the two. It is not hard, however, to see in this depiction the situation of the rabbis themselves. As leaders they loved their people and wished to ease their burdens, especially to reassure them, in the face of historical tragedy, of God's unabated love. Hence the projected Aspect of Mercy. But at the same time the rabbis were judges, upholders of the Law and administrators of its authority. As such they had to be bearers of an "Aspect of Justice" that surely brought them into tension with their desire to offer compassion and forgiveness, precisely the lens of conflict through which they came to depict God.

The *maleness* of God is also a part of this process of the monotheistic adaptation of the ancient Near Eastern legacy. Pre-Israelite religion did include the worship of goddesses as well as gods, some of them quite powerful and cultically significant. Rites of *hieros gamos*, or earthly reenactments of the coital union taking place between male and female deities, were also well established. But when the forces were unified under the aegis of the most powerful single deity, it was always clear that this deity would be male, reflecting the power situation in the human community. The oneness of God meant His essential maleness, even though some classically "feminine" personality traits, including compassion and the love of peace, would become manifest in that God. God's essential maleness, carried from ancient Near Eastern religion (the realm of Baal and Marduk) into the religious imagery of biblical and rabbinic sources, is key to that image, including its poignant descriptions of the typically male struggle to overcome an inner tendency toward violence and to strive for compassion, a point to which we will return later. Female elements of nearly divine character reappear in the figure of Mary in early Christianity, who becomes a quasi-divine figure, and in the *shekhinah* of medieval Kabbalah, also to be discussed more fully below.

Theology and Myth

The God of Hebrew Scripture as we are describing Him (and God is clearly a "Him" at this stage) is a God of myth, and there is no reason to object to that term. The absence of a pantheon of gods in the Bible, and especially the lack of a divine consort, led scholars a generation ago to speak of biblical religion as being without myth, a purely this-worldly faith that created linear history precisely as a counterpoint to the rejected worldview of myth. Mythology referred to the interrelationships of the gods in a transworldly realm. Israelite religion, and hence later Judaism and Christianity, elevated history to become the site of divine concern and action, leaving no room for myth. Today we think about myth in somewhat broader terms, and it is indeed possible to speak of biblical religion as containing mythic elements. The sacred history of Israel takes on mythical dimensions, especially as it is celebrated and recreated in an annual ritual cycle. If myths are *ancient and powerful narratives that contain deep truths reverberating through human life*, surely such tales as the expulsion from Eden, the 'aqedah or binding of Isaac, and the Exodus may be seen as essential myths of Judaism. I believe that myth is a positive and vital tool of religious expression, and understand our task as partly one of reinvigorating the mythic legacy of Judaism, depleted by a certain linearity or univocality of thinking characteristic of the modern era.[9]

There is nevertheless something distinctive about the mythic tales of Y-H-W-H in biblical and later Jewish tradition. Their setting is indeed this-worldly; they constitute a story about God's encounter with humans, featuring the seemingly near-total failure in this "experiment" of creating free-willed creatures. It is a mythology of relationship, a series of tales about how God, singular and independent, decides to create humans and enter into dialogue and relationship with them. The decision to bring forth these creatures in God's own "image and likeness," we should recall, came at the last possible minute. The chief object of creation for the sixth day was that of land animals, complementing the birds and fish that had been fashioned a day earlier. But after the beasts emerged, God seems to have felt that creation was still incomplete. Perhaps uncertain about this next step, He turned to some unspecified partner (the angels, the Torah, His own heart, the future generations of the righteous — to name but a few candidates offered by later interpreters) and said: "Let us make a human."

All this happened just before the Sabbath, when God would have to cease from labor. The first pair of humans had been in Eden, their intended home forever, just a few hours when they transgressed God's command and were ordered expelled. (They were allowed to stay for the length of the Sabbath, however, for a good host could hardly chase people out just before Shabbat when they had no place to go!)[10] They were expelled from Eden, said Franz Kafka (not knowing that the Kabbalists had preceded him by seven hundred years), not because they ate of the Tree of Knowledge but because they failed to join it to the Tree of Life.[11] With Adam and Eve's lifeless knowledge, perhaps the product of idle curiosity, comes the alienation that begins as we emerge from Eden, kept out by that ever-turning flaming sword (the sword of our ambivalence?) that guards the way behind us. Only at Sinai will the pain of that exile begin its long journey toward healing. But even this tale of expulsion, an attempt to explain human alienation, is a myth of relationship. Like many myths, it tells of trust betrayed, resulting in intimacy gone sour.

The first narrative after Eden is the tale of Cain, the Torah's hero of tragic rage. There is no difference between Cain's rejected sacrifice and Abel's, which the Lord accepts. Sacrifice was in fact Cain's idea; Abel was merely copying him, perhaps seeking to outdo his brother. But Cain's situation is all of ours; Scripture is shockingly frank in acknowledging it. That's the way it is once we are outside the fantasy garden of Edenic childhood. Life is tough and arbitrary; there is no reason why one flourishes and another suffers, none that has to do with justice, in any case. Cain is infuriated when forced to confront this truth. Unable to lash out against God, all he can do is kill his poor brother. But that's the other part of the story: his brother's blood cries out against him. Welcome to the real world, welcome to adulthood. Life is totally unfair, and you are totally responsible. How hard it is to come to terms with this essential unfairness of life! Perhaps this explains why so many adolescents contemplate or even commit suicide. How can you live in such a world? Our rage at God is also part of the divine-human relationship, a fact that needs to be explained by an ancient story.

How, indeed, can one live after Eden, after Cain? "Cursing and blaspheming" is certainly one understandable response to that question, a path chosen by many. The early generations, according to the rabbis, discover idolatry, a form of contrareligion, one that blasphemes by its very acts of worship.[12] You need something to worship in a world like this. But how could those generations revere the universal One when everything felt so fragmented? The original "natural religion" of Eden (we might think of it in Rousseau-like fashion as childhood's innocent embrace of life) was forgotten, so it is claimed, and "false gods" began to appear. But multiple deities only underscore human divisions, and represent tribes in continuing and worsening the aggressive, competitive behavior that is our evolutionary legacy, rather than checking it in the name of sacred oneness, which our shared humanity should give us the ability to do. By the time of the Flood, humans are so filled with violence that God nearly decides to end the great experiment, sweeping them all away. "This evolutionary path called Homo sapiens was nearly a blind alley," the tale of the Flood seems to say, bearing an implicit warning to future generations, including our own. Morally speaking, humanity was no progression over the apes. The best human that God could find in that generation was one who locked himself away in his own relative virtue. Noah does not plead for his fellow creatures, does not argue with God's outrageous plan; he merely builds an ark. Only his own family, among humans, will be saved from the Flood. Some hero![13] Ultimately the self-indulgence that gives the lie to his "righteousness" is revealed in the intentionally ugly story of Noah's drunkenness that follows the Flood. His successors are not much better. They build the Tower of Babel, a monument to their own religious delusions.

Taken collectively and sequentially, these mythic tales of God's ongoing encounters with this new human species, created and blessed in the closing hours of the sixth day, give us a glimpse into the personal growth and education of the Creator, the true subject of all biblical myth. The One who had been alone for countless ages now has sought to find a partner, one with whom to enter into the dance of mutual relationship. This is not entirely easy or comfortable, given the strong and willful creature who has come forth, perhaps in a process that did not happen altogether as anticipated. (How was He to know?) Only with Abraham, whom God loves so greatly, does the tide of failure begin to turn.[14] We will have more to say later about the patriarchal tales and the origins of Israel.

But the value of this process of divine involvement with humanity — and that is the core of biblical myth — will be proven only later, when God comes to redeem Israel from Egyptian bondage. God sees the suffering of Israel and "knows" (Ex. 2:25), as though He too had shared in their suffering. God comes down from the heights to learn what it means to enter into relationship with humans. Just as Israel is purified and transformed in the "iron furnace" of Egypt, so too has God, as it were, become prepared for a true and lasting covenant of love. Having accepted the right of his beloved Abraham to argue for the people of Sodom, God has learned to turn away from His own fuming anger. This will prepare Him to back down from His fierce intent to destroy Israel after the Golden Calf. He responds with compassion when Moses stands up for the people, and He remains faithful to His promise even through long periods when Israel seems undeserving of His love. Having to deal with mortals as His only love partners, God is ever learning what it is to be the parent of a wayward child or the husband of an unfaithful wife. A deity who had other outlets for relationship might well have given up on humans. Only One who is otherwise quite wholly and intolerably alone can be counted on to remain engaged in the enterprise of divine/human intimacy forever, no matter how hard it gets. Thus it happens that *relationship*, modeled on multiple forms of human interpersonal intimacy, forms the essential subject of biblical myth and becomes the essential truth of Jewish and Western religious life.

Metaphor and Divine Personhood

Here we necessarily open ourselves to a broader question. To what extent are all our humanlike images of God projections from the realm of human experience? The inevitable answer is that they indeed are, and the theologian does best who admits fully that such is the case.[15] Of course, the person of faith is tempted to turn the picture around, suggesting that the complexity of human personality simply reflects our own creation in God's image, and that it is God, rather than humans, who is to be seen as the primary figure of this similitude. The hall of mirrors may indeed be approached from either end, as the mystics have always understood so well. But the ancient rabbis already seem to have admitted that our images of God change according to the needs of the hour. When God appeared to Israel at the Sea of Reeds, said the rabbis, as the people confronted the advancing Egyptian armies, "He appeared to them as a youth." On the day of battle one has no use for a tottering old God. But at Sinai, in giving the Law, "He appeared as an elder." Who wants to receive laws from a mere youth of a God? On the day of lawgiving, only an elder would do.[16] The word "appeared" (*nire'ah*) in this Midrash of perhaps the third to fifth centuries, is a passive form, and it is tellingly unclear whether the text means that God willfully changed His appearance in accord with the people's needs or whether they just saw Him in multiple ways, reflected in the variable lens of their own needs and desires.

The God of Hebrew Scripture is both elusive and concrete, unknowable and yet firmly anchored in images of divine personhood. Even Moses, the most enlightened of all prophets, is not given a true understanding of divinity. When he is about to go into Egypt to redeem Israel, he asks of the voice that addresses him: "If they say 'What is His name?' what shall I say to them?" (Ex. 3:13). God's answer is at once a self-revelation and a rebuff: "My name is Y-H-W-H — Being — and I shall be whatever I shall be." In effect God takes God's own name, the mysterious and precious noun by which He is evoked, back to its verbal root. He then conjugates Himself, as though to say: "If you think you understand me, if you think you've *got* Me in the little box of nominal definition, I'll show you how I can fly away again." God's answer to Moses' request is something like the slap of a Zen master. This is the One who later again turns down Moses' "Show me Your glory," reminding him that "No man shall see Me and live" (Ex.

33:18–20). This is the God of whom the prophet says: "To whom may you liken Me that I be compared?" and "What image would you attribute to Him?" (Is. 40:18, 25).

All of this abstraction and questioning of images, newly central to the religious language of Scripture, exists side by side with a host of images for God, most of them taken over directly from the religious world that had long existed, in which gods are regularly portrayed as bearing a form similar, but superior, to that of humans. In the pre-Israelite cultures, these were represented artistically as well as verbally, as a great many surviving stone cuttings and bas-reliefs attest. Once the Torah forbade such depictions, only verbal embodiments remained, but these are ubiquitous both in Scripture and in the post-biblical writings of the early Jews. *Personal* metaphors for God are found throughout biblical and rabbinic sources, far outnumbering and overwhelming any other sort of image. The two most central of these, *God as Father* and *God as King*, provide the backbone of Jewish devotional life as reflected in our prayer book. They make their most dramatic appearance on the High Holy Days, when *Avinu Malkenu*, "Our Father, Our King," becomes the key refrain of our worship. A few words need to be said about each of these metaphors.

The parental metaphor for God is early and quite universal. It has to do with our human quest for origins. It is the "Who made me?" of those who know on some level that they are here because of their parents' union. God becomes a deeper parent or, to use Freudian language, a projected parent, one who can do in a perfect way all that parents are supposed — and so often fail — to do. This includes nurturance, protection from harm, teaching us how to live, and providing a proper moral and personal example. God is Father (rather than Mother) because we are the product of patriarchal societies, those where men had dominance and where men's spheres of action were the most highly valued. The fact that we are critical of such societies today and hope to change that bias should not keep us from acknowledging those historical realities. All of us, even those now born into several generations of feminist-influenced Judaism or Christianity, are products of many centuries of patriarchy.

The royal metaphor for God is as ancient as human kingship, and also much precedes the Bible. Royal households naturally supported the notion of kinglike gods. As one scholar of the ancient Near East put it, speaking of the Sargonic age (about 2300 BCE), "The new ideology of the deified king . . . worked both ways — the king became more like a god, but at the same time the gods became more like kings."[17] Depictions from widespread ancient sites show the gods crowned, dressed in royal raiment, or adorned with whatever other symbols glorified human kingship. This metaphor is chiefly about power and reflects the place within the religious mind that longs for submission to a supreme and trustworthy authority. It is tied to our acceptance of mortality and thus more broadly to our human sense of ultimate powerlessness. As the author of the book of Job might have said it (though he did so with considerably more eloquence), "You've got all the marbles in this game, O Lord, so I kneel before Your greatness."

In my younger years I used to rail against these images, treating them as whipping boys for all that was wrong with religion. Father imagery for God worked well, I would say, as long as we lived in stable communities where generations loyally followed one another undisturbed, when the shoemaker's son became a shoemaker, the rabbi's son a rabbi, and the finest thing you could say to a person was "Your father is a great man!" In an age like ours, however, where adolescent rebellion is taken for granted (and my own story was the case in point), God as projected father will have to be deposed ("kicked in the shins," I used to say, and "shins" was a euphemism), just as parental authority is questioned and rejected almost as a rite of passage in each generation. God as projected father, as Freud so rightly understood, was bound for a fall.

All this was quite convincing to me until, at the age of thirty-five, I suddenly found myself the father of a newborn infant. As I looked down at my daughter for the first time, the bonding was so complete (and this was a case of adoption, not biology, by the way) that I knew without question that this child would be with me forever and that I would give my life to protect her. This was before she could even smile or captivate me with eye contact. Then I understood that God as Father means just that: God loves me and embraces me in this total, uncomplicated, and wholly unearned way. I am loved just because I am, even though I have done nothing to "deserve" love.[18] The parental metaphor remains problematic in our age, but we do need to understand it as parents, not only as children.

The royal metaphor was also a favorite bugaboo of my youth. God as King, I would claim, may be read two ways in our day. Shall we choose England or Saudi Arabia? If God is king of England, He has no real power. We (the party in power) run the world, and that is what we essentially believe. But once a year, on Coronation Day (call it Rosh Hashanah, if you will), we dress Him up in all His finery and parade Him through the streets. A little pageantry is good for the soul, after all. On the other hand, if God is king as in Saudi Arabia, we're in really big trouble. Who of us is free enough from sin not to wind up on the gallows of such a ruler?

The image of God as King was "redeemed" for me by a famous Talmudic story.[19] Rabbi Yohanan ben Zakkai, the great master of the generation when the second Temple was destroyed, had a son who fell terribly ill. The rabbi sent a message to his disciple Hanina ben Dosa, well known as a miracle worker, asking him to pray for the lad. Hanina went upstairs in his home and prayed. He came down and told the messenger to return, because the lad was healed. When the messenger arrived, he found that the boy's crisis had passed just at the moment when Hanina had come downstairs. The only person not satisfied with this solution was Mrs. Ben Zakkai. "You are the great rabbi of the age," she said to her husband, "and you need this disciple to pray for you?" Rabbi Yohanan took her aside and explained it thus: "When I come before the King," he said, "I am like an ambassador from another land. We need to make an appointment as befits a state occasion. When Hanina comes in," he said, "he is like a servant in the throne room. Anything he wants to tell the King he can say right there." The little guy who dusts off the throne may have an easier time getting the King's ear.

What did this story do for me? It made me realize that the exaggeration of royal imagery may serve as a dramatic foil to emphasize intimacy, even with One who is none other than the mighty King of Kings, the blessed Holy One, Master of the Universe. When those awesome-sounding terms are used by pious Jews, I came to understand, they are spoken as though they were terms of intimacy and endearment. This single early rabbinic story is in fact one of hundreds in which the King weeps with His children, longs for their return when they go astray, and acts in every other way like a projected embodiment of loving grandfatherly humanity, rather than as a brutal ruler.[20]

At the same time, the potential for what may feel to us like brutality is never far away. Life can be that way (and the metaphor means that God can act that way). When it is, we have naught left but to appeal to mystery. We do not understand. Each time the ram's horn is blown in our New Year service, we respond to it with the following words: "We come before You either as children or as servants. If we come as Your children, be compassionate with us as a father is with his children. But if we come as servants, our eyes are turned to You." "Our eyes are turned to You" means that we recognize the ultimacy and the final arbitrariness of Your power. "All we can do is beg" is the thrust of the prayer. What can be seen as cold and arbitrary, evidence of total divine indifference, is reframed here as the mysterious decree of an inscrutable but loving King. "Our eyes are turned to You" because You ultimately are the One we trust at the same time that You are the One we fear.[21]

Historical Transformations

As the biblical images of God evolved into that which we call Judaism, the changes surely reflect both the history of Israel and some broader themes in the development of civilization. Although the tribal God became more consistently the universal Creator, His special love for Israel was something the rabbis needed constantly to reiterate and underscore. This was an especially important message in the face of Jewish historical defeat and powerlessness. Jews were subject to the constant pressures of triumphant Christianity's (and later Islam's) supersessionist theologies, insisting that history had proven how wrong the Jews were in not accepting Christ (or the Qur'an). The election of Israel thus remained a cornerstone of Jewish theology, even as the old tribal deity evolved toward greater universalism. A degree of inconsistency arose between these two, but the rabbis did not seem to feel much need to reconcile them. Yes, God is Father and Ruler of all the world, as the High Holy Day liturgy makes very clear. But that same prayer text, calling upon Him as "Our Father, Our King," clearly sees God as Parent and King to Israel in particular; it is our Jewish martyrs who "have gone through fire and water for the sake of Your name." The classical Hebrew poets often depict Israel in exile as a wounded child or a temporarily abandoned mate, calling upon God to vindicate his or her true position by again manifesting His love.

The fierce tribal God of Israel's wanderings who demanded that they slay every man, woman, and child of their foes is now increasingly transformed into the loving Father of all His creatures. This change takes place almost simultaneously in the emergence of Christianity and rabbinic Judaism, even though it is often still popularly associated with the New Testament. While described almost exclusively in male language, the God of the rabbis is, in admittedly stereotypic terms, a rather "feminized" male, bearer of *rahamim*, womblike compassion, unfailing nurturer, lover of peace. "Our Father, compassionate Father" is best worshipped by those who "dwell in tents," (like the rabbinic image of our father Jacob, Rebecca's favorite). Those "tents" are here converted to "synagogues and houses of study."[22] This is where faithfulness to Y-H-W-H may best be shown, rather than the terrain of those who go forth in conquest, be it military or adventurous. As the Jews were transformed from nomads and warriors into town dwellers, merchants, and increasingly "people of the book," their God too became one chiefly encountered in the study of Torah, "the best of all goods," as a Yiddish saying would have it. As the people Israel became politically powerless, remaining so for many centuries, they needed a God who could relate to their situation and even join them in a life of exile and wandering. This is the God who is with them wherever they are exiled, who longs for His wayward children to return to Him,[23] who knows how to mourn with them in their sorrows, both personal and collective, and who smiles at the thought that they have bested Him in interpreting His Law.[24] The royal and parental metaphors are affectionately united in the widespread notion that "all Israel are the children of the King."[25] While the call for ultimate vindication through triumph (and sometimes even vengeance) was not altogether abandoned, Judaism came to live with a God less manifest in power than in love for Israel's faithfulness to Him. This loyalty was expressed by life according to *halakhah*, the "path" of proper living, and their devotion to its study and practice.

The *humanizing* (and perhaps "feminizing") of God has much to do with His learning to love and forgive, rather than to destroy in great blowouts of anger. This process reflects a projection of human experience, particularly that of males. We now understand civilization itself as a product of that taming of inner aggression. The instinct to fight, conquering weaker species, sometimes for food, and fending off predators as best we can, is an essential part of our evolutionary legacy. Within a species, contests of strength among males, often as ways of attracting the potentially most fruitful female partners, are also part of what we bear within our extended genetic memory. The viciousness of this legacy lies buried within us, long outliving the time in our biohistory when its use may have been appropriate. Human history is punctuated with frequent reminders that perceived slights, challenges to "manhood," rival claims to territory, and the like can peel off the veneer of civilization quite rapidly and drag us down into the inner hell of beastly creature-against-creature struggle, revealing us capable of behavior otherwise beyond imagination.

The force that holds back these forces within us was depicted by Freud as the superego, the repressive but moralizing force that re-channels our energies into forces that make for civilization, its "discontents" lying beneath it like the gods of old, never quite fully vanquished. A more contemporary psychological model might look at an inner balancing of archetypically "male" and "female" energies within the self, affected by hormones that bear within them all the developmental legacy of human history. The "female" side of that legacy, borne within male as well as within female bodies, represents the "nesting" instinct, the fostering of home and family (hence tending toward monogamy), and cooperation with others in building a society. The "male," borne by both genders but more typically dominant in men, is aggressive and competitive, oriented toward conquest (manifested by some in sexual behavior), but protective and loving toward those a man has declared "his own." It is the inner balance of those forces, especially in the context of family living, that brings about a civilized order of humanity.

The God depictions of ancient Israel represent this ongoing human struggle. They do so from the point of view of males largely because it was males who created them. But in seeing Israel, the collective embodiment of Jewry, as female, they were reflecting on her role as a shaper of the imagination as well. This can be seen in the history of the most famous of all texts describing God, the words spoken by a mysterious divine voice as Moses stood at Sinai supplicating for the forgiveness of his people. Exodus 34:6–7 reads: "Y-H-W-H, Y-H-W-H, a compassionate and gracious God, long-suffering and magnanimous in true love, keeping that love for the multitudes, forgiving sin, transgression, and misdeed, but surely not cleansing them entirely, revisiting the sins of the fathers upon their children, down to the third and fourth generations." The early synagogue adopted this passage as central to its liturgy. All *selihot*, or prayers for forgiveness, are built around it as a refrain. But when read in the synagogue, the text is rather different: "Y-H-W-H, Y-H-W-H, a compassionate and gracious God, long-suffering and magnanimous in true love, keeping that love for the multitudes, forgiving sin, transgression, and misdeed, and cleansing!" The absolute form of the verb *naqeh* ("cleansing") is simply cut off from the negative it was meant to underscore, with its meaning totally transformed. This is truly an emasculation of the text (*sarsehu vedarshehu!*), one that documents like no other the transformation of a God who seeks retribution from descendents of uncleansed sinners into One who forgives and cleanses with unmitigated compassion. This bit of radical Midrashic surgery was created by anonymous liturgical authors within the early rabbinic community. It may be deemed likely that these authors were males. But we might also metaphorically understand that here it was *kenesset yisra'el*, the Community of Israel, God's "female" beloved, who defeated, tamed, or educated her Spouse.

The Missing Metaphor

In the corpus of classical Jewish writings (almost all either narrative or homiletical), images of Father and King are indeed essential to the ways in which God was depicted. These two images are to a degree variants of one another; both reflect an older male figure before whom one is to stand in loving awe. But there is another key picture of God widespread in the ancient sources that became almost unknown to later Judaism, for an interesting series of historical reasons. That is the metaphor of God as Spouse or Lover, first of the Community of Israel but then also of the individual.[26]

The history of this metaphor goes to the very heart of Israel's national saga, the tale of redemption from Egypt. Israel's most vivid recollection of God dwells on this moment, and it is here that this special relationship emerges. The ten commandments at the heart of the Sinai revelation open with "I am Y-H-W-H your God who brought you forth from the Land of Egypt, from the house of bondage" (Ex. 20:2). The *shema'*, recited twice each day, concludes with the dramatic assertion that "I am Y-H-W-H your God who brought you forth from the Land of Egypt to become your God; I am Y-H-W-H your God" (Num. 15:41). In redeeming Israel from Egyptian bondage, God acquired an eternally indebted agent in this world, alternatively described in the Bible as an adopted child or a young slave girl whom He redeems and takes as His bride. Recollection of this moment reverberates throughout Israel's long history, placing her in the role of God's beloved.

It is here that monotheism makes a crucial difference. The one God is, as we have noted, all alone. This means that God has no one with whom to be a partner, until He creates and allows Himself to love humans. The old pagan chief deities all had divine consorts. Marriages, love affairs, and romantic intrigues were common among the gods and goddesses of the Near East, as they were among those of Greece and Rome. Monotheism means an essential change to what may be called the erotic situation of God, who is left without a partner. God has no one to love except *you*. This means you, faithful servant or beloved child; you, Israel, or, in the Christian adaptation, you, the church or the Christian. At the Exodus God takes Israel to be His spouse (Jer. 2:2), and the history of Western religion is changed forever.

While textual "evidence" of God's spousal love for Israel may be found in a number of other biblical sources (especially Hosea's account of God's outcry as a husband wounded by Israel's unfaithfulness), those texts were all but sidelined by Israel's great love poem, the Song of Songs. The Song — attributed to Solomon, whose name Shelomo was later read as "King of Peace," making it "God's song" — was saved for Scripture by Rabbi Akiva ben Joseph (d. c. 135 CE), who described it as the "holy of holies" among the sacred books.[27] The allegorization of this Song is the heart of the erotic metaphor in the Western canon. The beloved people — the Community of Israel, the church, or the soul — is seen as God's chosen bride. It is God who knocks on the door of the beloved's heart, who stands behind the wall or peers through the latticework to catch a glimpse of her, and all the rest.

This reading of the Song of Songs as the hymn to God's passionate love for humans becomes linked to the God of Genesis, who followed each work of Creation by saying "Good! Good! Good!" He then looks at Adam and says, for the first time: "It is *not good* for man to be alone; I will make him a help-meet to be before him" (Gen. 2:18). Everything created in the opening chapter of Genesis comes forth as a member of a pair: day and night, light and darkness, upper waters and lower waters, land and sea, sun and moon, fish and birds, man and woman. Creation is thus a tale of the emergence of duality. Everything is paired — *except God*. To say it in the language of Jewish imagination, we would suggest that this is why the Torah begins with the letter *bet*, indicating the number 2. The *aleph* is reserved for the single and singular Self of God, revealed only at Sinai in the first letter of the opening word *anokhi*, "I am."

At Sinai there is a new pairing, that of God and Israel as Lover and Beloved. The erotic metaphor is then applied by the early rabbis to the old sacred narrative of Israel in Egypt, at the Sea of Reeds, and wandering in the wilderness. The biblical narrative is transformed by being "washed over"[28] with quotations from the Song, as evidenced both in Midrashic homilies and in the synagogue's earliest liturgical poetry, the sixth- or seventh-century *piyyut*. One might say that the "Passion" of Christianity has its parallel here, in the now eros-charged reframing of the Exodus/Sinai narrative. The account of Exodus and Sinai, reinvigorated by this Midrash, now becomes a collective or national "passion play," focused on the love between the blessed Holy One and His chosen mate, the Community of Israel. This entire Midrashic tradition is then adopted by the Zohar and other Kabbalistic authors, who use it in their own way.[29]

The erotic metaphor has its greatest impact on the Judaism of the mystical tradition. The Kabbalists reread much of prior Judaism, enabled by a number of subtle changes in their understanding of long-established symbols.[30] The oneness of God, for the Kabbalist, is dynamic and flowing rather than static and unmoved. Within this oneness is a series of ten graded manifestations, each representing another stage in the ongoing self-manifestation of the Deity. The tenth of these, called *shekhinah* (indwelling), *kenesset yisra'el* (assemblage of Israel), bride, queen, heavenly Jerusalem, and a host of other mostly female-associated names, is the inner divine resting place (hence "sabbath") where all the divine energies are gathered before flowing forward to animate the "lower," nondivine world. She is the bride, spouse, love object of the "male" aspect of divinity, the recharged blessed Holy One (now most identified with the "male" potencies *tif'eret* and *yesod*) of the old rabbinic tradition.

Kabbalah thus violates a seemingly essential part of the monotheistic revolution. Here the God of Israel has a consort, and the act of *hieros gamos*, the sacred marital union, takes place *within* the divine, rather than between the divine Spouse and His human beloved. Kabbalah may be described (like certain tendencies within Christian Trinitarian faith) as a religion of the love of God for God. We humans, the earthly manifestation of *kenesset yisra'el*, are both the *offspring* (souls are born of the upper union, as bodies are conceived by its earthly imitation) and the *facilitators* of the inner divine love match. Human actions have the power of arousing divine erotic energies in such a way that Bride and Bridegroom are turned toward one another, unite in sacred coitus, and thus renew the force of life and the fructification of all the lower worlds.

But while the mystics' *shekhinah* is the consort or female fulfillment of "God," the "blessed Holy One," she is also depicted as the love object of Israel. We are her devotees, seeking to arouse her to love. Since Kabbalah originates in medieval Western Europe, a bit of chivalric image enters the tradition here. The Kabbalist sees himself as a sort of spiritual knight, giving himself to *shekhinah*, particularly as She suffers in exile, much as the knight gives himself to his lady and, more to the point, much as the medieval Western monk devoted himself to the mother of God, especially after the great Marian revival of the twelfth century. The figure of *shekhinah* owes much to the surrounding Catholic culture and its discovery of a female semidivine figure. The way in which this female configuration is poised precisely at the border between the divine and the lower worlds, serving as the conduit of divine grace and energy as it pours into this world and of human energy in prayer and devotion as they rise to unite with God is very much parallel to Christian depictions of Mary as the "mediatrix" between Christ and the Christian.[31] A key difference remains between the traditions in that Judaism glorified neither celibacy nor virginity. *Shekhinah* is not the "virgin bride" of God but rather His Spouse in a fully sexualized way.

The erotic metaphor as a way of expressing the love and intimate bond between God and Israel has now been displaced by this reclaiming of the ancient *hieros gamos* myth, the union of male and female within the divine. While the Kabbalist's relationship to *shekhinah* is one of sonship and fealty, a measure of human romantic attachment to Her is also legitimized. We too may be described as lovers of *shekhinah*, in a menage that is considered entirely proper — indeed, as enabling fuller expression of our own love of God. In the Zohar, the key text of classical Kabbalah, the erotic metaphor is rampant; there is barely a page in the Zohar where the Song of Songs' influence is not to be seen. In the later Kabbalistic sources, surprisingly blunt sexual terms continue to appear, though they seem to have become so fully theologized that their original meaning goes almost unnoticed.

When Judaism was presented to the modern West, however, the erotic element was dismissed as an embarrassment, and Kabbalah was completely sidelined. A notion of "mainstream" Judaism was created by nineteenth-century scholars, largely for the purpose of discarding the mystical tradition. Freud was right, in other words, when he saw religion, as he experienced it in the Judaism of his day, to be little more than the revering of a projected superego, the God of the Jews being an obvious father figure.[32] But that was the Judaism the generations immediately preceding him had chosen to present to the world, one denuded of the eros of sacred passion. We can only wonder whether Freud, himself only one generation removed from Galician Hasidism, realized how much of repressed eros underlay the stern and sober *Vatergott* of Viennese Jewish respectability.

Apologetics and an emerging Jewish bourgeois sense of propriety had much to do with this elimination. It should be recalled that liberal-spirited Protestant and Deist elites were the first to champion the breakdown of the ghetto walls and to accept Jews into European society. A lot of effort was devoted among Jews to returning that great favor by showing those good people that our religious faith was much like their own. Neither the erotic terminology of the Kabbalist nor the devotional intensity of early Hasidism was acceptable in this setting, one that was carried over and taken to new extremes as American Judaism developed out of the nineteenth-century German model.

But there may also have been another reason why the language of religious eros was dismissed. The Song of Songs is clearly to be associated with the image of God as a youth, to which I referred above. "At the sea, He appeared to them as a youth": this is the young warrior-hero, defeating the Egyptians on the day of battle. But this is also God as young lover, the one who brought forth Israel the hand-maiden, she who "saw more at the sea than did Isaiah and Ezekiel,"[33] the greatest visionaries among the prophets. What did she see that even they were to miss? "She" saw God as Lover and youthful Re-deemer, the subject of her true love and devotion. In the later re-ligious imagination of the West (especially in Christian iconography), this figure of the young, attractive male deity comes to be fully identi-fied with Jesus, in his role as "God the Son." Christianity, especially in its monastic versions, indeed knows an eroticized religious passion in the love of Christ. The Jews, in some combination of distaste and envy at the constant visual reminders of the dying and reborn young God, wanted no part of him or of any language too readily associated with him. They chose, rather proudly, to be defined as a religion that worshipped God the Father. This choice by definition left them with-out sacred eros, creating a religion largely devoid of religious passion as well.

From Myth to Philosophy

But I have got somewhat ahead of myself. The evolution of religion does not take place in simple chronological lines. Until now we have been discussing myths and metaphors through which God was con-ceived and worshipped, especially metaphors that sought to express religious intimacy. But there is another trend in the history of theol-ogy, found in Judaism as well as in Christianity and Islam, which leads in a quite different direction. This is the philosophical piety that devel-oped in the Middle Ages. In Jewish history this tendency is most iden-tified with Moses Maimonides (1135–1205), but it in fact included a wide range of thinkers and schools, beginning in the ninth to tenth centuries, and played a significant role for perhaps half a millennium.

To begin our understanding of this development, we have to go back to the internal metaphor and trace a bit more of its evolution. We also have to examine how the vertical/internal axis works in rela-tion to Judaism's emphasis on personal relationship with God. Can one have an intense, emotionally stirring relationship with a God who is no longer seen as a "person" in the traditional sense? This question first occurs in the context of what we might call radical transcendence, as found in a number of medieval thinkers. Their God is so *elevated* — meaning abstract or rarified — that relationship becomes hard to imagine. But the question applies equally, though differently, to a theology of radical immanence, such as I am proposing. Here the question is not the *remoteness* of God but rather the *otherness* of God. Can you be in *relationship*, which somehow implies the *inter*personal, with One who is in no way separable from your own deepest self, the innermost Self of all that is? This challenge keeps the medieval theological enterprise — from which I stand quite far in some ways — germane to my own quest.

I have mentioned that Philo of Alexandria was the first postbiblical thinker to develop the idea of God as present within the self or soul. It is no coincidence that Philo was a Hellenistic Jew, writing in Greek and seeking to create a reading of biblical Judaism in a Platonic mode. Plato, you may recall, did not think highly of the old Homeric tales of the gods. He even thought of banning from his ideal republic the poets who wrote of them. God for Plato is already quite abstract, the highest ideal of truth known to the human soul. Philo is both a Platonic philosopher and a mystic. His religion is centered around a contemplative idealism in which the soul fulfills itself by discovering its identity in its divine source. In Neoplatonic thought, influenced by Philo, God is the ultimate source of being, symbolized by light, toward which all souls naturally turn and to which they long to be restored. For the Neoplatonists, who (unlike Philo himself) exercised considerable influence on Judaism throughout the Middle Ages, God is both a philosophical category and the object of deep personal desire, often expressed in the persuasive language of poetry.[34]

It took nearly a thousand years after Philo's first attempt for Judaism again to be transposed into philosophic terms. When this did happen, beginning in the tenth century, it was largely in the Islamic cultural realm. Jews first came to read the Greek (including the Neoplatonic) philosophers via Arabic translation, and the most important works of Jewish philosophy were composed in Arabic as well. One of the great goals of this philosophical movement was what has been called a "purification" of the Jewish views of God.[35] To the sophisticated medieval mind, the sacred stories of the Bible and especially the seemingly exaggerated tales of the rabbis were embarrassingly primitive and grossly anthropomorphic. Surely one could not believe these stories literally; their value had to lie in some other dimension, either in a moral message they contained or in some more obscure truth that could be unpacked only by means of esoteric interpretation. Philosophical Judaism was frequently accompanied by a massive effort at reinterpreting, and often explaining away, the anthropomorphic theology of the received tradition.

The God of the medieval philosophers was transcendent in a way very different from that of the rabbis or the old Merkavah mystics. Those early voyagers through the divine "palaces" transcended this world for the sake of a higher universe characterized by visual and auditory experiences of a most graphic nature. They lived entirely within a fantastic universe shaped by images and myths received from tradition. The apex of their inward journey, one that transported them beyond the physical realm, was an extension of visions articulated by the ancient prophets, texts that had been revered and expanded upon for centuries.

In the philosophical piety of the Middle Ages, the vertical metaphor was still in use. The new hierarchical cosmologies of the Middle Ages may have contained ten spheres rather than seven heavens, but verticality still seems essential to their character. The spheres that led to God were called "higher," even though they were also depicted as concentric rings encircling the planetary orbits that surrounded the earth. But essentially the divine world was conceived as an *order of being* different from the "sublunar" world in which we live. It was entirely immaterial and therefore could not be attained by any sort of physical or spatial journey, only by an opening of the mind (for the Aristotelians) or by the perfect and unimpeded longing of the soul (for the Neoplatonists). The true transcendence of God lay not in spatial distance but in the endless abstraction of God as a *concept* and the degree to which the mind had to stretch itself to gain even the smallest intellectual glimpse of the divine.

Where did the mind turn to get its idea of God? Scripture was an important guide, of course, especially when read through the lens of proper philosophic interpretation. But essentially the philosophers pursued an inward contemplative path. God was attained by a progressive abstraction of consciousness, an inner mental turning aside from all externals and "accidents," including the utter shedding of all anthropomorphisms, to discover the single abstract truth of Being. Thus, despite their seeming loyalty to a hierarchical and even "vertical" worldview, it was the God within their minds and souls who was the true object of philosophical quest. It may be said that both of the root metaphors, the vertical and the internal, were taken nonliterally by the philosophers, who saw no conflict between them. The ultimate divine reality was not clearly distinguished from the ultimately rarified *idea* of God. To purify the mind of all anthropomorphisms and other misconceptions was to come as close as humans might to *hassagah* ("attainment" or "understanding"; significantly, the word is the same) of the divine reality.

The techniques of attaining this abstraction are best known from Maimonides' presentation of them in his *Guide for the Perplexed*. The first section of the *Guide* is concerned mostly with dismissing any literal truth claim that might be made for either anthropomorphic (human-form-like) or anthropopathic (human-emotion-like) descriptions of God to be found in the Bible. Since it is clear that God has no body (based on a combination of Aristotelian metaphysics and quotations from the more abstract prophetic passages referred to above), seeming anthropomorphic descriptions of God must have some other meaning. Words like "hand" and "eye," when applied to God, cannot refer to physical body parts, since God has no body. These words are then taken to be homonyms, words that have one set of meanings when applied to corporeal beings and a second, unknowable (and therefore essentially dismissible) meaning when applied to God. The same is true of such actions as walking, seeing, hearing, and (most crucially in this case) speaking. This process of negation is then carried over to the realm of emotion, since such feelings would imply lack or need, compromising the supposed perfection of God. This "perfection" itself, we should add, is an assumption of philosophy, and does not represent a claim found in the biblical or rabbinic tradition. Once all concrete attributes are denied to God, the seeker may only use ongoing apophatic claims (negative assertions or denials) to speak about the divine nature. We come to know God best by denying all false and untenable claims that can be made regarding "Him."

It would be a misunderstanding of Maimonides and the whole school of philosophic religion to think that there was no possibility left of passionate religious devotion to such a God. When we read the climactic concluding chapters of the *Guide* (3:51 and 54), as well as certain key passages in Maimonides' other works, it is clear that he represents a deep piety, one in which the human soul is utterly drawn to the delights of sublime contemplation, remaining attached to God at all times, even while involved in the duties that bind us to this world. There are ways in which the term "mystic" might well be applied to the great philosopher, even though most students of Maimonides have balked at the term.[36] His is a highly refined philosophic piety, one that it is hard to imagine being shared beyond a rather limited intellectual elite.

From Philosophy to Kabbalah

The Kabbalists (and even if Maimonides may be termed a "mystic," he surely was no Kabbalist) represent a related, but quite different, elite vision of Jewish spiritual life. They shared with the philosophers the quest for a pure and abstract notion of divinity. Both sought to discover within the seemingly naive biblical/rabbinic heritage a font of profound truth about the nature of reality and the inner relatedness of God, world, and soul. Both understood that this would be accomplished by interpretation of Scripture in a new key, uncovering an esoteric layer of meaning. Like the philosophers, the Kabbalists believed it to be within their power to lift the veils of illusion that imprison the unenlightened mind and discover this sublime truth within Scripture. "Out of the depths I call You, O Lord" (Ps. 130:1) for the Kabbalist no longer means that he longs for God to rescue him from the depths of human despair; rather, it means that he, the mystic, calls God forth from His own inner depths,[37] those "places" in which divinity is hidden, and seeks to bring Him close. The person who was willing to walk the straight road of the disciplined religious life, including both the traditional commandments and the mental and devotional exercises prescribed by the particular school of thought, could achieve great gifts of insight, helping to redeem *shekhinah* from exile by restoring the divine presence to the lower world. While formally both Maimonidean philosopher and Kabbalist might have needed to claim that it was God who bestowed the gift of prophecy or enlightenment, they were united in their understanding that most of the journey to God was one of inward human training, the struggle to purify the mind and spirit.

The intimacy with God attained by such a process is not at all the same intimacy as that of the highly personal relationship with the Other that we discussed above. Here we are talking about absorption within an all-encompassing oneness of Being rather than the grace of being favored by the smiling countenance of the divine Beloved. The Maimonidean sought to align his mind perfectly with the Aristotelian Active Intellect, in order to attain the overflow of the divine mind into his, thus filling him with truth. The Kabbalist, through devotion to very specific esoteric forms of contemplation, sought to have *shekhinah* overflow with bounteous love, embracing him, drawing his soul "upward," and energizing the divine cosmos as a whole. There is an important difference between these two; it is only the Kabbalist, influenced by older and more mythic forms of religion, who sees his devotion affecting God and the cosmic order, not just his own soul. The Maimonidean would be quite horrified by such a claim. Yet the differences between them turn out to be quite subtle, shaded as they are by the fact that philosophers and mystics too are shaped by the contours of biblical and rabbinic imagery, which neither is willing to leave behind. The "Root of Roots" of the Aristotelian and the *eyn sof* ("the Endless") of the Kabbalist are supposedly not to be seen in personified terms. To do so would be to betray the most essential teachings of these schools of thought. Yet the works of both schools are replete with violations of that seemingly strictly held principle.[38] And surely the quest that leads one toward them is described quite passionately, either as fire within the soul or in the erotic language of the Song of Songs.

The Kabbalists resolved this tension between the abstract nature of God and the colorful and passionate religious life by describing a second aspect of divinity in which the endless and indescribable *eyn sof* reveals itself to contain ten *sefirot* ("numbers," stations, or stages of divine self-manifestation), which are filled with all the color, imagery, and mythic/erotic nuance that were lacking in God as "One of Ones" or "Primordial Nothing."[39] These represent the divine energy source in process, the stages of the flow that leads from abstraction to the constant reinvigorating of this world by the emanation of divine blessing (*shefa'*). Once the *sefirot* are in place, the strategy of the Kabbalist becomes the very antithesis of that of the philosopher, though leading to the same ultimate goal. If the Maimonidean seeks to purify one's thinking about God by questioning and progressively *removing* all anthropomorphic and anthropopathic images, the Kabbalist seeks to mentally flood the reader with an overwhelming *excess* of images, leading to the conclusion that the divine reality must ultimately transcend them all. Virtually *everything*, almost any noun encountered in Scripture and any object within the natural realm, becomes an image term that leads back to contemplation of some aspect of God. If the same element or stage of self-revelation within the Godhead may be called by a diverse set of names (the third *sefirah*, for example, is "mother," "womb," "jubilee," "fountain," "repentance," "upper Eden," "heart," "understanding," "palace," and a host more), it becomes clear that all of these are somehow pointing beyond themselves and that no single name, image, or symbol fully expresses just what this *sefirah* (or symbol cluster) is. "You are the One who fills all names," as the *Tiqquney Zohar* famously expresses it, "but You Yourself have no specific name."[40]

In Kabbalah too we find an interesting mix of vertical and internal religious language. Being medieval in its original formulations, the notion of hierarchy within the divine process is fully accepted, as indicated by the well-known Kabbalistic charts. The first of the ten *sefirot* is known as *keter 'elyon*, "uppermost crown,"[41] and is placed at the head of what appears to be a descending order. It is also referred to as *'atiqa*, "the ancient one," indicating that the flow of emanation, itself beyond both time and space, can be translated into either the spatial or the temporal order. But the *sefirot* are also depicted as circles within circles. Sometimes *eyn sof* is presented as the innermost reality, and the journey toward this abstract deity beyond Nothingness is a trek inward, toward the core of Being. Other charts show the divine surrounding all beings, with *eyn sof* on the "outside" of reality, the *sefirot* "descending" inward toward earth. Indeed, the original source of the term *sefirot*, *Sefer Yetzirah*, presents them as "their end linked to their beginning and their beginning to their end," most likely a series of interlocking circles. Later Kabbalists returned to this picture when claiming (adapting a well-known philosophic adage) that the final *sefirah*, *shekhinah*, was directly joined to the highest, "last in deed but first in thought."[42]

This is not the place to offer a full accounting of the *sefirot* and their many meanings in Kabbalistic symbolism.[43] For our purpose, some brief highlights will do. *Keter* or *'atiqa* stands at the head of the process, the first emanation out of the unknowable reservoir of Being called only *eyn sof*, "the Endless." From the viewpoint of human experience, it is the most recondite realm imaginable, the deepest Self of the cosmos, far beyond personality or relationship. *Keter* reflects only the desire of Being to become manifest, not yet bearing any specific or concrete content. Out of *keter* emerge the first primal pair, *hokhmah* and *binah*, "wisdom" and "contemplation." These conceive (in both senses of the term) the first point of reality, thus beginning the flow of energy that will devolve into all of existence. Their first offspring is the sixfold divine person known as the blessed Holy One, the male deity of biblical/rabbinic tradition. "God," in other words, is born out of the deeper, more mysterious realms within the Godhead. In the

Zohar's radical reconstruction of the opening verse of Genesis, *elohim* ("God") is the object rather than the subject of the sentence.[44] This personified deity, while made up of six elements, is centered in the locus called *tif'eret* ("glory"), and is often called by that name. The last of the ten, as I have already indicated, is *shekhinah*, the feminine consort or bride of the Holy One. In classical Kabbalah she is depicted as a truly liminal figure, straddling the "upper" (inner divine) and "lower" universes; she is the source in which all the divine energy is gathered, thence to be distributed to the lower worlds. In later Hasidism, however, the old rabbinic meaning of the term *shekhinah* is revived, and she is taken again to represent the immanent presence of divinity throughout this world. In that sense the world is understood to exist "within" God, rather than being entirely "other."

The Kabbalists chose to occupy themselves with a series of contemplative exercises that both described and taught one how to traverse an increasingly complicated realm that divided the fragmented consciousness of this-worldly perception from the unitive reality of God. The notion of four "worlds," each of them conceived in the same decadic structure, was one vehicle for this more richly elaborated cosmic picture. So too was the notion that each of the ten *sefirot* was itself divisible into ten, containing by implication all the others within it. This led, especially in the most fully articulated system of Rabbi Moses Cordovero (1522–1570), to an essential symbolic "grid" of some four hundred combined entities, rather than ten *sefirot*. Devotional exercises and interpretation of prayers all had to be fitted to a particular locus within an increasingly complicated cosmic map.

This complicating of the contemplative system or "filling up" of cosmic space went much farther in the new Kabbalah promulgated by the disciples of Isaac Luria (1534–1572).[45] Luria was a bold and innovative mythical thinker, one who focused devotional attention on the process of *tiqqun*, or the repair and restoration of the broken universe (or the exiled *shekhinah*), with much greater specificity than any previous Kabbalist. As his system came to dominate, this delineation of multiple cosmic realms and inner stages of "maturation" in each of these led to a virtual atomization of the spiritual universe, each step in the uplifting and restoration of the cosmos associated with intensive concentration on devotional exercises attached to the prayer book, to the commandments, to alternative spellings and vocalizations of the divine name, or to particular moments on the Jewish religious calendar. The mystical oneness of God that underlay the whole system, flowing through and nurturing the cosmos, was largely obscured by the "crowded" heavens and the great attention the worshipper needed to pay to the particular details underlying each "unification" of the upper realms. The essential insights of Kabbalah, soon to be weakened from within by mystical heresies and challenged from without by the rise of modern science, also partially collapsed under the weight of their own overelaboration.

From the late sixteenth century, Kabbalah became the dominating language of Jewish theology for some two hundred years. Hasidism, the next important stage in the development of Jewish God-consciousness, is both a continuation of and a rebellion against this growing Kabbalistic consensus.[46] The great teachers of Hasidism were religious revivalists, out to provide simple and direct access to the transformative vision of the Ba'al Shem Tov (or BeShT, 1700–1760) by which they had been captivated. That vision is best encapsulated by the ancient phrases that became daily watchwords of the new Hasidic piety: "The whole earth is filled with His glory! There is no place devoid of Him!" The BeShT described a world overflowing with the bounteous presence of God, accessible everywhere and at each moment to any Jew with inner eyes and ears open.[47] This vision, to be celebrated in joyous transformation of everyday life, was the essential message of Torah. All the rest of Jewish teaching was to serve as a vehicle for bringing about this awareness (*da'at*). The ensuing generations of Hasidic preachers, themselves raised in the Kabbalistic tradition, sought to strip it of what they saw as burdensome complexity and to turn directly to the task of describing the experience of intimacy with God, with an emphasis on the emotional side of that experience. If God was to be found within all things by a simple opening of the inner eye, there was no need for the edifice of symbolism. Most Hasidic teachings turned away from the Lurianic meditations; even the imagery of the *sefirot* themselves was mostly diverted to serve as a tool of religious psychology. They left in place only the "highest" and "lowest" of the divine manifestations, *hokhmah* and *malkhut*.[48] The former, described as *ayin* ("Nothingness") in the classical Hasidic sources,[49] stood for the utterly unknowable God, the One prior to all content or delineation. The latter was another name for *shekhinah*, the indwelling Godliness that fills the universe, or inside which the universe itself exists. God as *malkhut* is discoverable in each and every moment of existence.[50] This aspect of the Godhead is described as *yesh* ("Being"), divinity filled with worldliness, or world filled with God. The essential mystical task, as described in the school of the Maggid of Miedzyrzec, is to realize the unity of these two stages within God. "Being is Nothingness; Nothingness is Being!" is another early Hasidic watchword.

The metaphysical structure underlying Hasidism consists of a two-fold dialectical process. Divine self-revelation is constant, uniquely present in every being and in each moment, resulting in the ever-increasing variegation of being and thus in the seeming breakup of cosmic unity into ever-smaller fragments of existence. "Seeming" is the key word here, as the deeper reality of unbroken divine oneness is the ultimate truth that is to be rediscovered and restored as a visible face of reality. Both world and Torah are products of this intentional but ultimately delusive self-fragmenting of Y-H-W-H. It is in the realms of both daily life ("serving through corporeal things") and specific religious praxis, including prayer and study, that one is to seek out and reveal the hidden unity of Being, all roads leading back to the monistic truth. The illusion of cosmic fragmentation and distance from God is a "gift" given to the human mind in order to enable us to engage in the labors of restoration.

Philosophical sophistication or consistency was hardly the strength of these revivalist preachers, most of whose works are written in homiletical form. There are some relative exceptions to this rule, however, especially in the writings of Rabbi Shneur Zalman of Liadi, the founder of the HaBaD school, and his close disciple Rabbi Aaron of Staroselje.[51] These carry the insights of the BeShT and the Maggid forward into a clearly delineated panentheistic theology of Judaism.

While God as *eyn sof* remains utterly transcendent and mysterious, the light it gives forth shines through both in the *ayin* that surrounds existence and the *yesh* that fills it. The task of the religious mind is to understand that these make up but a single light, manifest in Torah and commandments (the self-revelation of God) as it is manifest throughout the world, since "Creation" itself is nothing but another self-manifestation of the divine glory. The pantheistic tendencies and insights found throughout the earlier mystical tradition are here presented in their most radical and systematic fashion.

With the elimination of all the intermediary *sefirot*, this Hasidism essentially gives up on the Kabbalistic faith in emanation. Instead it creates a theology that understands God as the eternal dialectical dance between presence and transcendence, between the revealed and the mysterious, *ḥokhmah* (sometimes parsed as *KoaH MaH*, a spiritualized Prime Matter) and *malkhut* or *shekhinah*, God's earthly indwelling presence. In a sense *ḥokhmah* functions here as a stand-in for *eyn sof*, considered too recondite even to be evoked in such a conversation. It is the deep and mysterious well out of which all existence is drawn. But the point of many an early HaBaD Hasidic homily is that these two are one; the seeming separation between them exists in our eyes alone. Essentially we are at all times fully at one with our Source. *Tsimtsim*, the alleged self-removal of God from cosmic space, is naught but the illusion of our existence as separate beings, though an illusion within which we are expected — even commanded — to live.

The Hebrew term used to speak of the intimate relationship between God and the individual, throughout both the philosophical and mystical sources, is *devekut*, often translated as "attachment" or "cleaving." The verb is used several times in the book of Deuteronomy to describe the relationship between God and His faithful ("You who cleave to Y-H-W-H your God are all alive this day" [4:4]; "to walk in all His ways and to cleave to Him" [11:22]), and it is from here that it enters the later Jewish religious vocabulary. But the term is also used in a very telling and well-known single instance in Genesis 2:24: "Therefore shall a man leave his father and mother and cleave to his wife, and they shall be one flesh." There has been much discussion among scholars of Jewish mysticism as to whether and how frequently *devekut* means actual union with God, entailing a loss of individual identity.[52] But the human experience that stands behind *devekut* is also that of marriage, including moments of great intimacy and even union, but implying as well the long-standing marital fidelity that leads a couple to see themselves as one. *Devekut* with God is entering into a similar state of oneness. In its highest form it may indeed be described as mystical union, a moment when the self is completely absorbed and overwhelmed by the reality of oneness, the climax of religious experience. Yet it also allows for the soul to return to itself, enriched and even transformed by the unitive moment but still able to live and act as a separate spirit — indeed, still able to maintain its existence within the body.

The classical Jewish piety of the Middle Ages and later, to which I am pointing here, is to be found within both philosophy and mysticism. It is characterized by what I would like to call a *union of intimacy and abstraction*. Abstraction demands that God be understood as nothing less than the unity of all being, the One that underlies all the infinitely varied and changing faces of reality. It is the One after which there is no "two," a One that knows no other. The power to describe such oneness was not generally native to the language of the ancient Hebrews. It was only in borrowing and adaptation from the Greeks that it could be articulated. But the *longing* for this abstract One was ever described in language taken from the personalist terminology of ancient Jewish tradition, both the paternal imagery of the old liturgy and the erotic passion of the Song of Songs.

Mystical Judaism Lost and Reclaimed

In popular Judaism, and especially in the religious education of ongoing generations, the philosophical edge of that language was intentionally dulled, and the old personalist language of the biblical and rabbinic sources overwhelmed it. As modern Judaism emerged, beginning in the eighteenth century, Kabbalah was hidden away and proclaimed "outside the mainstream," as I have indicated. The profound theology of Hasidism was completely unknown to Westernized Jews, who had been taught to dismiss this form of Jewish piety as the senseless jabber of ignorant Jews still living in the Middle Ages. Maimonidean philosophy nominally fared better in the modern era. It was praised by the post-Mendelssohnian generations as the apex of enlightened Judaism.[53] But while it may have been taught in rabbinical colleges and graduate seminars, it did not filter down into popular Judaism in either Orthodox or liberal circles. The intellectual difficulty of Maimonides' tour de force combined with an old fear of the heretical implications of some of his teachings to keep him out of the hands of most Jews. What dominated instead was a Judaism of rather simplistic rabbinic faith, the religion, to say it in capsule form, of RaShI rather than that of either Maimonides or the Zohar. Here the God-idea was carried in the most ancient of metaphors, those of Father and King, stripped of all the later subtleties and refinements. The liturgy, mostly derived from a Judaism that historically preceded both philosophy and Kabbalah, retained its key role in shaping the popular Jewish imagination. Knowing little of either the philosophical or the mystical tradition, most modern Jews thought of Judaism's God in rather naive and childlike terms. Once they came to reflect on the faith they had inherited, this Judaism unsurprisingly was rejected. Jews came to be among the most highly secularized populations of the modern era.[54]

Yet the ever-evolving and ever-revealing One finds its ways. Awareness of the One burrows through the labyrinth of the human religious imagination across all the cultural divides that once defined us. The story as I have told it up to this point is entirely a Western one, running from the religious world of the ancient Near East, through the Hebrew Bible, and thence into Judaism, also shaping both Christianity and Islam. These three religions exist in an intertwined relationship throughout history, influencing and borrowing from one another in more irregular and complex ways than had once been imagined. For today's picture, however, we have to step beyond this Western-dominated view and notice other streams of influence. In our times the borrowing and adaptation that once came into the

Jewish imagination through Greco-Islamic channels seems to be taking place again in the very fascinating and new encounter between Judaism and the religious languages of India, Japan, and Tibet. Westerners, including many Jews who think they cannot "believe in God," meaning that they reject the naive images of the deity absorbed in childhood, find themselves attracted to deep meditations on the oneness of Being adapted for Westerners from both Buddhist and Vedantic teachings.[55] These insights are being brought home by returning Jewish voyagers and integrated into our tradition much as the garbled teachings of Plato and Aristotle were, so many centuries ago. So far this has been taking place mostly in the personal practice of theological amateurs, but the time has come for serious thinkers to take note of it and find the proper language for what I believe can be a welcome renewal of deeper Jewish faith, one coming about through influence from unexpected quarters.

In this context, the time has arrived for Jewish panentheism to step out of the closet, as it were. This faith that understands *yihud ha-shem*, the divine unity, to refer to the underlying oneness of all being has long existed in Jewish circles, though clothed in the earlier and scripturally reinforced language of personalism. Implicit in the Zohar, where the energy of existence is constantly flowing into all creatures from the inexhaustible source of Being called *eyn sof*, a Jewish panentheism is described most fully in the early texts of Hasidism that I have mentioned. There it is quite explicit in the theological literature, though again often obscured in the more popular face that Hasidism tried to show. As the movement survived initial persecution and grew to find acceptance as a form of ultra-Orthodoxy, it jettisoned its more daring and innovative theological stances.[56] Hillel Zeitlin (1874–1942), the neo-Hasidic thinker whose work has so influenced me, tried to revive it. His contemporary Rabbi Abraham Isaac Kook (1865–1935) was quite close to him in this matter. More recent Jewish theological voices, much consumed with other "local" and pressing Jewish issues (Holocaust and survival, statehood and diaspora, law and authority), expressed little interest in this essential question of reconceiving the relationship between God and world.[57]

Today, in the face of the newly emerging dialogue between classically "Eastern" and "Western" modes of religious thought, there is a new focus on the quest for alternatives to personalist theism. I understand this as yet another moment in the ongoing call from within to push our understanding forward, to participate in the evolving process of divine self-manifestation in the human mind and spirit. We are now witness to a renewed discussion of states of mind that were well understood by Jewish mystics of prior ages, though discussed in abstruse Kabbalistic language. Now they are presented to us in Indian or Buddhist religious categories, another set of culturally unfamiliar garments. We need to build bridges that will allow contemporary seekers to overcome these problems of language, much as Hasidism once did in rendering the Kabbalistic tradition accessible through simplification. The Judaism emerging from such a process would clearly assert the holiness of all life, seeing the face of God both in the uniqueness of each individual creature and in the underlying and mysterious unity of all. The worship of the personified "God" needs to be clearly described as a symbolic way to express this truth and to deepen its expression through the rich echo chambers of a traditional religious language.

Here too I turn to Kabbalah for a way to say this within the context of Judaism. The Zohar understands well that the personal God-figure, in both its male and female articulations (*tif'eret* and *malkhut*) is a series of symbolic constructions, less than the divine absolute. In encouraging speculation that goes beyond the God of biblical memory and even seeks out the origins (in fact, the "birth") of that God in the recondite mythology of the uppermost *sefirot*, the mystics were creating a theological position that they rarely dared to articulate clearly.[58] The personal God is a symbolic bridge between transcendent mystery (that which by definition the mind cannot grasp) and a humanity that constantly reaches forth toward it. Because that "reaching" needs to be undertaken by the whole of the human self, including emotion and body as well as mind, the "bridge" needs to be one to which we can most wholly respond, a projection of our own form. The mysterious reality beyond, that which the Kabbalist would call *'atiqa*, "the Ancient

One," or *eyn sof*, "the Endless," exists before and after our reaching out, and is none other than the underlying oneness of Being.

At long last, I return to the urgency with which I opened this discussion. I am indeed a neo-Hasidic Jew, and the insight of the Ba'al Shem is one that has become my own. The intimations of holiness I encounter in both time and space serve as windows through which I catch brief glimpses of an underlying cosmic unity, insights into a deeper truth about being. The panentheistic reading of Judaism I offer here is a theology that seeks to be honest to such moments of experience. But I offer it also as a vehicle through which to transform the way we live on earth. All of existence is holy. Every creature, whether alive and sensate or "inanimate," is nothing other than the sacred presence of Y-H-W-H, hidden and revealed through yet another of its endless masks. No creature is truly separate from my own self, since I too am but one of those masks of God. My "self" is nothing other than a manifestation of the single Self of being, having ever so temporarily arranged its molecules in a pattern that allows for this particular manifestation. My love and reverence for all creatures, including all the human and nonhuman others I encounter, derives from the awareness that we are all one in Y-H-W-H. This awareness calls upon me to know and to care for those others, as I partake in and celebrate the diversity through which our shared inner Self becomes present in the world.

But to become fully at home in Judaism these insights into *qedushat ha-hayyim* (the sanctity of all life) and oneness will have to adapt themselves to the Jewish language of intimacy as well. Even though I understand that God is no true Other to the soul, and I see us on the path toward a monistic consciousness, I continue to speak the Jewish language of love. This language includes both "Behold, thou art fair, My beloved" (Song of Songs 1:16) and "Blessed are *You* Y-H-W-H, our God, eternal and universal Ruler." My call for devotion to this language is no mere traditionalism or nostalgia for a naive faith once held. I write as a mystic and a monist, one who believes in (and in rare and precious moments has come to know) the essential truth that there is only one Being, and that all distinctions between self and other and between God, world, and soul represent partial betrayals of that truth. In my liturgical and communal religious life, however, I continue to speak this dualistic religious language. I do so because I remain a Westerner. I continue to live most of my life, as we all do, on a plane of duality, in a life experience where the distinction between you and me and the borders between us are pretty important things to remember. My task is to educate and awaken *that* self (the "lesser" mind of *qatnut*, to use the Hasidic term), in my own being as well as in others, to the reality of the single Truth. It is the self who lives on that plane who has to be taught and reminded, day by day and moment by moment, that the world of multiplicity and fragmentation is not ultimate reality. That self is the one who has to be brought across the bridge. In order to do that teaching, I need to employ a language that such a self can understand, one that will seduce and uplift the ordinary human mind. Simply to proclaim and repeat the monist abstraction to one who lives in duality will not do. For this purpose we have been given the great gift of human intimacy, the "mirror of love," if you will, to hold up as a bridge between the worlds of the two and the One. To remind the self of the greatest moments of intimacy and expansion it has known, to take the passion and longing that are such real parts of our shared humanity and to use them as channels toward that deeper truth, is to follow a path taken by mystics over many centuries. The God who is the object of our love, precisely because we bring ourselves forward in that love with such openheartedness and vulnerability, is the One who can lead us beyond the duality that "I love you" implies, toward that place where there is only One. Who more than the Ba'al Shem Tov stands to remind us that all love, even all of eros, is the fallen fruit of the great single love of God that animates the cosmos?[59] The language of love is a way in which soul and mind can address one another, each calling the other along to the great journey. "Deep calls to deep" (Ps. 42:8), to say it in the language of *midrash*: one aspect of human depth calls out to the other.

This same phrase, "deep calls unto deep," also offers us a hint as to how a contemporary understanding might view the old struggle between vertical and internal religious language. We would see both of them as aspects of consciousness, the highly complex human mind pushing and churning within itself to attain a higher (or more profound) grasp of being, both in its oneness and in its infinite complexity. To do this the mind has to combine its most sophisticated tools of abstract analysis with its most primitive instinctual rootedness in the One, its "reptilian brain." (In Kabbalistic language, where it is much easier to say this, the united male/female person, *tif'eret/malkhut*, has to go back to his/her deepest contemplative roots in *binah*, the inner womb of being, in order to receive the infinite grace of *'atiqa*, the ultimate source of divine light, the God beyond all "gods.")

The union of intimacy and abstraction I have described above is expressed in Judaism's special devotion to the name of God, the four-letter name referred to as *shem ha-meforash*, which I have represented here by the letters Y-H-W-H. God's "explicit" name is one that may never be written or pronounced. The name, as I suggested earlier, is an impossible configuration, a pseudo-noun, created out of the verb "to be," and should probably best be translated "was/is/will be." But the sounds that form the name also indicate abstraction. There is no firm consonant among them; the *y*, the *w*, and the *h* are all nothing more than shapings of the breath. Indeed, these letters are also used in ancient Hebrew to indicate vowel signs, showing that they are only marginally to be seen as "real" letters. The God who is ever blowing the breath of life into Adam's nostrils in the ongoing renewal of human life now turns out to *be* that very breath. The name of God is but a breath, nothing you can hold onto very firmly. Indeed, if you try to hold onto it, if you think that Y-H-W-H is a noun that indicates some substantial and definable entity, Scripture laughs at you as God becomes a verb again.

But at the same time that this word bears within it the Bible's most abstract notion of the deity, it also serves as a *name*. Names are fraught with both power and intimacy, in the ancient world as well as in our own. To know someone's name is to stand in relationship, to be able to call in such a way that the other must respond. "I raise him up because he knows My name" (Ps. 91:14). A pious Jew refers to *ha-shem yitbarakh*, "God's blessed name," in an intimate, familiar way of speaking. To call out God's name in prayer is to transcend all other words one might speak. In fact, a Hasidic teaching claims that in true prayer *every* word becomes a name of God.[60]

We do not fully speak the name. Y-H-W-H is too holy a word to be spoken. We for whom words come and go so easily are not allowed to pronounce this word, lest it be profaned by us. Instead we sheathe it in the pious garb of *adonai*, "my Lord." But each time we pronounce that word in prayer, the Kabbalists tell us, we are to see the letters Y-H-W-H standing before us, a sort of verbal icon, visually filling us with an intensity of divine presence that we dare not permit our mouths to speak.[61]

The great calling out of God's name is the recitation of *shema' yisra'el* — "Hear O Israel, Y-H-W-H our God, Y-H-W-H is One!" The Torah tells us to speak this verse twice each day, upon rising at dawn and before going to sleep. It is a first prayer taught to young children and it has graced the lips of martyrs from Rabbi Akiva in Roman times to pious Jews in the Holocaust. No act of piety is more characteristic of Judaism than this calling out of *shema' yisra'el*. It is a statement of intimacy, devotion, and abstraction all at once. Its recitation is referred to in our sources as *yihud ha-shem*, the proclamation (but for the Kabbalist "the *effecting*") of God's oneness.

The daily recitation of this verse has been the object of a remarkable wealth of reflection throughout Jewish theology. The Zohar contains a particularly wide array of readings of the *shema'*.[62] But here I will content myself by quoting the rather simple mystical confession of a Hasidic master, Rabbi Yehudah Aryeh Leib of Ger (1847–1904), author of *Sefat Emet*. In a letter to his children and grandchildren he spoke with unusual directness about the *shema'* and its meaning: "The proclamation of oneness that we declare each day in saying *Shema' Yisra'el* . . . needs to be understood as it truly is. That which is entirely clear to me . . . based on the holy writings of great Kabbalists, I am obliged to reveal to you. . . . The meaning of 'Y-H-W-H is one' is not that He is the only true God, negating other gods (though that too is true!). But the meaning is deeper than that: there is no being other than God. [This is true] even though it seems otherwise to most people.

. . . Everything that exists in the world, spiritual and physical, is God Himself. . . . These things are true without a doubt. Because of this, every person can become attached to God wherever he is, through the holiness that exists in every single thing, even corporeal things. . . . This is the foundation of all the mystical formulations in the world."[63]

three

TORAH: WORD OUT OF SILENCE

Sacred Language Then and Now

To find this message — that God alone exists — at the heart of Judaism is to read Torah with the mystics' eyes. You may find God wherever you are. Everything — "even" the corporeal world — will lead you back to God, since none of it has existence outside God. There is only One. This is the essential teaching of mystics in every tradition; their task is to read tradition as a vehicle to convey this message. Although the core teaching seems on the face of things to be entirely simple, it cuts so deeply against the grain of ordinary human perception and daily life experience that it needs to be reinforced with all the power that tradition can muster.

For Jews, this process leads first to Torah. The sacred text of Judaism has to be reread to convey this singular message. But how could one even imagine this? On the face of it, Torah seems to be a very this-worldly document, filled with human stories, laws, commandments, and not a word about God alone existing. The transformative effort is indeed a massive one. Every word of Torah, every letter, even the vowel points and the musical notations, has been taken by the Kabbalists to point to the hidden inner realm of the *sefirot*, a symbolic accounting of how multiplicity in all its forms emerged (and continues to emerge, in each moment) from the mysterious and unknown One. That is Kabbalah's essential truth. The "world of the *sefirot*" is a mediating realm between the One and the many, a network of chambers through which the simple energy of the One is constantly radiated into myriad diverse forms. Torah too is such a mediating realm, standing (and flowing) between the One, beyond language, and the human community, constituted by speech. Hence it is given the role of transforming our consciousness through its own transformation into the mystical mode, something that seems quite far from it (as from us!) on first encounter.

The seekers of former generations, especially those living in the three great ages of Jewish mystical creativity (thirteenth-century Spain, sixteenth-century Safed, and Eastern European Hasidism of the late eighteenth century), so fully inhabited the language of tradition that it seemed completely natural to them to appropriate it in this way. It was, you might say, their only garment, and they fully and quite unselfconsciously adapted it to serve their own spiritual needs. For the Spanish Kabbalists it was obvious that a particular ritual prescribed in the Torah effected the union of divine "male" and "female," opening the upper (I would say "inner") channels so that the infinite energies could flow through them and constantly renew all of life. They understood prayer as a way of "returning all things to their root" in the highest of divine realms. All of these exercises are hierarchical expressions, later shaped into endless refinements and gradations, of the assertion that all things are one with their Source and can be restored to it. Any *perud*, or separation, from the One (whether taken as real or illusory) is to be overcome by the spiritual efforts of the pious (read: the Kabbalists), who are constantly reinfusing all of being with the energy of the One. This is in effect a new Judaism created by the mystics, who saw their own task as one of clearing cosmic channels and bringing about "unifications" between hidden divine realms. The Safed Kabbalists, especially the followers of Isaac Luria, endlessly sought to identify these channels and formulate specific remedies for the clearing of each. While the channels are described in ontological terms and are thought of as actually existing in the "upper" realms, there was a parallel claim that the same exercises offered a purification of the devotee's own soul and inner life. Hasidism stands fully within this tradition. It turned most of its interest to the inner human channels, changing cosmic activism into a devotional psychology, a way of transforming the inner life. As a popular religious movement, it taught that God can be worshipped — and God-consciousness attained — through the most ordinary human activities. But the Hasidic *tsaddik* is still depicted as the "channel" through which divine blessing flows into the world.[1] This flow of blessing is nothing other than *shefa'*, the lifeblood of the constant renewal of being, without which nothing could exist. As it comes into the world, it blesses all, especially the community surrounding the *tsaddik*, in both material and spiritual ways.

In thinking about a mystical theology of Judaism for the current age, our claims will be somewhat different, less sweeping and more modest. We need to assert them with a combination of *spiritual openness* and *intellectual honesty*. When we do this, we will find ourselves with a religious life unlike that of the past, though one deeply nurtured by its legacy. As postmoderns we cannot simply appropriate a premodern system and expect it to work for us, even if the terminology and metaphors are updated.[2] We do not, and should not expect ourselves to, believe in the same way as our premodern forebears. We do not have, and are not about to have, all the "answers" to the nature and meaning of human existence that our ancestors used to think they possessed.

Spiritual openness means the humility to acknowledge that we do not understand all of existence. In ways renamed by modernity, we share this admission with earlier generations. Despite the great gains in scientific understanding, we are all too aware of modernist hubris in thinking that we have "it all" figured out. There are realities semi-acknowledged by scientists (Other dimensions of being? Senses unknown to us? "Dark matter?" "Channels" and "charges" of unknown sources of energy?) that we do not comprehend, but that may shape existence in very profound ways. These possibly account for many phenomena that cannot be otherwise explained; they may be part of the mysterious and unknown realms frequently invoked by the religious language of prior eras (the "other side," "worlds without number," and so forth). We do not claim knowledge of these, but we understand that they may play some part in mystical insight and teachings. The channels that lead back and forth between *nothingness* and *being* surely belong to these hidden realms. Our own experience and the accounts by mystics in many traditions help us to know that the distinction between "Nothing" and "nothing" is surely no mere semantic game. The turning away from externals toward inwardness, from variety and multiplicity toward inner oneness, exposes us to dimensions of reality unknown to the superficial senses. These hidden realms may exercise great influence over our psychic lives, in ways we are hardly able to articulate. Our "Kabbalah" includes our acknowledging these mysterious aspects of existence. When we appropriate Kabbalistic language, we have an eye toward these domains of the unknown.

On the other hand, we cannot claim, as the Kabbalists once did, to have *mastery* over these realms. Intellectual honesty demands that we admit to being Western-shaped. This includes a commitment to open-mindedness and the importance of questioning dogmatic assumptions, no matter where they originate. We are seekers of a new postmodern path into areas neglected by the rationalist and scientific mind that has so dominated thinking in recent centuries. But that does not mean that we can or should leave all of our modern baggage behind us. We understand the power of myth and symbol, their ability to transport us to deeper states of mind, to realities not given to discursive or scientific description. We accept and embrace those realities as such, but we also do not submit to them fully, which would require giving up our critical faculties. However attractive these deep insights may be, we do not make a literal or historical truth claim for the sources that proclaim them. A literalist or simplistic reading of the premodern Kabbalistic maps and teachings makes no sense in our day. We do not have an infallible guide to those unknowable aspects of existence. Rather, we have a set of tools (or perhaps multiple sets) by which we can struggle to achieve *insight* into these unknown realms as well as into ourselves. The distinction is an important one. Kabbalah as a "science" or an all-embracing truth system was rightly trounced, along with alchemy and other prior cosmologies, in early modern times. Many of the claims once made for Kabbalah, including those that veer close to the edges of magic, should be questioned in the context of our contemporary religious path.[3] We do not possess a set of theurgic keys that will sustain or transform the cosmic order. We are not certain that any person has the power to bend the divine will (whatever we might mean by that term) to our own. What we believe to be of greatest value in the Kabbalistic legacy is largely psychological, in the broadest sense of that term, having to do with *psyche*, or "soul," as well as mind. Especially in its insights into deeper levels of human experience, reflecting on aspects of the contemplative mind that are still little understood, the mystical tradition has much to teach us. Insofar as we then come to see each of our individual minds as a subset or a manifestation of a single collective Mind, coursing through all of existence, we may move to another level of truth claim. But this is still far from the old view that Kabbalah contained all the "secrets of Creation." In our day, if we want to understand how the universe originated, we will most sensibly turn to nuclear physicists and astronomers, not to Kabbalists. But if we want to appreciate the depths to which humans can enter into transtemporal states, including the attempt to open the mind to identify with Being as it first emerged, we might do well to study the testimony of the Zohar. When we then discover that the Zoharic language around contemplation of the uppermost *sefirot*, based on experience of inner mind, bears a striking resemblance to some of the language used by today's scientists in talking about the first few milliseconds of existence, we can only stand in silent awe. There is indeed much that we do not know.

But here we need to restate the goal. We seek a Jewish spiritual language that will serve us as a reminder and a gateway to the oneness of Being. Torah can still serve in that role, raising our spiritual awareness and guiding us into these mysterious aspects of existence, as it has done for so many generations. We continue to revere the profound mysteries that so many teachers have brought forth by delving deeply into the text of Torah, and we seek to carry that process forward, revealing old — or new — secrets appropriate to our current era. Like the natural world, Torah too may contain entire dimensions that are not yet apparent to us. These may disclose themselves to us through new interpretive tools, or by fresh new uses of the old ways of reading. Or we may find that simple concentration on the Hebrew letters themselves can lead into deeper states of mind.[4] Study of the Hebrew language's system of roots and the patterns of association that emerge from it can also serve as a powerful source of insights, used by the masters of Midrash over many centuries. All of these methods of reading, deeply anchored in tradition, remain accessible to us, and none of them requires a literalist or naive view of revelation. We should strive to remain open to learning on as many levels, and by as many methods, as we are able to. In this way, Torah will become for us, as it was for earlier generations, a way to navigate those mysterious channels of existence. To put it differently, Torah — both its study and the life it calls forth — is our way of reshaping mystery into meaning, of rendering the Silence articulate, without losing our sense of awe as we stand before the great Unknown.

Rereading Judaism as a vehicle for mystical consciousness requires that we enter into the ancient stream of Torah interpretation, the creative lifeblood of the Jewish tradition. We need to become *intimate* with the Torah text, an intimacy that combines familiarity and open-heartedness. Knowing and loving the text in this way permits us to turn to the tools of interpretation, both old and new, allowing them to do their work of seducing the spirit, of awakening our minds to the deeper truth of the One that underlies all being. These readings of Torah are *poetic* attempts to reinvigorate our spiritual lives through a contemporary remythologization of Judaism. They will all lead us to the Torah beyond the text, the word that embodies all of divine silence, that Torah of which it is said that "God looked into Torah and created the world." But to approach this goal, we first need to achieve some understanding of Torah itself and where we stand in relation to it.

Reflection on intellectual honesty and its role in articulating a contemporary theology requires another few steps. As I said at the outset of our journey together, my own naive faith was challenged by critical study of Jewish sources as well as by personal struggles around questions of providence and theodicy. In the coming discussion of Torah I make no literalist assumptions about the historicity of the text or its revealed origins. I speak out of deep relationship with the Torah text as we have it, out of unceasing engagement (including moments of outrage and frustration), but not as a believer in it as resulting from divine dictation. The biblical scholar's understanding of the text's complex origins and editing are a level of truth that I recognize as valid. In my religious life, however, I continue to embrace the text as a whole, as sacred artifact rather than as historical document. I enter into the text as a participant in an unending conversation among generations of Jews, enriched but essentially unfazed by critical perspectives. I recognize this as a postmodern perspective. I rejoice in my renewed freedom to be a living participant in the hearing, articulation, and constant reinterpretation of Torah that has been the creative lifeblood of our tradition for many centuries. Liberated from modernity's insistence both on the literal truth/untruth test (Spinoza's legacy) and on the demand for critical distance, I am able to reenter the stream of tradition uncrippled by the sense of detachment and alienation that stood as modernity's hallmark.

I have been able to make the leap from modernity to postmodernity across the bridge of a mystical faith, one that roots itself unabashedly in the ground of collective human inner experience and in the assumption that the mind can stretch to embrace realms of consciousness and reality beyond those ordinarily considered, even in philosophical discussions. The ability to transcend the ego-self (and hence to escape the prison of self-consciousness that so characterizes modernity), to accept the coincidence of opposites, and to glimpse realities that cannot be expressed in ordinary language are all widely attested in the teachings of mystical masters throughout the world, including our Jewish sources. In placing my own feeble moments of mystical insight in the context of these, I find myself liberated to enter fully into the serious and committed gamesmanship of *talmud torah*, or to respond positively to the invitation of the Ba'al Shem Tov to "enter, you and all your household, into the word" (a reading of Genesis 7:1). Everything I say below should be understood in this spirit.

What Is Torah?

Torah means "teaching." The word is found numerous times in the text of the work we call the Torah, referring to various specific teachings ("This is the teaching of the sin-offering" [Lev. 7:2], and so on) or to groups of teachings given to Israel on a particular occasion. It can be used in the broadest sense in the world; any teaching, instruction, doctrine can be referred to as *torah*, a term that in itself contains no judgment as to truth or legitimacy of content. In modern secularized Hebrew it is used in just that way. A Hebrew book about "the documentary hypothesis" regarding the Pentateuch was called *Torat ha-Te'udot* (literally, "the Torah of the Documents"), with no irony intended. In classical Jewish parlance, *torah* retains a more specifically religious meaning. "If they tell you 'There is wisdom to be found among the nations,' believe them. But if they say 'There is Torah to be found among them,' do not believe."[5] Torah in this old rabbinic epigram is distinguished from *hokhmah*, the more neutral and universal "wisdom," which the nations do possess. It is specifically Jewish teaching, whose source, unlike mere human wisdom, lies in divine revelation and in the covenantal bond between God and Israel. "Moses received Torah from Sinai and passed it to Joshua, who passed it to the judges," says the superscription of the Mishnah.[6] Within this context, the meaning of *torah* can be as broad as "Jewish tradition," including all the teachings, practices, commentaries, law codes, homilies, and so forth, produced through the ages, or as narrow as *hamishah humshey Torah*, the Five Books of Moses. Pushed a bit harder, it can be so broad as to incorporate *hokhmah*, all of divine/human wisdom (since we are hardly in a position to distinguish between these two) and so narrow as to be squeezed into a single word or even a single letter. Both the broad expansion of Torah and its narrowing or concentration may serve to reshape Torah into a vessel of mystical understanding.[7]

"Upon commencing study of what body of material is one obligated to recite the blessing over Torah-study?" the Talmudic masters ask.[8] This is as close as they could come to what we would call a "definition" of Torah. Over Scripture? Surely the blessing must be recited! Over *midrash*, the rabbis' reinterpretation of Scripture's meaning? Yes, this too requires a blessing, because *midrash* is itself a sacred process. Over *mishnah*, the codified teachings of the sages? Indeed, recite the blessing; these too are holy. Over *talmud* (remember, this discussion takes place among the rabbis before there is "a Talmud!"), meaning our own ongoing discussion around the *mishnah* code? Yes, our discussion too requires a blessing. As the sages say of themselves in another context, "Are we mere reed cutters in the bog?"[9]—an old Babylonian idiom that would come out in Brooklynese as "What are we? Chopped liver?" By extension, if we keep the process open as it was meant to be,[10] "Oral Torah" is to be seen in its most expansive sense, including that which you and I are creating in this moment. All of it is part of revelation.

What do we mean by "Torah?" The Five Books of Moses seem to be a straightforward starting point. Weren't they all given at Sinai, as later tradition—certainly as insisted upon by Orthodoxy in recent centuries—seems to claim? But were they? Does such a claim, not mentioned in the Torah itself, make any sense? What about the last eight verses of Deuteronomy, beginning: "And Moses the servant of the Lord died there?" Were these too dictated by God on the mountain and written down by Moses (as one *midrash* suggests) in tears instead of ink? Or were they, as some early rabbinic voices already propose, added by Joshua after his master's death?[11] But then what of the whole book of Numbers, filled with tales of Israel's wanderings and rebellions in the years that followed Sinai? Were these too dictated and written down before they happened? How could that be? What would such a notion imply about human free will and determinism? Does it make any sense? All these questions arise prior to and independently of current understandings of the literary origins and editing of the Torah text. They are questions much discussed in earlier generations, but widely ignored by the pious and would-be pious of our own day. Remember that the three questions "What was spoken at Sinai?" "What is the Word of God?" and "What is Torah?" are not identical. God spoke both before and after Sinai, as the Torah itself clearly tells us, and "Torah" may include all of our commentaries, not just the written Word.

Common sense seems to force us toward the school of Rabbi Ishmael among the Tannaitic masters, teachers of the second and third centuries. "Torah speaks in human language," he insisted, and "Torah was given scroll by scroll,"[12] some of it indeed at Sinai, some of it from time to time spoken by God to Moses in the Tent of Meeting, and some of it (the entire book of Deuteronomy, Moses' final speeches) revealed only before Moses' death, on the plains of Moab.[13] This view is closest to what the Torah text itself seems to say. The view that it was all spoken at Sinai belongs to the school of Rabbi Akiva, a man of *uncommon* sense. Akiva is a mystic who sees Sinai as a moment beyond time, a revelatory/apocalyptic event. The eternal and transtemporal God for a moment crashes into linear, temporal history, transforming it totally. All the rules are suspended in that great mystical moment: past, present, and future are fused into eternal presence, making it an event that can thus be relived forever. The multiple moments of ordered time reveal themselves as a single one in the presence of the transtemporal reality of Y-H-W-H. It was in this sense that Akiva saw all of Torah given at once, all present at Sinai. *Akiva's view is not a misguided pseudo-historical claim but rather a mystical apocalyptic vision.* Akiva is speaking on a different level of reality, if you will, from an inner "place" where the ordinary linear sequence of time does not exist. In this spirit his disciples went on to say that "everything a faithful disciple is ever to teach has already been given in the path revealed to Moses at Sinai."[14] Later generations lost sight of the mystical character of that claim, and what had once been vision was transformed into dogma.

What, then, is the essence of Torah? What is truly revealed by God, however we might define that process? Is it only those passages that open: "The Lord said to Moses," containing law as distinct from narrative, *halakhah* but not *aggadah*? Jewish tradition was wise enough to avoid such a claim, knowing that the tale and the message were so deeply interwoven as to be inseparable, that legal precedent was often derived from the unpacking of narrative texts, and vice versa.[15]

Some early sources apply the term *torah* specifically to the ten commandments, that which the text itself quite clearly reads as the content of divine revelation at Sinai.[16] All the rest of Torah, it is then taught, is rooted in these. Both the spiritual truths and the moral imperatives needed to found community are rooted in these few words. There was once a tendency in Judaism to downplay the importance of the ten commandments. When the church fathers said that of the "Old Testament" Law only these commandments were still binding, defenders of rabbinic Judaism needed to insist that we follow all 613 commandments of the Torah, not merely ten. But then a poetic and exegetical tradition emerged to claim that there was no real difference between these views, that all the commandments could be derived from those original ten.[17] We will come back to the ten, which I believe should still stand as the basis of a contemporary religious and moral vision, one that both encompasses the best of Jewish teaching and reaches out beyond its borders, precisely because they are so well known and accepted throughout the Christian-influenced world.

The ten commandments. They were spoken by God and heard by all Israel. Surely *this* the text tells us plainly enough: "The Lord spoke all these words, saying" (Ex. 20:1). But a well-known Talmudic source tells it differently. All that God got to speak were the first two commandments, "I am the Lord your God" and "You shall have no other gods besides Me and make no graven image." Then Israel, stricken with terror, cried out to Moses and said: "You speak with us and we will listen, but let God not speak with us, lest we die."[18] The rest of the commandments were spoken by Moses, and thus are presumably fraught with the possibility of human fallibility.[19] Nevertheless, these first two, it is claimed, contain the entire Torah. "I am" bears within it all 248 positive commandments, and "No other gods . . . no graven image" is the basis of all the 365 prohibitions. All we need to accept, one might say, is God's "I am" and the notion that this alone is to shape and limit our behavior. All the rest will follow.

Franz Rosenzweig, at least in one of his formulations, went farther still, though possibly with similar intent.[20] In admitting " 'He came down [i.e., "Y-H-W-H descended upon Mount Sinai" (Ex. 19:2)]' already concludes the revelation; 'He spoke' is the beginning of interpretation, and certainly 'I am,' " Rosenzweig is saying that the *fact* of divine self-disclosure, before there is any speech at all, surpasses any content the words could possibly have, that the reality of God, hence the basis for all religion, is present in (and, indeed, precedes) the divine speech act itself.

Another version of this idea that God's revelation is without or beyond specific content is found in a Hasidic source quoted in the name of Rabbi Mendel of Rymanow.[21] Perhaps it can be seen as the final step in this progressive narrowing of revelation's funnel. Only the first letter of the commandments, the *aleph* of *anokhi*, "I am," was spoken by the divine voice alone, Rabbi Mendel claims. All the rest was revealed through Moses. Aleph signifies the number 1, referring to the unity of all in Y-H-W-H. That sufficed for the message. The *bet*, or number 2, of *bereshit*, the birth of duality in Creation (since "creature" appears to be other than its "Creator"), is now replaced by the all-embracing *aleph*. All the rest is humanly transmitted commentary.

But the perceptive reader will note (with Gershom Scholem)[22] that the letter *aleph*, if unmarked by a vowel point, is utterly silent, nothing more than an intake of breath. Is this all God has to say? Or does the divine voice in fact only make room, through an act of *tsimtsum*, self-limitation, to allow the human voice to speak and articulate the teaching in the human tongue? Here we are taken through the eye of the Kabbalist's needle, back into the realm of divine silence, or to the font of a divine speech that cannot be fully translated into our all-too-human languages, where its essence and purity would surely be lost. Thinking in words and letters, we have gone back to the mysterious name Y-H-W-H, the most abstract and yet energy-filled of all words, the root of all language. This name is nothing but a breath, yet it will animate all of speech. On the Kabbalistic chart we have here "ascended," or, as I prefer, turned deeply inward, proceeding from chamber to chamber. We have made the journey from *malkhut*, or Oral Torah, as wide as the seven seas, taking in all the world and its wisdom, back to her mate *tif'eret*, Written Torah, containing just so many words and letters, each of which has to be written and pronounced perfectly. (The *textus receptus* is a kind of verbal embodiment of God's presence in our midst, an icon in language. Hence the insistence on perfection in its form.)[23] But now we continue along on the journey, slipping through _hokhmah_, the primal point of divine self-disclosure. _Hokhmah_ is symbolized by the letter _yod_, the smallest of all letters and the graphic beginning point in writing them all, the shape of the needle's eye. As we pass through it, we stand in _aleph_, the realm of _'atiqa_,[24] the Ancient of Days, the God of primal unity before Creation, before differentiation, before sound, and we strive to listen to its silence.

Language and silence are here engaged at the high point of their eternal dance with one another. Poets have always used language to bring their readers to the edge of silence. The interplay between the two is the great poet's stock-in-trade. _Shetok; kakh 'aleh be-maḥashavah_: "Be silent; only thus may you ascend to the divine mind," said Rabbi Naḥman of Bratslav, intentionally misreading a famous Talmudic quotation.[25] Leave words behind as you enter the divine palace, a place of silence. As long as you still have with you language and the questions it inevitably brings, you will not be able to break through to God's silent, awesome realm. But then another voice enters. "No," cries the prophet, "_Take words with you_ as you return to God" (Hos. 14:3). You cannot leave language utterly behind. Uplift and transform language; use it in a different way. Create the sort of language that will always feel like it is brimming with divine silence. Be a prophet, or, at very least, a poet, one who knows how to infuse words with silence. This is the voice that dominates in Jewish culture (differing from Eastern traditions here), one that ultimately depends upon the possibility of sacred language.

"All of Torah contained within the letter _aleph_" means that all the many words that will come to exist, both within the Torah text and in the onflowing stream of conversation about it in all generations, constituting the Oral Torah, are present in the divine silence that precedes and underlies them. In that silence there is not yet any division between words and letters, between schools of thought or points of view on any question that will ever emerge within Torah. I would expand this to claim that the divine silence also reaches beyond the divide between religions, taking us back to that inner place that precedes and underlies them all. It is important to recall that _aleph_, as the first letter of the alphabet, also represents the number 1 in the Hebrew counting system. Here Torah, as the divine word that is one with its Source, takes us back to that which we were seeking: a Jewish language for expressing the oneness of all that is. God is the underlying One behind and within all existence. Torah is the underlying One behind and within all language. The oneness underlying "Creation" and the oneness underlying "revelation" are the same One.

The Torah of Eden

What could it possibly mean to speak of Torah as "God's word" or "revelation" in the religious context I am offering here? I challenge myself yet again, as I do frequently, asking whether my mystical language is not merely an obfuscation of my disbelief. God is Y-H-W-H, the wholeness of Being, the energy that makes for existence, the engine that drives the evolutionary process. This is a God of silence, not a speaker, surely not of the Hebrew text of Torah as it stands before us. The Hebrew language is a late dialect of West Semitic, a part of the human evolution of language, not the sacred tongue as our ancestors knew it, employed by God not only for the giving of Torah but for the creation of the world itself. The text was written and edited by human beings over the course of centuries, rather than dictated from the mountaintop. The personified God, I have admitted quite clearly, is a mythical projection. A literal belief in a God who speaks the words of Torah is indeed far from what I have in mind.

And yet I have already identified God as a speaker. In saying that the creative force within Being calls out "Where are you?" to every human being, surely a call that is not in words and comes from a place deeper than language, I have already begun to build the bridge that will carry us from silence to Torah. Let us return now to the accounts of "Creation," old and new. In the old tale, God calls out to Adam: "*Ayekah?*" — "Where are you?" Making the shift from the old to the new "Creation" story, I have chosen to read this as the call of God from within, the animating spirit of the whole great evolutionary journey, calling out to every human to participate fully in it, each in our distinctive way. It is our ability to hear and respond to this call, transformed because of the evolution of the human brain, including conscience, that lets us dare claim to be *tselem elohim*, the image of God, in a way other than the rest of creation. "The power of the Maker is in the made," say the Hasidic masters, referring to the stamp of God on all of Creation.[26] As a panentheist or radical immanentist, I would go farther still. All beings are part of the indivisible One, each a unique manifestation of HaWaYaH, the force of existence. But the distinctiveness of humanity and the unique way each human reflects divinity[27] also needs to be maintained. In one pocket, to paraphrase a Hasidic master, carry the message: "We humans are animals: flesh and blood, dust and ashes." But in the other pocket: "For You have made us little lower than the angels" (Ps. 8:6). Soaring spirits, ever climbing ladders to an inner "heaven."

The rabbis long ago noted that the *ayekah* ("Where are you?") of Eden needs merely to be revocalized to produce the mournful *ekhah* ("*How* does the city sit solitary!") that opens the book of Lamentations, which is to say that all the destructions, holocausts, and lesser sufferings of human history could be foretold from the moment of Adam and Eve's wayward turn.[28] God is thus at once calling to human conscience and mourning the ultimate ineffectuality of that call, realizing that in the face of human freedom there is nothing more God can do than call upon us to change our ways and weep with us at our failings. But is it also possible, in the Zohar's spirit, to see in this word "Where are you?" the move from God's primal *aleph*, the silent and undisturbed oneness of being, through *yod*, reversing the journey through the needle's eye, the birth canal of speech, into *KoH* of "*Thus* says the Lord," the language of revelation?

I am suggesting that the silently spoken divine "Where are you?" is the essence of revelation. To be a religious human being is to recognize that call and to seek to respond to it. It is given new iteration in Sinai's two commandments "I am" and "Worship nothing else," but it essentially remains unchanged. All the rest of Torah (here used in the broadest sense), with all of its shaping and patterning of our lives, with all its intricacies and ambiguities of language, is a traditional storehouse out of which we form and enrich our *response* to that challenge. The question addressed to us is indeed a silent one, but it calls forth from us all of our most refined and subtle uses of language.[29]

In speaking this way, I need to remind the reader, I am not proclaiming the existence of a silent divine realm "somewhere" other than *everywhere*, throughout existence, manifesting itself deep within the human psyche, perhaps also in the collective memory of humanity. Where is language born within the individual? Is there some memory cell, not yet discovered or known to consciousness, that can take us back to infantile memory, to the time before we had language, before we were able to shape the cacophony of our shouts into words? Might the same be possible for humanity as a whole, as we follow the links in our newly revealed DNA maps back to ancestors who could not yet speak? Is there a preverbal human locked away within us, hidden behind our complex, civilizing masks of language? Might this be what leads to the profundity of primal scream therapy or, as read by many a Hasidic master, of the wordless *niggun* or the *shofar* sound, penetrating to places deeper, more *ancient* within us than words can reach?

Those who practice meditation come to taste the profundities of inner silence. This is an age in which we seek silence. The louder and more deafening the din of our fast-paced lives, the more we hear of people signing on to silent weekends or even thirty- or forty-day silent retreats, reminding us of Elijah's time on Mount Horeb. The *ta'anit dibbur*, or "verbal fast," is an old Jewish tradition that waits to be revived in our day. Only amid our own silence will we be able to "hear" the silent call that comes from the beyond that lies within us. The recovery of silence is probably the greatest gift that we Jews have to gain from our contact with the sacred traditions of the East, where silence has been cultivated so well.

Mitzvah: Responding to the Call

All of religion can be seen as a series of ongoing and evolving human responses to the silent "Where are you?" that we hear or feel welling up inside us. In this sense I understand the silent Self of Being indeed to be the immanent, indwelling "commander" of the *mitzvot*, "commandments" that make up so much of Jewish life.[30] But this claim is in need of some serious examination and unpacking. What does the innermost One *"want"* in calling out to us? (Yes, my rereading of our post-Darwinian reality as a quest for meaning demands such a seemingly unscientific question. To put it perhaps more comfortably for some readers: "In the economy of the natural order, is there some reason why human beings should feel a sense of demand to reciprocate for the many gifts of life?") First, it wants us to be aware, to attain the deepest understanding we can of the evolving oneness of being, and to live in faithfulness to that awareness. Only in this way can we do our assigned work of continuing evolution, of moving the process forward. Its primary "commandment" is to know, to awaken to the presence and the call of the One within us. Religious teachers as varied as Valentinius the Gnostic, Maimonides, and the Buddha have (in different ways) understood this: there is a deeper truth that calls out to us to know it; hearing this call and responding to it is the beginning point of religion. But in order to succeed in this ongoing quest, both individuals and societies need guideposts and reminders. We may have moments of great insight, but we are humans. We backslide, we forget. The oneness of Being is not immediately obvious to us on the plane of existence where we live most of our lives.

Religions emerge to create forms that serve as such reminders. I do not know a God who "commands" or cares about the fulfillment of specific rites. I understand that all religious practices are of human origin and evolve within religious communities through history. But I am suggesting that the creation of such ritual forms is indeed our human *response* to an authentic single *mitzvah*, a divine imperative of the immanent presence, a wordless calling forth within us that says: "Know Me!" "Wake up!" "Be aware!" "I am Y-H-W-H your God."

The word *mitzvah* is usually translated as "commandment." As traditional Judaism meets the modern world, it often founders on the question "Who commands?" Do we believe in a personal God who demands that we perform certain rites, recite certain words, acknowledge "Him" in established ways? If not, the fear is that nothing will be left of Judaism, that the authority that stands behind tradition will be shattered, and with that Judaism will come to an end.

Here too, as in the case of the traditional Creation story versus evolution, we need to understand that the past century's battle is over. Having studied the history of religion, including the specific contexts in which biblical and rabbinic religion emerged, we understand that the forms we know as Judaism developed over a long period, often in response to circumstances now lost to us. Some practices were magical in origin, given a more historical or "spiritual" meaning only by later interpreters. Some of these transformations reach back so far that they are already found in the Torah text, where they are presented as the word of God. Others emerged only later, codified by the rabbis in explaining either obligatory laws or optional customs. But all of the forms came about at one time or another as products of human innovation and the ensuing evolution of religion, rather than as dictated by the will of God.

Such an admission need not spell the end of Judaism, however. As I said with regard to evolution, our religious task is not to fight a rearguard battle against the scientific (in this case historical and literary) evidence. Here again the challenge is that of *reframing* the issue, lifting our discussion of it to a different level or state of mind. Torah remains Torah, even after we digest all of historical criticism. We, the community of Israel, continue to accept it as our canon; we live in relationship to it. The form remains a *mitzvah*, a sanctified religious deed. Doing the *mitzvah* is the will of God, in the sense that it is the way we as a religious community respond to the One that calls out to us, that seeks to have us know it, ever awaiting our response. This particular form of response rather than another is sanctified by the canonizing power of the Jewish people, an ancient community that bears much wisdom about how to bring divine awareness into everyday life. The *mitzvah* is holy because Jews do it, because they have done it for such a long time, and because they have invested it with a depth of *kavvanah*, or spiritual energy, that is never lost but only builds in intensity over the course of centuries. The fullness of that

energy is the divine presence that lies within it, waiting to be un-
covered anew in each generation. *Mitzvah* is more than a custom, not
merely a folkway. We have declared it holy, and so it is.[31] Hasidic
tradition reads the word *mitzvah* to mean "a place of encounter," a
form in which the divine and the human meet and are joined together.[32] Its mystery and power, reinforced by antiquity and the very
absence of obvious meaning, remain in force despite the fact that it
originates within history. It is an act in which we open ourselves to
Y-H-W-H, a moment, a "place," or a deed of awareness and response.
Each *mitzvah* is an *opportunity* for encounter between the silent divine
presence and the human soul that seeks to articulate it.[33]

But there is a second commandment implicit in this same "Where
are you?" following immediately upon the first, "Be aware." Our
second task, needing no further language, is to share this realization
with others. The One needs and calls upon us to become aware, each
in our own way. But it is through the great *collectivity* of human consciousness that the One drives forward in its goal of being known,
manifest, and loved. We share this awareness best not by preaching
but by our deeds. This is the part of "Where are you?" that calls for
*com*passion and moral action. We let others know that we and they are
part of the same One when we treat them like brothers and sisters, or
like parts of the same single universal body.[34] We are called upon to
proclaim the oneness of Being throughout the world and to welcome
all human beings into the chorus of exulting in the One, in whatever
language and style best suits them.

How do you help to enable another person to become aware of the
One that fills and surrounds us? First, by helping him or her reach a
condition of self-love and self-acceptance. We will open our eyes to
the beauty and sanctity of life only when we attain the inner peace and
wholeness needed to do so. There is much of this work that each
person has to do on his or her own. But others can and must help to
provide the right conditions. We cannot expect a person to reach that
place as long as he or she is hungry. Or as long as he or she is homeless
or oppressed or addicted or condemned to a life of meaningless labor.
We fellow members of the human community, limbs in the single

body of Y-H-W-H, therefore have to act in love, in *caring* for one another, in support of one another's many struggles, and in empathy with each other's pain. Only then do we earn a right to the messianic dream that sustains us, our hope and faith that we will *all* open our eyes and see that Presence.

In this way all the *mitzvot*, both those called "between person and God" (the ritual forms) and those called "between person and person" (the moral/ethical realm) can be seen as our response to that single silent word, the divine *Ayeka?* — "Where are you?" — that echoes within every human heart. They are sacred forms, bearing the special potential for encounter with the One, a truth not diminished by our acceptance that they are all of human origin. To the question "Are the *mitzvot* divine or human?" I can only answer, "Yes."

Ten Words, Twice Spoken

The tradition insists that the world was founded by an act, or a series of acts, of divine speech. "God said: 'Let there be . . .'" is Torah's opening myth.[35] But there is also a silent God, the One before or underlying that first act of speech. The silent God does not disappear as divine speech begins. In this too we exist in God's image. The speaking or articulate person, so much emphasized and encouraged in Judaism (Homo sapiens is defined in Hebrew as *medabber*, "speaker"), both expresses and masks the silent inner self.[36] So does the pregnant divine silence ever underlie divine speech.

The phrase "Let there be," by an early count, occurs ten times in the opening chapter of Genesis, leading the Mishnah to proclaim that "the world was created by ten utterances." The Talmud already objected that there are only nine such statements in Genesis 1, resolving the difference by the strange notion that "In the beginning" is also a sort of utterance.[37] The Kabbalists quite naturally identified these ten with the ten *sefirot*, the historical origins of which are in fact quite different, having more to do with number than language. The first divine manifestation, *keter*, was thus identified with this most primal and essentially preverbal speech act, the "In the beginning" that opened the way for "And God said. . . ." This figure, also called 'atiqa, the Ancient of Days, is the silence behind all speech, the place to which every speech act returns to draw its strength.

The value of this tradition of the ten utterances is in its insistence that divinity lies hidden within the perceptible world. The mystic understands that the true relationship of God and world is not that of "Creator" and "creature," separate from one another, but rather one of deep structure and surface appearance. God is the underlying reality of being; peel off the surface or lift the veil of our divided and multifaceted reality and you will begin to peer through to the singularity of truth, the One that lies within and behind the many. So too may you peer through the multifaceted text of Torah to discover first the ten, then the silent One. The use of "utterances" regarding Creation is of course premature, if they are to be thought of in terms of human speech. But perhaps in order to understand the claim we have to leave prose behind, hearing in the rabbinic formula nothing more or less than the Psalmist's magnificent "The Heavens declare the glory of God, the skies tell of His handiwork" (Ps. 19:1). The "David" of that Psalm, whatever his real name, was already taking "speech" other than literally.

It is possible, in other words, to know God prior to and without religion. Awareness of the One who "peers through the lattices," waiting to be discovered within the variety and beauty of the evolving natural order, does not depend upon the existence of religious language. If evolution is indeed the greatest sacred story, perhaps the most vital knowledge of God exists prior to all religious forms. It is that which is to be discovered in simple encounter with nature and its wonders. The celebration of Creation, so central to the Psalmists, calls out for revival in our day. We need not fear it.[38] On the contrary, the urgent need to transform human behavior in relation to the environment will be best supported by a religious life that returns to the Psalmists' consciousness of our human place within (not above) the great symphony of Creation.[39]

But the ten utterances, which we might call the *voiceprint* of God within the natural world, are also linked to another ten, the ten commandments of Sinai. (In Hebrew they are called not "command-ments" — *mitzvot* — but *dibberot* ["words"], essentially another way of saying "utterances.")[40] This is to say that God speaks twice, once in creating the world and again in giving the Torah. Creation itself, in the form of ongoing evolution, is the great self-revelation of God.[41] There "speech" must be taken metaphorically; the world is an expression of the hidden One, of the divine Self. But Torah as text takes that reality and recasts it in a language to which we can respond. "Torah speaks in human language," as the ancients taught.

What is changed by Sinai, using "Sinai" as metaphorically as you choose? On one hand, nothing is changed. The earth is as filled with divine radiance as it was before. The face of God is to be seen, as always, in the face of every creature. The *dibberot* add nothing to the *ma'amarot* that were there from the beginning. Yet everything has been changed, because awareness has been given to us as a gift. "You have been shown to know," says the Deuteronomist in recalling the event at Sinai, "that Y-H-W-H is God; there is naught besides Him" (Deut. 4:35). You have now been shown this in your own human language. We can certainly still hide our eyes, still turn away from the light. But it is considerably harder to do so, requiring an act of willful denial. Now it is right there before us, "in black and white," as it were, in a language we cannot help but read.

Another change: the ten utterances of Creation have now been restated, but this time in *imperative* form. Life in the world after Eden might seem like a life without responsibility. Our exile from the Garden might be seen as a flight from God's "Where are you?" or at least as a loss as to how to respond. It might not be clear just what our ability to discover God within the natural world calls upon us to *do*. Too much have we humans approached this world with a sense of ownership and privilege rather than with obligation. But Judaism is all about responsibility. "If Israel are not prophets, they are the children of prophets."[42] The prophetic call to action still rings in our ears. We know instinctively that no religion is serious unless it makes demands on our lives, until it asks the question: *"How are we supposed to live* in response to this truth?" All the imperatives of Sinai are our ways of responding to the divine "Where are you?"

We humans are pilgrims on the road of life. We want to respond to that call and challenge. But how do we undertake the journey? How do we set out on our way? What do we need to take along with us? What is the vessel in which we are to travel? What will protect us from hardships and temptations along the way? Human societies have created religions in response to those questions. As the word indicates, a religion is a regimen or a set of rules. These rules tell us how to live, how to act, how to conduct our lives in such a way that they become fit vehicles for our great journey back to our Source. The Hebrew term closest to "religion" in this sense is *halakhah*, "the path" as set forth by the ancient rabbis' understanding of the biblical commandments.

Religion is thus a language, a set of symbols, that seeks to address itself to the soul. Its truest purpose is to direct both individuals and human communities to turn inward, to focus attention toward that deeper level of mind where the journey takes place. Traditions claim, of course, that their particular sets of rules are revealed by God, concretized expressions of the divine will. It is this claim that lends authority to Jewish *halakhah*, Islamic *shariyyah*, Catholic canon law, or any other laid-out form of religious behavior. But it is also true that such systems are created and evolve in response to historic need and circumstance and are most effective when they retain a proper balance between discipline and flexibility.

Knowing and admitting this, we still struggle to think of *halakhah* (or its parallels) as "the will of God." I have tried to point a way toward doing this, understanding *halakhah* as our response, our "filling in the spaces" of the wordless divine call. This does make the sacred act a fulfillment of God's will, but only in the very broadest and most abstract sense. In order to examine this crucial question further, we need to return to our discussion of Torah, and to the first two of the ten "commandments," those that are supposed to contain all the rest. "I am Y-H-W-H your God" and "Have no gods besides Me."

Let me try to translate these into the theological language I am speaking here. The underlying One of the universe seeks to be known, manifest through the mechanism of our evolving awareness. Its "Where are you?" spoken within us calls us to that knowledge. That call to constant awareness both *liberates* and *obligates* us. This is the secret of the first two "commandments" of Sinai.

"I am Y-H-W-H your God who brought you forth from the Land of Egypt, out of the house of bondage." "Freedom is carved into the tablets," say the sages.[43] At Sinai the slave chains have been broken, by the great breakthrough in human awareness that we call "revelation." That revelation began in Eden, at the moment when the challenging "voice" first called to us. But we fled Eden (Was that exile not self-imposed?) and spent countless generations in flight from that voice, running away from that which calls us. Now, having been through the trauma of bondage and liberation, we have come to a moment of maturity, of facing truth, of *recognizing* that a claim is made upon us by the One who set us free. The voice goes forth from Sinai every day, say the sages.[44] It is only on *this* day, the day of the great revelation, that we are ready to hear it. That voice was present in our collective infancy in Eden, much like the angel who supposedly teaches us before we emerge from the womb. But it is only here at Sinai, the culmination of a liberation struggle filled with doubt, growth, and wonder, that we are ready to hear it as adults.

That first *mitzvah* is joined by a second, but one that is really only a reverse side of the first. "Worship nothing else." Beware of idols, of false gods in all their dimensions. Do not be led astray by venerating anything less than Y-H-W-H, the wholeness of being. The temptations range from the "sticks and stones" as the Bible presents "idolatry" to the much more sophisticated distortions and limitations of truth that constitute most of religion, even in our own day.[45] All of them lead us to turn away from the singular task of *sacred awareness without limits*. Each of them narrows our vision, keeps out part of the light. The Ba'al Shem Tov said it clearly and sharply, commenting on "Lest you turn aside and worship other gods" (Deut. 11:16). "As soon as you turn aside," he said, "you are worshipping other gods."[46] Humans are never without *something* that they worship. Turn away from the whole and you are worshipping but a part, causing *perud*, fragmentation of reality, the beginning of all evil. This *mitzvah* is an admonition against false religion in the strongest sense. Any religion that makes exclusive claims and still plays on the field of "my god against your god" is by definition such an idolatry. You are turning away from the whole, worshipping one part of reality as though it were the All. Narrowness of vision, exclusion of large bodies of human experience, means that one is likely worshipping less than the whole, effecting division or "separation" within God. The One is always bigger than we imagine, beyond all our attempts to fence it in or out. The One, the only One, is always "in" wherever we try to post signs that say: "Keep out!" And that One is always *out there*, whenever we try to put up fences that say: "Keep within these bounds!"

Our first task as humans is to be aware, to expand both mind and heart. In seeking to carry out this task, the memory of slavery is a particularly valuable portion of our Jewish legacy. We know from experience that you cannot worship God without freedom. This means a deep inner freedom, the ability to turn inward and bring forth awareness, appreciation, and gratitude from the most profound places toward which the self can reach. We need to be free from all that which would block us in this inner turning, which is also the great prerequisite of our ability to love. Only after coming out of "Egypt," those places that constrict us and keep us from that wholeness, are we free enough to stand before God's mountain.[47]

In the course of this discovery, the danger of idolatry is constant. Hence the need for the second commandment, immediately following the first. How easy it is, when you think you are "doing God's work," to be sure that you have found the true and only way, to be convinced that others have more to learn from you than you from them. The Golden Calf is built in the very moment that Moses was receiving the tablets. If we take seriously the mystical claim that Moses' mind contained those of all Israel, we were at once on top of the mountain, receiving the word, and (in the very same moment) at its base, constructing an idol. Might we have been fashioning the revelation itself into an idol? One of the great Torah interpreters of the last century explained Moses' smashing of the tablets in just this way. When he came down from the mountain, ready to give God's Law, he saw the Golden Calf before him. "Oh my God!" he cried, "They're idol makers! Think what they'll do if they ever get their hands on *these*!" And so he smashed them, leaving only fragments of broken tablets.[48] Those broken tablets, I like to say, were placed in the Ark for our generation, one that can receive them in only that way.

The second commandment, including its prohibition of idols, needs to be taken with great seriousness in any religion we seek to promulgate today. I have spoken freely here of the power of myth, calling for a reinvigoration of Judaism by drinking deeply of the mythic and mystical traditions. I understand the God-language of the Torah itself to be essentially of a mythical sort, and in appropriating it as freely as I do (while being clear that I am not a literal believer), I propose a religion largely based on *remythologization*. But here we encounter a serious moral problem. The veneration of myth can itself become an idol. We are not the only ones in modern or postmodern times to have recourse to myth. Most notoriously, the Nazis and other fascists of mid-twentieth century Europe turned back to so-called Aryan myths to buttress their murderous ideologies. How do we justify our own turn to myth while firmly rejecting theirs? How do we morally differentiate one myth from another? As inhabitants of the Western world, living for so many centuries as a minority within Christendom, we Jews bear a deep awareness that we are the villains in the tale that for so many in the society around us is "the Greatest Story Ever Told." The founding myth of Christianity, already in the gospels, was told in such a way as to implicate "the Jews." I fully respect the attempts of many sincere and well-meaning Christians to cleanse their myth of anti-Semitism, but it is not an easy job. I do not know how to help my Christian friends and readers get by the fact that "Judas" and "Jew" just fit too well together, short of emending their Scripture. Despite the recently found and much-acclaimed "Gospel of Judas," historical Christianity chose a different and often pernicious path. In the neoliteralist world of contemporary Islam, the worst selection of ancient sources is sometimes made, those demonizing the Jews in ways more redolent of medieval Christianity than the much more tolerant history of Islam. New "Africanist" mythologies have emerged in our time, seeking to combat old and venal myths of African inferiority. Are we then left with nothing more than a battle of myth against myth, my myth against yours? Can I reject the truth claim of your myth without your feeling that I am rejecting you as well? If myth *in itself* is to be celebrated, we are indeed going down a dangerous path. Claims of racial superiority and ancient ethnic rivalries, causes of renewed bloodletting in our own day, are most often rooted in venerable myths. The rise of fundamentalist religion, such a dangerous force in the world today, may be ascribed to myths that are being taken *too* seriously, even if they are not recognized as myth. Are we not aggravating those dangers, or at least weakening our ability to stand up to them, if we celebrate the power of myth?

Here we go back to the universalism of the vision with which we began. We need to go beyond our separate and divisive tales, back to the single great story that unites us all. The story of evolution, including the ongoing evolution of humanity, is bigger than all the distinctions between religions and their myths. The One I seek to address, that which I (perhaps recklessly) allow myself to call "God," is also bigger than all that. Awareness of it is the call to all of us. Worship is our human response to that call, one that each of us necessarily hears in his or her own language. The worship of that One, in a way that does not diminish or constrict it, requires that we stand open to the full chorus of human naming and worshipping of that same One. "*Everywhere* there is incense burnt and offering made to My name," says the prophet (Mal. 1:11). All of human worship belongs to the One. Any religion less open than that in its claims — whether under the banner of "Judaism" or any other — is precisely a "turning aside," a lopping off of a certain part of human experience and taking it for the whole. *That* is idolatry, the worship of "other gods," meaning the taking of something less than the whole for God, which is the all-embracing One.

The basis of Jewish moral teaching is universal. " 'Why was Adam created singly?' So that no person say 'My father was greater than yours.' "[49] I turn to the myth of the call to Adam precisely because that is a universal myth, one that will be inclusive of all humanity. In journeying from that myth to the account of Sinai, my intent is to read the latter as well in an open and universalizing way. Once "Egypt" is read symbolically, the religion of the first two commandments of Sinai, "I am Y-H-W-H your God" and "Worship nothing else," is not limited to Judaism or Jews. Fully cognizant of myth and its powers, including its dangers, I am suggesting that the moral test for the legitimate use of myth is its universality or our ability to read it in a universalizing way. A myth that explains something about the universal human situation, that deepens our understanding of some aspect of what it means to be a human being, is indeed enriching to human experience and may be worthy of embracing. But a myth that divides, that tells us why Jews or blacks or women or Gypsies or Canaanites — or any other particular group — are cursed, are excluded from the camp of the Lord, or anything of that order, is a myth to be treated with suspicion, whether it exists within our tradition or any other. The universality of the Creation tale (especially in its Genesis 1 version) sets the standard. The possibility that idolatry, with all the worst of its implications, can lie within the myth-making center of the human mind, should come as no surprise.

Sinai and Covenant

When we approach Sinai, however, we stand directly in the face of Israel's myth: its faith in its uniqueness and its singular covenant with God. How can a religious universalist live with these, and how can one imagine a Judaism without them? I remain an affirmer of both Sinai and covenant, but in very carefully defined ways, including both restriction and expansion of their meaning.

We Jews began our life together as a sacred community by an act of covenantal engagement. That is the original community of Israel, gathered at the base of Mount Sinai, a gathering that takes place throughout all eternity, one at which each of us (including all who choose to join the people Israel) is ever present. This is when we become "a kingdom of priests, a holy nation" (Ex. 19:6). Priesthood makes no sense without a laity, in this case one that includes the entire human family. The task of the priest is to teach and to serve in such ways as to help others come close to God. The teaching this family of nations is to receive (not only from us) needs to be a universal one, applicable to them all. Its most basic principles are two: *all of being is one in Y-H-W-H, and every person is the image of God.* This is our message, the reason we continue to exist. All the rest is commentary.

As a religious Jew, I remain fully committed to this priesthood. I understand, in the language of tradition, that "Israel stand under oath since Mount Sinai."[50] The covenant is one of joy as well as burden. Sinai is the moment in which each heart leaps forward and says *na'aseh ve-nishma'* ("Let us do! Let us hear!" [Ex. 24:7]), committing us to live in response to the Word even before it is fully uttered. Because that covenantal moment is so central to the life of Judaism, I need to offer some clear statement as to how I understand it in the context of the theology I am proposing.

First I need to remind us that we are living within the story, dwelling in the land of myth. I make no claim for the literal historicity of Sinai. Like the seven-day Creation, it is a sacred tale around which our lives are woven, representing a truth that resides in the realm of myth and symbol, a deeper truth than that of history, but one that should not be confused with it. Even though we are talking within the story, however, some distinctions can be made as to how we understand it and are committed to it. The key chapter that describes Sinai as covenant is Exodus 24, where the covenantal ritual is described in a few verses inserted within the account of Moses' and the elders' ascent and vision at the top of the mount. Moses creates a very powerful ritual of binding, in which he takes the blood-offering of sacrificial bullocks and sprinkles it, half on the altar, representing God, and half on the assembled throng of Israel. God and the people have thus "shared blood" and are bound together as one. This is the covenantal moment, that by which we are bound forever, since we were all there.

Interestingly, the Torah does not claim that Moses is *commanded* to perform this rite. It seems to be his innovation, a humanly conceived ritual with which to impress the people, perhaps even a bold human act that attempts to bind God. I take this obvious "lack" in the text as a hint, telling us that covenant is indeed a human idea. No, I do not know a God who makes a covenant with Israel, One who from the heavens, or even from those "heavens" deep within the heart, chooses this people from among all nations to be His own. Even in the internalized version, I would find such a formulation both too personifying and unduly particularistic. I believe that the One is revealed in all hearts, to all people, in much the same way. The variation comes from our end, from the cultural settings and responses we offer to that universal call. Israel is unique among the nations in the way we have heard and responded, not in the fact that we are called. The covenant is our act of choosing, our response to Sinai, creating the religious civilization that begins at the base of the mountain and evolves through history.[51] I thus do accept the covenant, but understand it as quite human in origin and affirm it as such. In response to the unfolding event at Sinai — a Sinai of mind and heart, to be sure — we Israelites said "Yes!" in a firm and committed way. We agreed to respond to the inner call by means of *Torah* and *mitzvot*, by accepting a sacred text, the basis and font of eternal reinterpretation, and by committing ourselves to the commandments that were revealed to us at Sinai, those engraved on the tablets and within our hearts. To stand in covenant with God is accept a challenge to regard one's entire life as a channel for bringing divine presence and blessing into the world. We as a Jewish people, the people of Sinai, made such a commitment, one to which we remain bound forever. To understand us Jews is to realize that we are eternally devoted to that vision. No matter how secular we may declare ourselves to be, something within us remains priest at that altar.

Does my claim that covenant is a human initiative serve to exclude God from it? Am I saying that it is *merely* human? Hardly! As God is present within the human heart, God is there within us as we say "Yes" to Sinai. (Indeed, God is also present in that part of us that says "No.") *Semolo taḥat le-roshi vi-yemino teḥabbeqeni*: "His left hand is beneath my head as his right embraces me" (Song of Songs 2:6). God is present to us from more angles than we can see.

But is the covenant *mutual*? Are we promised anything? Is God "bound" by the covenant as well? Does God give to us, open to us, in response to our loyalty to that covenant? As long as we keep our expectations on the spiritual plane, I can answer with a wholehearted "Yes!" Here is the great lesson of love: the more you give, the more you receive. To open yourself to serve others as a channel of divine grace, to bring light and blessing into their lives, is endlessly rewarding. The more light you shine forth, the more comes pouring through. The inner Wellspring is one whose "waters do not betray" and never run dry. This is all I have by way of faith in reward. *And it is plenty.*

From that pre-Sinai moment of *na'aseh ve-nishma'* ("we will do and we will listen"), when commitment is made and we become fully engaged to it, all of our accounts of what actually took place at Sinai, both in the Torah text and in millennia of ensuing Midrash, become wholly subjective. They are statements of the committed heart, hardly to be taken as objective truth. We would not have got that close to God's mountain had we been concerned with maintaining critical distance. There is thus no *evidence* for Sinai, either in the historical or the philosophical realm. There is rather only *testimony*, which I take to be quite different. Evidence is impersonal, betokening impartiality, an objective claim that no rational mind could deny. Testimony is all about engagement; it is wholly personal, indeed can only be spoken with the entire self.[52] It does not exist for the sake of argument, in order to convince others. It exists for itself, though others may be impressed by it and their hearts may be turned. We Israelites as a faith-community are those who see ourselves as having stood, as still standing, at the base of that mountain. "My soul went forth as He spoke" (Song of Songs 5:6) is the watchword of that experience. We indeed fainted, as the Talmud interprets that phrase,[53] as God began to speak. All the rest that we heard was in a swoon.

How do we go about creating a society where the message of Sinai is universally upheld and revered? At the mountain the people of Israel committed themselves to seeking an answer to that question. It is the answer to which we said: "We will do and we will listen!" affirming our commitment even before the words were spoken. It is the answer we then received engraved on the tablets. Those first tablets, the story tells us, were more than we could bear. They are described as "made by God and written by God" (Ex. 32:16). They had to be smashed because (contrary to our first outcry) we were not really ready to receive them. The second tablets were said to be fashioned by Moses, in his own human way, and inscribed by God. These we were ready to receive; the wording on them was essentially the same.

Those ten "words" form the constitution of the Republic of the Hebrews, to borrow a phrase from Spinoza. We also designate it as "the Kingdom of Heaven" here on earth, refusing to make any distinction between those two. But it is a constitution made not for us alone, defining the life of this particular people. It is also the curriculum or the catechism that we as "a kingdom of priests" are to teach and give to the world. It is time for us to return to these ten, to explore them deeply and to ask what it would mean to make them the basis of all that we seek to teach and give.

The essential principles, as I have suggested, are contained in the first two commandments, "Know the One!" and "Worship nothing less!" The remaining eight are there to define and shape the way we do this, to help that transcendent message enter safely into the lives of real, fallible human beings and societies. I offer just a few words of comment on each, interpreting them in this way as themselves refining, exemplifying, and commenting on those first two commandments that contain them and all the rest. I understand these latter eight commandments as embodying Moses' first attempt to take the two, those all Israel heard directly (or, in my language, those that proceed directly from this respoken "Where are you?"), and I try to embody them in the reality of human life and community. Because Moses is known to us as Moshe Rabbenu ("Moses our teacher") and, not incidentally, since I have spent my life as a teacher, I understand them mostly as admonitions to teachers, though they would apply to other sorts of leaders as well. Israel's priesthood is one mainly devoted to teaching. Here are some things we as *teachers of humanity* need to remember along the way. Let us turn first to the remaining three commandments on the first tablet:

> *Do not raise up the name of Y-H-W-H your God in vain.* Honesty is an essential virtue in religious teaching. Hypocrisy is the "sin crouching at the door," as God says to Cain, of every would-be teacher. Do not speak glibly. Do not preach things you do not believe. Do not lie, even to yourself. At the same time, do not be unduly certain of yourself. Certainty too often allows us to neglect the experience of others, keeping us from acknowledging their part of truth. If you are sure, you are probably wrong. It is in moments of self-assurance that you are most likely to betray God by taking the part for the whole, and thus taking the divine name in vain.
>
> *Remember the Sabbath Day to keep it holy.* Maintain the ability to cease your labors, even those you consider the most holy. Stop the train; get off the treadmill, even if you think your treadmill is a "righteous" one. The ability to breathe deeply, reflect, and even be inspired to change course may be more important than anything else you have to say. For this we were given the great gift of sharing in God's own Sabbath. Use it well. "Remember" the Sabbath means to have it in mind always, even on Monday and Tuesday. Do not become so involved in your work, whatever it is, that you do not also long for the possibility of letting it go, of "being" rather than "doing."
>
> *Honor your father and your mother.* You are not the font of all wisdom. Recognize the gifts of prior generations, the evolution of their thinking that has helped to shape your own. This may have begun with your childhood education, shaped on your parents' knee, but it includes much more. Both intellectually and spiritually, we are the products of all that came before us. Be humbled by this, and grateful.

The five commandments on the second tablet need some further words of introduction. They are all about interpersonal relations, the ways one human being acts and feels in the course of interacting with others. I pause before these because there is a misreading of mystical religion that sees it as wanting to sweep over the distinction between self and other, sinking it in the depths of the oneness that underlies us all. Nothing could be farther from the truth about mysticism, as taught and practiced by the enlightened of our tradition and others. This misperception derives from a spiritual impatience in taking on mystical teachings, one that confuses levels of reality with one another. Granted, there is a level on which nothing but the One exists, Y-H-W-H that underlies and animates all of being. But we come to know that One, and to manifest our devotion to it, only by embracing its manifestation in the infinite variety and diversity of beings, those into which it continues to pour its Presence. Insight into Y-H-W-H comes through appreciating the fullness of this Presence (*shekhinah*), not through a premature attempt to dissolve it into Nothingness. We live is *this* world, one in which the distinction between self and other, and the need to respect the other, is bedrock. Yes, hovering over (or buried within) this world is *'olam ha-ba'*, the "World to Come," at the deepest level of which there is only One. But Moses is not giving us a Torah to be lived there, a "place" where there is no need for Torah. Torah is for this world, where self and other meet with all their differences revealed and yet have to find a way to live in peace. The subsequent five commandments are all about our grounding in the real world of humanity.

> *Do not murder.* Each human being has a right to live. Every human life is sacred. The shedding of blood is always tragic, always a diminishing of God's image. There may be circumstances in which taking a life is justified or necessary, but there are no circumstances in which the taking of life is less than tragic. Make sure your teachings do nothing that encourages the tragic taking of human life. Our fate as Jews has forced us to learn how to defend ourselves, even by taking life. But we may never let our Jewish teaching be used in a way that lessens the humanity of others, making it easier to kill them. This transgression has already occurred in our day and we need to be especially vigilant and courageous in standing up to it. The same applies to teaching that diminishes any person's right to live a full, productive, and self-respecting life. To lessen another human being in his or her own eyes can also be a form of murder.
>
> *Do not commit adultery.* Would-be spiritual teachers, "priests" of Sinai and its powerful message, always need to be aware of human weakness, their own before that of all others. Sexual energies are always

there when we flesh-and-blood humans interact with one another, anywhere this side of Eden. Check yourself always. Be aware; know your boundaries. Precisely because good teaching is an act of love, the teacher is always in danger. Make sure that all your giving is for the sake of those who seek to receive it, not just fulfilling your own unspoken needs, sexual and other.

Do not steal. Do not use your teachings or your cleverness to diminish another or to take away what belongs to another. This may be something as subtle as a person's pride or self-definition, or as concrete as relationship, home, land, or property. Even if you think you are right, think again before you take, claim, or demand. The more you are in a position of power, the more you need to question yourself. This applies to nations as it does to individuals.

Do not bear false witness against your neighbor. Here we return to the question of honesty. It is not only God whose name we may take in vain. Do not betray others by bearing false witness, by not acknowledging what they have to offer. Do not define others in ways that are comfortable to you but may not fit who they really are. Do not caricature the views of others, avoiding confrontation with the real truth they may speak.

You shall not covet. How much beauty and wisdom there is in other peoples' teachings and traditions! "If only we had the Christians' ability to speak of God's love! The silence and patience of the Buddhists! The body-soul integration of the yogis!" Learn from others, appreciate what they have to give, but do not covet. Be satisfied with your lot, content with your own heritage and its message. We have *plenty* to offer. So does each of the great traditions.

The ten commandments need to stand as the basis of a reinvigorated Judaism.[54] Ritual life, observances, the sacred calendar, are all part of our response to the first commandment, Sinai's restatement of the original "Where are you?" As such they are no longer absolutes but rather our tradition's means toward the end of becoming and remaining aware. "Between man and God" the only absolutes are the great call to be aware and our need to respond. In the "between person and person" realm there indeed are moral absolutes. The last six of the commandments are a good starting point for such a list. These too, of course, need to be redefined in each age, but their essential claim on our conduct is constant. The *metzavveh* (I prefer "the one who brings us together" as a translation, rather than "commander," but there is an imperative here) of both categories of *mitzvot* lies deep within the single Self of the cosmos, manifest within each of us, calling upon us ever to stretch and to know, to open the heart and to act accordingly. These are the basis of all *mitzvot*.

Reflecting on Our Journey

Does such an approach suffice? To recapitulate our discussion in Kabbalistic language, we have made the journey from *malkhut* or oral Torah, where teaching was to be found everywhere, back to the single *aleph* of *keter*, the realm of inner divine silence. We gave rather short shrift to *tif'eret*, the written Torah, which stands at the midpoint between them. How would we know what Torah is, after all, were it not for the very concrete and defined text that we read each week, the specific aggregate of words and letters, narratives and laws, that fills the parchment held between those two poles that we call the Trees of Life? This is the text about which Rabbi Ishmael (or perhaps Akiva) said to the scribe: "Take care, for if you add or detract a single letter, you may destroy the entire world!"[55] But that text is not without its problems, and there is good reason why we flee it in both directions (toward the utterly expansive and toward the totally reduced) at once. We understand the Torah text's complex historical origins, the process of editing that gave it this form. We rejoice in this knowledge that allows us the relief of admitting its fallibility, or at least the need for drastic reshaping through exegesis. Some parts of that reshaping are already ancient; others, too long neglected, are taking place before our eyes. We do not have our rebellious or overfed children stoned to death (Deut. 21:18–21). We will not kill a betrothed woman who has relations with another man, despite our high regard for marital fidelity (Deut. 22:23–24). "Honor killings" are not the Jewish way, *despite the text*. To these already ancient modifications of tradition, we add our own. We do not believe any person may own another, male or female, Jew or Gentile. We are horrified at the examples of massacre or even genocide that the text seems to prescribe for certain nations that resisted the people of Israel on their journey into the Promised Land. In an era when Jews have regained power, including military rule over others, we shudder to think that such passages might be treated as precedents for deeds no Jew should contemplate. We do not believe that homosexual acts are an "abomination," and will not accept treating gay people as though they were. We do not delete those Leviticus verses from the text of our Torah, but we rise up regularly "to preach against them."[56] When we are convinced that our struggle with the text demands the courage of radical rereading, we stand ready. There is a real danger, however, that all of these discomforts might serve to push us away from the text and make us prefer those versions of Torah that are infinitely larger (all of wisdom) or smaller (a single *aleph*).

But we are Jews and this is Torah. The text simply will not go away. This is the Torah we read in the synagogue each week, bless, kiss, raise up, and march around. As loyal Jews we *love* this text, even as we give vent to considerable anger and frustration with it. It is the place from which we come, something like ancient childhood memory, partially repressed and reshaped by sublimation, but nevertheless present within us, not to be denied. Fortunately we inherit the text together with a highly developed apparatus for reinterpretation, offering our generation, like all generations that have preceded it, a chance to participate in that text's ever-evolving meaning. The *textus receptus* may indeed be a verbal embodiment of God's presence in our midst.[57] Yet the text is never read without commentary. *Khumesh mit RaShI* ("the Pentateuch with commentary") was the subject of elementary education in the traditional *kheydr* (Jewish elementary school), not the Torah text alone. We may add to eleventh-century RaShI at least sixty-nine more commentaries of our own choosing to make up the Torah's "seventy faces" as we present them to the reader.[58] It is not the specific *content* of RaShI that is most important to convey; it is the *example* of RaShI, the tradition's daring to reinterpret. The Hasidic masters insist that the Torah *must* have new interpretations in each generation, in accord with the generation's spiritual character.[59] Only in this way, they clearly state, does Torah, eternally belonging to God, historically belonging to Moses, become *our* Torah.

In choosing to live with an ancient text in this way, keeping it alive through a constant process of creative reinterpretation, we stand in open conflict with Spinoza's insistence that the Bible must be treated just like any other document, its words meaning what critical scrutiny seems to indicate, and nothing more.[60] As a community still committed to a sacred canon, we privilege those texts to bear, and to transport us to, infinite other realms of meaning, the "inner palaces" of Torah. *We thus make the same claim for Torah that we make for the natural world itself: remove the veil of surface impressions, go deeper, and you will find there something profound and holy.* To get there we may use all the methods suggested above, and perhaps some newer ones as well. In doing this, we should realize that we are using the text as a pathway to insight that leads beyond text, and ultimately beyond language itself.

It may seem surprising to hear a heterodox Jew — that is, one who does not claim to believe literally in the revealed nature of the text — make such assertions. The right to interpret so daringly was classically defended on the basis of text as revelation. God in "His" infinity, after all, intended all the meanings future generations might ever find behind the text. Hence they were all "given to Moses at Sinai." We cannot make such a claim in a literal sense. But I deny — and here I am arguing with Mordecai Kaplan, Gershom Scholem, and others — that this means that the game is up. God *gives* Torah — wordless, airy, revealing itself to be nothing other than God's own name, or thundering in our ears as a single-word challenge: *Ayekah?* — "Where are you?" We, the Community of Israel, *receive* Torah, dressed in the finery of tales, traditions, impossible commands. Something happened, to be sure, between the "giving" and the "receiving." That "something" is translation into human-generated and evolving forms of religious life, embodiments of the elusive spirit. But this is the form in which we have that hidden Torah; we have no other. Only by digging deeply into the outer Torah, its sometimes harsh "shell," spurred on by the pain it causes us, will we find our way into the secret places where the experience of generations tells us that insight into God's presence will be found.

Spinoza is, of course, a founder of modernity. By asserting the rebirth and legitimacy of Midrash, we are making a postmodern claim. The text bears a multiplicity of meanings, and we, its readers, have an active hand in creating them and selecting among them. We make this claim, however, in carefully defined ways. We apply it only to the canonical text of Hebrew Scripture, sanctified by the rabbis of Yavneh and by the Jewish people over two millennia of religious life. Because we are postmoderns and not premoderns, having bitten into the apple of historical criticism, we will always know the difference between *peshat* (the critical, historical meaning of the text in its original context) and *drash* (the host of fanciful explanations we find hinted at in the text), and must be honest in distinguishing between the two. But with this honesty in place, we understand that *drash* is where the ever-evolving spirit wants us to put our energies. The renewal of *aggadah*, as Hayyim Nahman Bialik so powerfully reminded us, is the real creative challenge.[61] The power to reinterpret, the ability to expand meanings, is itself a divine gift or testimony to the divine presence within us. Listen to a Hasidic reading of the concluding Torah blessing which, recited after each portion, reads: " . . . who has given us the Torah of truth and implanted eternal life within us. Blessed are You Y-H-W-H, giving the Torah." The Torah, given once to the ancients, can only become "Torah of truth" when each reader takes that "eternal life" implanted with us and uses it to reread Torah in a way that speaks to his or her own life. We make Torah come to life. Only then may we say that God is "giving" the Torah, in the present moment, not only in the past. God resides not only behind the text as guarantor of its infinite elasticity but also within *us*, in the innermost chambers (*nequdah penimit*) of our endless creativity. We, through the living divine presence within us, make the text come alive. The text is a way into our own deepest selves, a tool for examining our inner lives. The king of Israel is to write a Torah and "read in it all the days of his life" (Deut. 17:18–19). The Hasidic reading of this is: you become a "king" in Israel when you learn to read (or "discover") all the days of your own life within the Torah.[62]

Such a licensing of interpretive freedom is not without its dangers. If we believe that the earliest transmitters of Torah tradition were human and fallible, how much more fallible are we in our readings! But we have no choice. We are blessed by history and community, which stand by our side, like Yakhin and Boaz, the two pillars of the Temple, to help see that our interpretations do not lead us astray. "Drink responsibly," as they say in those TV ads, of the "wine of Torah."

A Tree of Life

"She is a Tree of Life to those who take hold of her," says a verse that we recite after each public Torah reading (Prov. 3:18). The relationship between Torah and her interpreters—one that develops over the course of a lifetime, as well as across the centuries—is hardly a one-way affair. I said at the outset, trying to understand our relationship to the evolving truth of the natural/divine order: "We discover, it reveals; it reveals, we discover." The same is true in our ever-growing relationship with Torah. The text is not a passive object upon which we work the cold magic of interpretation, bringing forth meanings that are nothing but our own conjure. We fully believe in the *mutuality* of this relationship. To "take hold of" Torah, *le-haḥaziq bah*, is to hold "her" strongly, but also to gain strength from her. *She*, Torah, divine wisdom—described by the Zohar as a beautiful maiden hidden away in a palace[63]—reveals her face (indeed, her many faces) only to the one who loves her. We do not impose interpretation upon the text; we seduce the text to reveal her endless meanings to us.

The text is a living presence in our midst, a Tree of Life. Learning and interpretation are assertions of our own vitality, our attachment to that ever-renewing font of life. As we do with "God," so we do with Torah. Our religious need causes us to personify "her," to see her as one with whom we enter into intimate relationship, one to whom we give our love in gratitude for the endless love we have been given.

How could she *not* be "person" to us? If God is Father in much of Jewish imagery, Torah is both Mother and Bride. She charms us with the beauty of her subtle language and endless meanings; we respond to her charms and seek always to unlock her secrets. "Open to me, my sister, my love, my dear and perfect one, for my head is filled with dew, my locks glisten with the night" (Song of Songs 5:2). Interpretation and teaching of Torah assure that both the *giving* and *receiving* of Torah go on through the night.

Returning to the Torah of a single word, the Talmud notes that *anokhi* (consonantally A-N-K-Y), the "I am" of the first commandment, can be read as an acronym for the Aramaic *Ana Nafshai Katvit Yahavit*, "I Myself wrote it and gave it."[64] Later interpreters read the phrase differently: "I wrote and gave Myself."[65] What God gives in Torah is nothing other than God's own Self, but now in verbal form, so that we mortals may "read" God in the garb of language. This is what all sacred teaching needs to be: the divine presence parleyed into words. Since we accept that language is a human institution, we are the ones who can and must effect that transformation. The Hasidic author understands this well when he reads Deuteronomy 26:17, *et ha-shem he'emarta*, as "You have brought God into speech." But he is also wise enough to understand that when we engage in this work of articulating divinity, we mere humans are also transformed and uplifted, so much so that we humans become the voice — indeed, the only verbal voice — of God in the world. The verse goes on to say (26:18): *ve-ha-shem he'emirekha* — "God [or the silent divine presence within you] has caused you to speak, has transformed you into language." Make us Your Word, Lord, and speak us in truth.

ISRAEL: BEING HUMAN, BEING JEWISH

Response

"Where are you?" We are being called. The voice calls out to us from every corner of the natural world. *Mi-kenaf ha-arets zemirot sham'anu*, as Scripture says (Is. 24:16). "We hear singing from the corners of the earth."[1] But that same voice calls out to us from within the Torah, text and tradition also serving as *mikra'ey kodesh*, "holy callers," calling us to a life of holiness, dedicated awareness of the One that stands behind the multiplicity of our lives.

The voice calls out to every person, but we hear it uniquely as Jews, a people from the start constituted as a religious community that seeks to live in response to God's voice. How will we respond to the call? The challenge is addressed to every generation, but to ours in some unique and dramatic ways, given the high-risk times in which we live.

To begin to respond, we turn first to the universal questions, to ask: "Who are we? Why are we here? What does it mean to be a human being?" Today's universal human challenges are too great for us to allow ourselves to consider them *only* as Jews. How does seeing ourselves as religious human beings help us to respond to those questions? How is a God-seeking person supposed to live in a world threatened by destruction? Life in the early twenty-first century addresses these questions to every thinking person, whether or not that person uses the word "God." The "Where are you?" challenge calls to us all, bringing forth our shared fragile existence on this beautiful but threatened planet. Only as we face this reality, seeking out terms in which to respond, can we begin to ask: How do my humanity and my Jewishness speak to each other? What does being linked to the covenant of Sinai have to do with my self-understanding as a person and my role in the world? How do we construct a religious community (or build a *mishkan*) for our generation that embraces the best response we have to the great challenge ever before us? Because the first questions are always universal, we have to go back not just to Sinai but indeed to the first revelation, to *bereshit*, "In the beginning," and specifically to the creation of humans. We then will have to ask how such thinking works in the age of the new "Creation" story, that with which we began this inquiry. Only in this context can we address the specific questions of Jewish identity and continued Jewish existence within the "global village" culture of this new century. In doing so, we will have to complement our discussions of God and Torah with a full discussion of the term "Israel" and all that it implies, in both classical and contemporary contexts. God, Torah, and Israel are the classical Jewish trinity, the three poles around which any Jewish religious self-understanding is constructed. Dealing with each, as well as the interrelation between them, cannot be avoided. But in our day we can only get to the particularism of "Israel" by opening with the universal question: "What does it mean to be human?"[2]

Judaism's moral voice begins with Creation. Our most essential teaching, that for the sake of which Judaism still needs to exist, is our insistence that each human being is the unique image of God. "Why was Adam created singly?" asks the Mishnah. "So that no person might say: 'My father was greater than yours.'" "How great is the Creator! A human king has coins stamped out in a press and they all look alike. But God stamps each of us out in the imprint of Adam, and no two human beings are the same!" Each of us humans is needed as God's image and can be replaced by no other. It's as simple as that.[3]

"Why are graven images forbidden by the Torah?" I once heard Abraham Joshua Heschel ask. Why is the Torah so concerned with idolatry? You might think (with the Maimonideans) that it is because God has no image, and any image of God is therefore a distortion. But Heschel read the commandment differently. "No," he said, "it is precisely because God *has* an image that idols are forbidden. *You* are the image of God. But the only medium in which you can shape that image is that of your entire life. To take anything less than a full, living, breathing human being and try to create God's image out of it—that diminishes the divine and is considered idolatry."[4] You can't *make* God's image; you can only *be* God's image.

The Genesis account begins with two words for what we call "the image of God." *Tselem* is "image" in a representational sense, and it originally referred to the human form, both body and face.[5] Some versions of the early Aramaic translation of the Torah occasionally render *tselem* by the Greek loan-word "icon"; every human being is God's icon.[6] The icon was well known in the Christian art that by the fourth century was part of the dominant culture amid which Jews lived. The icon is a depiction of God, a saint, or a holy scene that comes to bear within it the presence of that holy being, and hence is revered in itself. To call each person an icon of God is to say that each human both *resembles* and *contains* the divine form. Each person is to be held aloft, revered, and kissed, as we have seen the Christians do with *their* icons. (No wonder we have no icons in the synagogue. The synagogue is filled with icons as soon as we walk in!) The second term, *demut*, is somewhat more subtle. "Likeness" is probably the right word for it. To be "like" something is to be comparable to it. But here we have a great problem. The prophet says quite clearly, speaking in God's name: "To whom will you compare Me, that I be likened?" and "To whom will you compare God? What likeness can you offer to Him?" (Is. 40:18, 25). Can we indeed be "like" God? Even if our form is theomorphic (the reversal of God as "anthropomorphic"), does that mean we are ipso facto Godlike beings?

Tselem refers to our hard wiring. We each embody a soul or a spark of inner divinity that is absolutely real and uncompromised. The entire macrocosm, the Self of the universe, is there within each human self, along with the ability to discover that truth, each in our own way. But *demut* is all about potential. To use computer imagery, it is the program we create on the basis of our hardware; it is the life we live. We *are* the *tselem* of God; we can choose to *become* God's *demut* as we work to live and fashion our lives in God's image. "I am Y-H-W-H your God who brought you out of Egypt to *become* your God" (Num. 15:41). We are both in process, somewhere along the path. Y-H-W-H is becoming our God; we are becoming God's image.

Our Most Basic Message

Rabbi Akiva and his friend Simeon Ben Azzai, sometime in the early second century, debated the question "What is the most basic principle of Torah?"[7] What is the teaching for the sake of which all the rest of Judaism exists? Akiva had a ready answer: "Love your neighbor as yourself" (Lev.19:18). Akiva was Judaism's greatest advocate for the path of love.[8] He was the one who insisted that the Song of Songs was the "Holy of Holies" within Scripture, spoken by God and Israel at Sinai.[9] The tale of Rabbi Akiva and his wife's love is one of the few truly romantic tales within the rabbinic corpus.[10] So too the account of Akiva's death; when he was being tortured by the Romans, he supposedly said: "Now I understand the commandment to love God with all your soul — even if He takes your soul."[11] Thus it is no surprise that Akiva is depicted as considering love to be the most basic rule of Torah.

But Ben Azzai disagreed. He said: I have a greater principle than yours. "On the day when God made human beings, they were made in the likeness of God; male and female God created them" (Gen. 5:1–2) is Torah's most basic principle. Every human being is God's image, says Ben Azzai to Akiva. Some are easier to love, some are harder. Some days you can love them, some days you can't. But you still have to recognize and treat them all as the image of God. Love is too shaky a pedestal on which to position the entire Torah. Perhaps Ben Azzai also saw that Akiva's principle might be narrowed, conceived only in terms of your own community. "Your *neighbor*," after all, might refer just to your fellow Jew. Or your fellow in piety, in good behavior. How about the stranger? The sinner? How about your enemy? Ben Azzai's principle leaves no room for exceptions, since it goes back to Creation itself. It's not just "your kind of people" who were created in God's image, but everyone.[12]

Once we have a basic principle, or even a set of basic principles, we have a standard by which to evaluate all other rules and practices, teachings and theological ideas. Does this particular practice lead us closer to seeing the divine in every person? Might this interpretation of a Torah verse be an obstacle toward doing so? Here lies an inner Jewish basis for raising some important questions, one that should be more in use among those who shape *halakhah* for our day.[13] Judaism may indeed exist independently of such extraneous ideas as participatory democracy, egalitarianism, and feminism. But it does not exist separately from its own most basic principle. I take the *kelal gadol* to mean "that for which all the rest exists," the animating principle behind our entire Jewish life. Then any Judaism that veers from the ongoing work of helping us allow every human being to become and be seen as God's image in the fullest way possible is a distortion of Judaism. That ongoing challenge requires us in each generation to widen the circle of those seen by us as fully human, as bearing God's image, as we seek to expand the bounds of the holy. As we find God's image in ever more of humanity, we open ourselves to ever more of God's presence. To find God in every human being is no small task. We could spend a lifetime at this art and still not perfect it. How much we have to learn about it from those who work daily with the suffering, with the dying, and especially with those so degraded by shame or societal status that they are unable to see the divine image in themselves! The greatest gift we can give to another human being is that of treating him or her as one who embodies God's presence. The greatest harm we can do is to rob a person of that sense.

Later Perspectives, Contemporary Transformations

As notions of God evolved in the course of history, so too did the concept of what it means to be "in God's image." The ancient understanding was that human beings somehow *looked* like God. You had to respect each person because that person reminded you of God, quite physically. The early sage Hillel, encountered by his students on his way to the bathhouse, told them that he was about to fulfill a divine precept. When questioned, he offered a parable of an emperor who set up statues of himself around the empire. Wouldn't he expect, Hillel asked his students, that his subjects should wash those statues and keep them clean?[14] Here it is clearly the bodily form that represents God's image, a notion found widely in early rabbinic teaching. God commands us not to leave the body of an executed criminal hanging overnight, because that body looks too much like its Maker (indeed, like His *twin*, suggests RaShI),[15] and God will be belittled by the desecration of that look-alike corpse. The death penalty is almost totally eliminated from practice by the sages because they do not want to be involved in shedding blood, something too close to the "lessening of divine image." On the other hand, the divine imperative to "be fruitful and multiply" is explained precisely as an attempt to make ever more of the divine image come into being in the world.[16]

Once Judaism and philosophy were wedded in the Middle Ages, it became clear that some other understanding of the "image" was essential. If God was to be conceived in strictly noncorporeal form, God's image had to be interpreted outside the realm of physical appearance. The simplest move was to turn to the soul, already analogized to God in older tradition. "Just as God fills all the world, so does the soul fill the entire body. . . . Just as no one knows God's place, so does no one know the location of the soul," and so forth.[17] But intellect and capacity for moral choice were also brought into the redefinition of ways in which man was uniquely to be likened to the incorporeal Deity. In all of these, of course, God was Creator and man His willfully designed creature.

The mystical tradition modified this tendency in two important ways. The Kabbalists were not so sure that "body" could not be ascribed to God,[18] even though they did not mean that in a completely physical sense. They retained the ancient awareness that the bodily form of the human being was sacred and refused to explain away the Scriptural passages that spoke about the hand, eyes, or face of God. These referred to some unknowable mystical essence, but one witnessed in the most basic symbol structure of Kabbalistic teaching. The casting of the ten *sefirot* or channels of divine energy in the form of a human body was a transformation of Judaism, or maybe a reclamation of its ancient truth in a new form of expression. In sefirotic symbolism, one could speak of God's right arm or left hip as having a particular meaning. Even more daringly, one could (and the

Kabbalists often did) speak of God's phallus and vagina, seeking to bring them together so that a cosmic birth process might take place, bringing more of divine energy into the world.

This reference to coupling and birth brings us to the second innovation of the mystics. In some of their teachings, including the highly influential Zohar, it is not clear that God "creates" a world entirely separate from the divine Self. Behind frequent masks of apologetics and denial, one gets a sense that the mystics' true faith was in emanation, the constant outflow of divine energy into all of being, linked to a needed backflow of sacred energy, through the human and specifically the Kabbalists' own channel, to replenish its source in the One. God and person are linked by something much more than a human sense of "creatureliness" and gratitude toward our Creator. They are rather two antipodes in a closed circuit of energy, each of them sending the needed charge back to the other in order to sustain the cosmic system that embraces them both. Viewed differently, one might say that existence is a great adventure. It is the One who "embarks" upon that journey or adventure, leading to existence as we know it. In that process, the One comes to be present in iconic (today we might say "holographic") form and is present within each step of the process and each being that comes to exist along the way. But the goal of that process, which we could easily depict as taking "evolutionary" form, is the emergence of humans, those who can, through their covenanted and devotional activity, channel the light back to its Source.

All of this language belongs to the old tale of Creation. But as moderns we are far from being literal "believers" in this still-beloved tale. I began this book by recognizing the length and complexity of our evolutionary journey. Our civilization has been transformed over the past century and a half in no small part by our acceptance of a new tale of origins, and today it is in the context of this account that we need to find a language for human dignity and the unique value of each human life. The history of living creatures, beginning with the origins of life itself, has been the object of both scientific research and quasi-scientific speculation over the course of the entire period since the Darwinian revolution began to take hold. An area of special interest has been physical anthropology, focusing on the evolution of our human ancestors out of those primates to whom we are most closely biologically related. Part of this work involves defining the "human." At what point, and in which skeletal remains, do we recognize some- one we can clearly call a "human" ancestor? Do we consider Homo erectus a "human" ancestor? Homo sapiens? Or only what is now called Homo sapiens sapiens? What are the criteria for defining this "humanity"? Is there a clear line we can draw between our regard for fellow members of our own species and that which we feel — and what we do — for the rest of the natural order?

I once again address this question within the conceptual framework that I laid out in the first chapter, one that seeks to reframe contem- porary scientific understanding in language and insight drawn from our mystical tradition. On the biblical verse "[God] blew the breath of life into [Adam's] nostrils," the mystics comment: "One who blows into something blows from within his own self."[19] The cosmology I outline here understands "God" as the One, the inner force of all being, present within each thing that exists, as it is present within each moment of time. It extends (or "blows") its own Self, if you will, into each of us. The emergence of each new life form, or even existence form, is a new "garbing" of the eternal One or a new breath blown forth from the inexhaustible Source. In that sense all creatures are the "image" of God, for they all embody the divine reality. But the human developed, in the course of our own evolution, a distinctive way of being. We possess unique measures of higher consciousness and self- awareness.[20] We are capable of abstract thought. We therefore bear within us the possibility of knowing the One, of mentally "seeing" the unity that binds all existence, and a degree of self-transcendence in response to this knowledge. As I said above, we may be standing on the edge of great breakthroughs in that awareness, especially as we do not yet understand how the development of artificial intelligence will interface in the future with the ongoing process of our own species' mental evolution.

Several hundred thousand years of human development and collec- tive self-assertion over other species have made us indisputable masters of this planet and its fate. From an evolutionist's point of view, we have *taken* that role by dint of human cleverness, communication, social organization, and all the rest. To an extent previously unparalleled in biohistory, a single species has outsmarted its predators (now largely microbic), cultivated (and ultimately domesticated) its prey, and adjusted to its environment. Now we have even tampered with that environment itself to suit our needs. But once again I pose the question of reframing. Is there another possible way of viewing this whole process, if we open our eyes a bit wider? Might our mastery over the fate of the planet, including the way we control and threaten the survival of so many other species, be understood as something other than a role we have taken by force of our many talents? Might we say that we have been *given* that role, precisely the one presented to us in Genesis 1:28: "and have dominion over the fish of the sea, the birds of heaven, and every living creature that roams upon the earth"? If the One is ever experimenting, pushing existence forward and seeking out new ways of being, we are but a part of that search for ever more complicated, interesting, and diverse forms of being, a process that by its own inner logic, the drive for self-manifestation, leads to the emergence of higher consciousness. As such, we need to see our existence as part of a great unfolding mystery, one we cannot fully fathom and yet one of which we are deeply aware. It is that very awareness that makes us human.

Something different, indeed unique, has happened in the course of evolution. This human species has emerged to dominate all of being on our planet. It is our actions, more than anything else, that determine "who shall live and who shall die" among the many species of plant and animal life. This fact gives us awesome responsibility. It is now clear that we could readily destroy this planet as a habitat for any but the most simple forms of life, sending it reeling backward millions of years in the evolutionary saga, perhaps never to recover. Is it coincidence that this same superefficient miner of resources and polluter of air and water also has built within it the mechanisms that make for conscience, sense of responsibility, and potential for an awareness of the One that underlies and unifies all of being? We are the "image of

God" not because of our superiority to other beings but because we can articulate the notion that *all* beings bear God's presence and we can create ways to *respond* to that presence. If we have been placed in a situation where human actions will determine the fate of all creatures, we surely have the obligation to act out of our deepest understanding of what that terrible responsibility means.

The fact that we are in that role, determining the future of the planet and all that dwells upon it, requires that the One, the force of Being that inhabits us all, relate to us, its own human self-manifestation, in a different way. God *has to* be revealed to us in our own way, Torah *has to* "speak in human language," because we are creatures who demand dialogue, who need to be addressed in order to respond, who need to be asked "Where are you?" in order to act as partners in helping the planet to survive.

Thinking about the Soul

When we speak of human uniqueness among the diverse creatures of our planet, the term "soul" rises up from the legacy of our ancient religious language. Never mind that the Hebrew *neshamah* connotes nothing other than "breath" in its original meaning. It certainly was taken by postbiblical tradition to refer to something distinctive about humans, a kind of divine presence within us (as indicated by Genesis 2:7, quoted above) that made us human and gave us a form of life that belongs to us alone.

I hesitate to use the word "soul," because it is so widely thought of as a "thing" or an entity that exists (or does not exist) "somewhere" within the person, and as an entity that survives (or does not survive) after the person is dead. But "soul" as I understand it is precisely not an entity, any more than "God" is an entity. Just as Y-H-W-H is not a "thing," but refers to the transcendent wholeness of Being that both surpasses and embraces all beings, so is the soul to be seen as the transcendent wholeness of the person, a mysterious essence that is more than the sum of all the characteristics of that person that we could ever name.[21] As the "breath of God" that exists within the person, *neshamah* or soul represents the link between our individual self and the great Self of being. It is the aspect of us that was not separated from our Source, that has never let go of its divine root in the long process of individuation and alienation that constitutes human life. The soul is that "holy being" within us that remembers the One and seeks to "re-member" us to it, to re-join us to our Source.[22] Difficult as it is to find that place of inner connection to the cosmos and all that is, I believe that it is present within each of us.

The quest for that aspect of ourselves is one way of depicting the core of the religious journey. We sense within us a "place" that joins us to the force of life itself, or to the Being that unites us with all other creatures. That part of us has been covered over, hidden from us, by the "grime" created by our fast-paced and high-risk ways of living.[23] Being the most sensitive and vulnerable part of us, it is covered with layers of self-protective gear that we develop over the course of our lives. Our fragile inner core, that of which we say each day "My God, the soul You placed within me is pure," is surrounded by a hard shell.[24] For many of us, that protective layer keeps the innermost self hidden, even from ourselves. Various things that happen to us in life — especially in childhood — cause us so to harden our shell that it becomes nearly impossible to break through it. The "journey" to God is thus nothing other than a return to our deepest self, a reclaiming of our own soul. Our task is to seek out that innermost reality, to find it, and to reshape the rest of our lives around that journey homeward.

As for the "immortality" of the soul, I can only affirm that the breath of God never dies. As we breathe out, for the final time, that which the One has breathed into us, the divine breath is already busy entering new life-forms, new human babies, new saplings, flowers, birds, and bees all over the world. I know nothing much about rebirth or reincarnation, only that the divine breath is eternal. The real religious question for me has always been: "Is there life *before* death?" As to the other question, surrender to the mystery of existence is the only truth I know. Among the many teachings I associate with reciting the daily *shema'* is its ordering of divine names. "Y-H-W-H *eloheynu* [our God] Y-H-W-H" means that endless Being was there before each and all of us came into existence. It is *our* God for the brief instant we flash across life's screen. But then we let go, and it is Y-H-W-H, endless Being, once again.[25]

Species and Tribe

The paradox of Jewish existence is that this universal message is borne by a very particular people, one that has been struggling to preserve its own existence, often not an easy task, for the past two thousand years. We exist in order to teach and bear witness to our primary values, the oneness of Y-H-W-H and the creation of each person in God's image. In order to do that, however, we Jews need to survive, to live with a certain security and respect. Having lived so long in societies where our own full humanity was questioned, we naturally became busy with issues of self-preservation and defense. Even today, in an age when we are less threatened than in almost any prior age, we bear the burden of historical memory (reinforced a thousandfold by the all-too-recent Holocaust and now by the promulgation of Nazi-like views in parts of the Islamic world) that makes us think and act defensively.

Having shared with you so much of what I mean by "God" and "Torah," I now need to turn to the third leg of the classical Jewish triad and address the question of "Israel."[26] I begin with what is bedrock for me, the verse from which I very nearly chose this book's title: "I will dwell amid the Children of Israel and become their God. Then they will know that I am Y-H-W-H their God who brought them forth from the Land of Egypt *to dwell within them.* I am Y-H-W-H their God" (Ex. 29:45–46). Israel is a dwelling place for God in this world. We are a living parallel to the *mishkan,* a wandering sanctuary for the divine presence. Our task through history is ever the same: to constitute a human community in which God is present, in which that presence is felt from within and seen from without. As each person is the image of God, an embodiment of divinity, so are we *as a people* to bear that living presence within us. This is the purpose of the whole enterprise, the reason God brought us forth from Egypt. We are liberated from human bondage in order to become an earthly familial home, a dwelling, for Y-H-W-H, the ever-living force that redeemed us.

To understand Judaism and the Jewish mindset, one needs to understand that our most basic statement of faith involves this collective experience of liberation from bondage. The full text called the *shema'*, recited morning and evening, concludes with the sentence "I am Y-H-W-H your God who brought you out of the Land of Egypt to be your God; I am Y-H-W-H your God" (Num. 15:41). The ten commandments are introduced by "I am Y-H-W-H your God who brought you out of the Land of Egypt, from the house of bondage" (Ex. 20:2).[27] These verses are two of many, scattered through Torah and the prophetic writings that repeat this theme. In this way Judaism differs from both Christianity and Islam, where the most essential faith message is directed to the individual. Jewish faith is about belonging to this liberated community of former slaves. Being "Israel" means identifying fully with that experience, as though it had just happened yesterday.

Although we were victimized in Egypt as members of a particular clan, we came out of the experience with a universal message. What was done to us, the dehumanization and degradation wrought by slavery, must never happen to another person or group anywhere. (The wisest survivors of our more recent trials know and proclaim this as well.) All of being is one; each human is the image of God. We, Israel, have been lifted out of slavery to bear witness to that truth.

Whom do we mean when we say "Israel?" The classic definition, those born into the Jewish people plus those who properly convert, is too simple, begging too many vexing questions. Is it all those who identify with this liberation from bondage? That seems too broad, for the story of Egypt has indeed become the property of all humanity. The fact is that there are many Israels. "Who is *my* Israel?" I ask myself. Who constitutes the community in whose midst I seek to share both my struggle for liberation and my joy in celebrating that freedom? *You* indeed are my Israel. You for whom I write, you whom I teach, you with whom I feel a deep kinship of shared human values and love of this Jewish language. Are you all Jews, in the formal sense? I'm not much worried about that question. In fact I am especially happy there are non-Jewish readers, especially Christians, with whom I share so much, along on this journey. But such readers might want to know on what terms you are welcomed, in what sense *we* together are collectively constituted as God's this-worldly home. Are you fellow sojourners, non-Jews sympathetic to this theological language, or members of a newly defined "House of Israel"? Or does the ancient category of "Israel" make no sense any more, in an age when we so urgently need to share our message with all of humanity? Is it time to shed our tribal identity for the sake of our universal values?

Such a current of thought was widespread among liberal Jews in America a few generations ago (think of Felix Adler, the founder of the Ethical Culture movement, among many others). This way of thinking became discredited after the Holocaust, when we all took on the responsibility of preserving very threatened Jewish survival. I belong to that generation of newly reinforced commitment to continued Jewish existence. We want to survive as a distinct human family among nations. Without that distinctive identity, who would remain as bearers of our hard-learned values into the next and future generations? Would not all the painfully gained insights of the Jewish experience be lost if we simply merged with all the many others who share our essential truths? Yet I am still concerned that we Jews, now free to preach our truth to the world without harassment, devote much more energy to our own survival than to the message that is its purpose. As one raised as a loyal Jew, and as one who has given much energy to the training of leaders whose efforts also will be largely devoted to Jewish continuity, I sometimes find us erring on the side of too much insecurity about our own existence, distracting ourselves from our more ultimate goal, that of being and building God's *mishkan* in the world. Such efforts are completely understandable in an age that still recalls that a third of us were brutally murdered in an event that remains within living memory. We also live in an open and embracing society that serves, in a completely different way, to further diminish our numbers. Still, we need to remind ourselves that the Jewish people was brought forth from Egypt and continues to exist for a purpose, and that is one that reaches beyond ourselves. I live and work within a framework that struggles daily around balancing these values, and I cannot ignore that struggle.

Dealing as I do in myth and Midrash, I will have to express this agony around the universal and the particular by sharing with you some further readings of Genesis. Earlier we walked the journey from Eden to Abraham, tales of the near-failure of the human experiment. Now we must go from Abraham to Jacob/Israel, saying something about the rise of Jewish particularism and how it still embodies the universal message. From there, after an important detour, we will turn once again to Exodus and Sinai, asking ourselves "where we stand" in facing that mountain and how Israel's covenant might be renewed for our day.

The religious path I am describing here might well be called a Judaism for seekers. It is all about challenge and response, one that by definition has to change and grow in each generation and even in the course of single lives. I like to think of it as a Judaism faithful to the journeys of Avraham Avinu, our father Abraham, who is the original figure of religious quest in our tradition. Abraham did not live his religious life out of faithfulness or loyalty to tradition. He was anything but a nice Jewish boy, making his parents proud. On the contrary, he models a radical break with all that came before him. He is a seeker and a no-holds-barred experimentalist, daring to challenge each stage of his own religious development. Thus we are told that (after smashing his father's idols) he worshipped both sun and moon until he discovered a power greater than these. The biblical text portrays God's call to him as unearned and spontaneous — almost as arbitrary, one might say, as God's rejection of Cain's offering.[28] But later tradition sees it quite differently. Abraham is the paradigmatic seeker in Judaism. Philo, the Midrash, the philosophers, and the Hasidic masters all depict him as engaged in a journey of discovery, one in which God answers him, rather than initiating the dialogue.[29] Abraham is unique among humans because of his courage and defiance; it is these qualities that attract God to him as one with whom to covenant. The term *'ivri* ("Hebrew") is first used to describe Abraham.

The rabbis read it to mean "contrarian" — "the whole world stood on one side ['*ever*] and he on the other."[30] Swimming against the stream will be essential to the Abrahamic legacy.

When I say that God "answers" Abraham, you may wonder just what a believer like me could mean by that word. I do not take it in a literal or personifying way. The Midrash compares Abraham to one wandering about the world and encountering a tower engulfed in flames[31] (or, as Heschel sometimes chose to read it, "a palace full of light"). "Can it be that the tower has no owner?" he cried. Then the owner looked out and said: "I am the owner of the tower." Abraham was a seeker. He confronted the tough nut of trying to understand life's meaning. "Can it all be for naught?" he asked. "Can all this pain — or all this beauty — have no meaning?" And life responded to him, opened up to him, *spoke* to him, saying: "It all has a purpose." He chose to follow the voice that spoke within him. That One of the inner voice needs these rare contrarian types. Who but they will push forward the evolution of human thought?

This "choosing" of (or "by") Abraham does not imply the rejection of others as God's children.[32] If reality "reveals" itself to Abraham, this by no means implies that it does so for him alone. Abraham's search becomes our doorway into the mystery; we have no need to deny the existence of other doors. Abraham and Sarah's wide-open tent flaps point to an intent to convert as much of humanity as they encounter to the monotheistic vision, but not to "Judaism" in a specific sense. Future Christians and Muslims can easily find room for themselves in the original big tent that our first ancestors worked so hard to create, ever expanding on "those souls they had acquired in Haran" (Gen. 12:5).[33] Melchizedek, outside the tent, is still a "priest to the most high God" (Gen. 14:18). In standing up for the people of Sodom and Gomorrah, Abraham challenges God not for members of his own tribe or faith community, just for fellow humans.[34] His defining cry of outrage ("Will the judge of all the earth not do justice?" [Gen. 18:25]) shows how far we have moved from the times of Cain. Now God, partner in a covenant, can be called to live up to certain expectations.

These expectations, however, have to do not just with "members of the tribe" but rather with ordinary, sinful humans and the "righteous" (by their deeds, not creed or lineage) who live among them.

But Judaism does not remain a religion of lone seekers. It is the religious legacy of a tribe, a people, who sees itself as a covenanted community. That covenant begins with Abraham. However we conceive God, the legacy of standing in the line of generations, all of whom carry forth the ancient covenant of faith, is central to our self-understanding. We celebrate the human advantage of building and living in community by passing down a strong sense of inherited faith from one generation to the next. How does this process begin? The question is historical, but it applies as well to the life of the individual in each generation. How do we go from one to the other, from seeker to tribe? Abraham is to be not just a seeker of God but the founder of a clan. What happens to us and to our very private quest when we decide to pass it on, to build the spiritual legacy of a family around it? Many seekers today are asking that very question. For more than a few, it is this challenge that brings them back to our shared tradition. Judaism is made for families. To be a Jew is to see oneself as a link between generations, passing down an ancient legacy.

The question of progeny becomes central when we seek to create a clan, immediately raising the question "Who is in and who is out?" as clans necessarily do. Here the rival claims begin, and the pain that has so long accompanied the Abrahamic legacy first asserts itself. Ishmael is the first rejected child (or the second, after Cain) of the biblical narrative. God (and the narrator) "hear his voice" (Gen. 21:17) to be sure, but Ishmael is defined as outsider. He is not cursed like Adam or Cain; he will sire a great tribe and ultimately a new covenant with God. But the resentment of his exclusion from the tribe will not be forgotten, as we know so well.

Isaac, risen from the altar of Moriah, carries forth the legacy. He knows and embodies the *fear* of God just as fully as Abraham is the bearer of God's love. Isaac carries with him the constant awareness of mortality; his brush with death at God's whim and his father's hand is not forgotten. He sees God's face as one sees it lying face-up while bound on the altar. The "laughter" that is in his name ("Isaac" means "he laughs") does not succeed in masking his burden of terror before God. Isaac again has two sons, seemingly repeating his father's pattern, but this time they are twins, born together of the same womb, underscoring their closeness. Esau is a hunter, like his uncle Ishmael. Isaac admires this, perhaps fulfilling through a son his own secret longing to have been more like his brother. Jacob is a man of the tents, his mother's favorite. He stakes a claim to the birthright in obvious acts of duplicity, even though he is the younger son.

Again progeny, tales of the clan, the need to choose. Biblical scholars claim that these tales reflect the insecurity and self-justification of the ancient Israelites, latecomers to the Land of Canaan, who nevertheless insisted that the country was theirs, the covenantal gift of God. God chooses the younger son. (Really? Always? What will we say today? Who *is* the younger son in today's Land of Israel?) Whether or not we accept this historical interpretation of the displacement of the firstborn, the discomfort Jews have long felt with the Jacob texts shows our awkwardness in being proclaimed God's chosen tribe. How else to explain the Midrashic discussion of Esau's tears after he loses the blessing? How else to account for the sages' need to protect themselves from sympathizing with Esau's embrace of Jacob on his return, depicting it instead as an attempt to bite his neck?[35]

But the key moment of transformation in the midst of this difficult narrative is Jacob's wrestling (or is it lovemaking?) with the angel (or is it God? or Esau?) after he crosses the Jabbok. Jacob refuses to give in to the one who challenges him. He emerges from the struggle wounded, but having wrested a blessing from the other. It is in that encounter that *Israel* is formed, a word said to mean "wrestler with God" or "divine struggler." Israel is defined as such by that struggle, one that has to balance the legacies of father and grandfather, the love and the terror in facing the God with which we humans live. "Israel is holy unto Y-H-W-H" (Jer. 2:3), knowing both of these, love and terror, to the fullest.

So Jacob, the most beautiful human since Adam[36] (and perhaps just as multigendered as Adam/Eve before the fall), already husband and father, has an all-nighter, fighting, loving, and struggling with a nameless stranger who knows him better than he knows himself. If Jacob and Leah are the source of our Judean/Jewish bodies, our Israelite souls are born of *this* encounter between Israel and the One beyond name.

The tribe has always insisted that Jacob and Israel are one. It was Jacob's sons, "the Children of Israel," who went down into Egypt and there were forged into a people, the ones who were to receive the Torah. "Moses commanded us the Torah, the legacy of Jacob's clan" (Deut. 33:4). The name belongs to us, all of us, and we to it. It belongs to us across history, no matter where or when we live. We have earned it by lots of suffering. *'Aseh le-ma'an ba 'ey ba-esh uva-mayyim 'al qiddush shemekha:* "Do it for the sake of those who have gone through fire and water to sanctify Your name."[37]

As part of that Israel I stand before God together with all my ancestors and those who will come after me, each with our own relationship to the sacred legacy of that name. This Israel includes many with whom I feel little in common. Our views — religious, political, social — may be deeply in conflict. But we all know that we are Israel. We know it in the synagogue on Yom Kippur and we knew it in the days before the 1967 Six Day War and again in the 1973 Yom Kippur War. We know we are all Israel because of the Holocaust, because of the Nuremberg Law that required every Jewish male to take the name "Israel" as a middle name, in order to distinguish us from the "Aryan" population. We bear it with pride.

The fact that I belong to this sacred community does not establish my only religious landscape. Living in our era of both an open society and a previously unimagined awareness of other cultures and civilizations, I feel a sense of fellowship with seekers, strivers, and doers everywhere. This fellowship does not depend upon whether they have any interest in being considered part of my Israel or share any relationship to the legacy of that name. While I may experience them as "Israel," to declare them such would be a sort of spiritual imperialism. I recognize my fellowship with them without needing to make them over into my own. They may be Buddhist monks or "secular" ecologists, jesters in the marketplace who make people laugh or great musicians who make their spirits soar. When I pray for God to "bring peace to us and to all Israel," I find myself wanting to include them as well.

Between these two groups, the historic Jewish people and the world community of seekers and strugglers, there lies a third, no less important community. We need to find a special place for those who revere and feel attached to the spiritual legacy of Israel without belonging to the historically defined Jewish people. Israel, "wrestler with God," is too big a name to belong just to a single people. We need a way to share it with others, welcoming them to feel like participants in this legacy, without ourselves being threatened, without fearing that we will lose our uniqueness.

In the first two centuries of the Common Era, historians tell us, the boundaries that separated the historical people of Israel from the "godfearers," Gentiles who frequented the synagogue (especially in the diaspora) and supported its worship, were not entirely rigid. Access to Torah and its message was little restricted, and newcomers were welcomed to an expansively conceived community with various levels of association. The very notion of *giyyur*, or "conversion," to Judaism arose out of this situation, along with the emergence of what we call "Judaism" itself.[38] Historical factors, including rivalry with the growing Christian church and then a long history of persecution, sealed our borders quite tightly for many centuries. "Israel" consisted of Jews by birth, defined by the more certain maternal line (in the face of all those marauding Crusaders and Cossacks), and a very small trickle of outsiders who chose the difficult — and in many eras dangerous — path of conversion. With rare exceptions, no one else wanted or dared try to be part of Israel. We were, after all, a historically defeated people, as supersessionist preachers, both Christian and Islamic, continually reminded us. Who would want to join a community of such historic losers?

This situation has changed drastically within the past several decades, due to a complex series of historical factors. The borders of Jewish peoplehood have become open again: Ethiopian Jews of questionable historical lineage, Russian Jews of mixed background, non-

Orthodox converts, adoptees, patrilineal Jews (recognized by some and not by others), and unconverted spouses of Jews are all finding their way into our community. Groups we'd never heard of—in Africa, India, and Latin America—are seeking to reclaim some tie they believe they have to the House of Israel. The instinct of our most traditional Jews, especially of the Orthodox rabbinate, has been to suspect all these as potential incursions and seek to build a high wall against them, making the rules for conversion tougher than ever. But perhaps we need to see this historic moment as an occasion that calls us to a different way of thinking. Perhaps we are being "told" something by this sweeping and somewhat shocking change in our historical situation.

Jewish existence remains a *covenanted* existence. We know that we are not "like all the nations," tempting as the thought of such normalcy might sometimes be. We go on throughout eternity for the sake of our message, in order to teach it, exemplify it, and bring it to others. Once we recognize that our essential message is a universal one, defining ourselves so narrowly as its exclusive bearers does not suffice. We *want* others to pick up the banner that proclaims all creatures sacred embodiments of the One, all humans the image of God. If our struggle is to share our insights with all humanity, we *need* a broader band of fellow travelers to bear this message. How will we make room for it to flourish? Some would want to become Jews, if we would make them more welcome. It is time to encourage and greet with open arms those who want to share our home with us, rather than drive them away. If Jewry was reduced by a third through the horrors of the Holocaust, it is time to replenish our numbers by opening the gates to make conversion more accessible. That will certainly make for a new and different Jewish people in this new and different age in which we live, but we should have sufficient faith not to be afraid of that. Those who choose conversion in this age, accepting Judaism's essential teachings and practices, ready to join themselves to the Jewish people, should be welcomed rather than driven away by ever more demanding requirements.

But we also have to find a place alongside the historic Jewish people for a bigger and broader "Israel," an Israel of Noahides, Abrahamians, New Israelites, or whatever they will choose to be called. These are people who partake of the legacy of biblical Israel and accept our most basic Jewish teachings as their own, without being ready to fully share our history, language, identity, and fate. What might be required for membership in such a broader "Israel?" A spiritually wounded thigh, to show that one has wrestled with God? A forswearing of anti-Semitism? A monotheism/monism that lives the Torah's sacred story? Can we imagine re-creating in our time a kind of extended faith-community of Israel, a large "outer courtyard" of our spiritual Temple? For non-Jews wedded to Jews and others considering but not yet ready for full conversion to Judaism, might this also serve as a sort of spiritual antechamber?[39]

In making this proposal, I am not unaware that I will quickly be accused by many Jews of giving in to that sinner Saul of Tarsus, the one who welcomed the uncircumcised heathen into his New Israel, as the church was to call itself. No, I am not here announcing my apostasy or the rejection of my own very deep commitment to the specific and ethnically defined heritage I received from my Eastern European Jewish grandparents. But I am pushing against the borders of my own community, and admitting (partly in sadness!) that it no longer suffices for me to limit my sense of spiritual fellowship to those who fall within the ethnic boundaries that history has given us. In a way that is significant to me, I have more in common with seekers and strugglers of other faiths than I do with either the narrowly and triumphally religious or the secular and materialistic elements within my own Jewish community. Yes, I am quite aware that Hitler and his henchmen would have herded us all together. But that does not suffice as a standard by which to set the bounds of my own sacred community, at least not on every level.

Would membership in this broader Israel require a leaving behind of other faiths? Should Islam, a completely "kosher" faith for non-Jews from a *halakhic* point of view, be treated differently from some forms of Hinduism or Buddhism, where the issues of both polytheism and the worship of "graven images" stand between us? The more significant question here, however, regards Christianity, which stands upon an ancient claim to be the "New Israel." There is no question that Christianity has historically served as the much broader mouth-piece for proclaiming Israel's prophetic message, including the values and literary treasures of what Christendom calls the "Old Testament." Many of these values are echoed in Christian Scripture, including the Sermon on the Mount and other key texts. Christianity, being so directly based on Hebrew Scripture, is less entirely "other" to us than any other tradition. The church certainly considers itself "Israel" in its liturgical use of the Psalms, for example, where "Israel" is clearly taken to refer to Christendom as the "people of God." Jews and Christians are indeed sibling communities, fellow heirs to the same legacy of ancient Israel. One of those heirs insisted that ethnic, mostly biological, descent from Israel was key to that heritage, while the other did not. But both created new ways of "being religious" in the early centuries of the Common Era. When the first Christians were mostly Jews, the emerging rabbis referred to the Nazarene faith as *minut*, a "sectarian" version of Judaism, rather than as another religion. But Christianity is also the tradition with which we have such a uniquely long and tortured historical past. Early Christian rivalry with rabbinic teaching, evidenced already in the gospels, set us up as the villains of Christianity's sacred story. This ancient rivalry was reinforced by later Christian insecurity in the face of Israel's stubborn survival, causing the churches to be major instigators of anti-Semitism throughout history, ranging from Crusades to blood libel to pogrom to Holocaust. Many thoughtful Christians, including the wing of the Catholic Church that most fully accepted Vatican II, have come to understand and acknowledge this fully.[40] Christian contrition for the church's role in the demonization and persecution of Jews, and particularly for the Holocaust, touches me deeply. While we Jews should never place ourselves in the role of judge ("Was that statement by the pope sufficient? Did he mention Auschwitz enough times?"), we should also not have to bear the burden of willingness to forgive. The gulf of historic pain that divides our two Israels is ancient and real, not to be overcome in the course of a single generation.

We two Israels will best build trust by sharing the work we need to do. Humanity's need for our shared message is too urgent, and we have far too long been distracted from sharing it. "The day is short, the work is great" is more true in our day than ever before in human history. Our work today lies in spreading the message of Ben Azzai's teaching, reconceived for an age of open borders and environmental crisis, as far and wide as we are able, welcoming cooperation with and help from all who want to join in that work. We understand that when we say: "Every person bears the image of God," Christians may prefer to say: "Every person contains the presence of Christ." We will learn to translate and continue the dialogue; the work is too important to be derailed by such differences of language and symbol.

Of course, "Israel" too can be seen as symbol as well as historical reality. Just as "God" or "the blessed Holy One" stands in for all that my monist soul means by the underlying oneness of being, and "Torah" represents the silence that both transcends and fills all language, so too "Israel" gestures beyond itself toward that broader representation of humanity. This point is made beautifully by a Hasidic rereading of an argument that originates in the exegesis of Jewish law. An ancient Midrash opens with a list of thirteen hermeneutical principles by which Torah is to be interpreted. One of these reads as follows: "Anything that belonged to a particular category and then became exceptional to that category did so in order not only to teach about itself but also to instruct with regard to the entire category." The *Sefat Emet* was in the habit of applying this purely technical legal argument to broad issues of theological content as well. *Shabbat* was within the category of days, he taught. When it became exceptional, it did so not only to teach us of the Sabbath but to show us how to regard time during the week as well, how to make the weekday sacred. The Land of Israel is within the category of lands; when it was proclaimed holy and thus made exceptional, we were to learn also about the holiness of land itself, not just this particular one. So too the people of Israel: our election comes to indicate the potential holiness of all peoples, not just our own.

Another "Israel"

Any discussion of "Israel" in our day is incomplete without reference to a relatively new claimant to the title, and that is Israel the state, established in our holy Land of Israel in 1948. Its citizens (Jews and non-Jews) are *Israelis*, which I am not, though I am a supporter, albeit often a loving critic, of Israel the state. I visit Israel frequently, I read Israeli literature, some of my own books are published there in Hebrew translation; I thus feel myself a distant participant in the rich Jewish cultural life of Israel. Nonetheless, I am an outsider to that society and place, an outsider by choice, as are all Jews today who do not live in Israel. While I take great pride, as do most Jews of my generation, in Israel's founding and achievements, part of me is unhappy that the state has laid claim to that name, one that belongs to me as well as to the Jew who lives in Tel Aviv or Jerusalem.[41]

Had I shared with Franz Rosenzweig the luxury of living and dying before 1933, I too might have shared his distance from political Zionism, questioning whether Jews should abandon their transtemporal sacred calendar-based identity for one that grapples fully with the reality of history. I surely would have seen myself as a cultural Zionist, partaking fully in the revival of the Hebrew language and Jewish culture, but probably would not have seen the need for a Jewish state. Suspect as I am of nation-states and their motives, and an internationalist by inclination, I would have supported another path. I would have shared the concerns of Judah Magnes, Martin Buber, and others for the rights of the Palestinian Arabs in their own land, as indeed I still do. But the realities of history did not offer that luxury. After Hitler came to power and the world evaded responsibility for the gathering storm, it became clear that we Jews needed both the protection and the pride offered by having a state of our own. The political Zionists were made right by the history we all dreaded. Israel as a place of refuge and the ingathering of exiles became a necessity after the war, and it is still unthinkable to me not to have Israel as a Jewish state, which on the most basic level means a defender of the Jewish people in the international forum and a refuge for Jews facing persecution.[42] I hesitate to comment further on the state of Israel in the context of a Jewish theology because I accord the state no theological meaning. I am a *religious* Jew and a *secular* Zionist, which is to say that I do not believe the founding of Israel to be "the first flowering of our redemption," as the chief rabbbinate's prayer puts it. I accord no messianic or protomessianic meaning to the existence of a Jewish state. The scourge of anti-Semitism, a deep blight on the Western, mainly Christian, moral conscience, reached a point at which Jewish life in Europe became impossible. The Zionists were right in seeing this crisis coming well before 1933, a reality hotly denied by others at the time. We Jews needed to create a society of our own. We did so both for both negative and positive reasons: as an escape from prejudice against us and as an opportunity to develop our own language, culture, and tradition in a society where they would be completely at home. It seemed natural to us to do this in our people's ancient homeland. Perhaps we did not fully realize how deeply our values would be put to the test in employing them to bring forth a new social and political reality.

To say that I accord the state no messianic status does not mean, however, that I refuse to find meaning in the fact of its existence. Perhaps here I should say a more general word about my attitude toward history. I am not, as should be clear by now, a believer in traditional views of providence, meaning that God consciously rules over the historic process and causes certain events to come about. Once confrontation with the Holocaust caused me to lose that faith, I was not able to resurrect it for the sake of Israel or its rather astounding victories in 1948 and 1967. I mostly found the attempts of others to do so rather shallow and jingoistic. But my disbelief in a God who causes these events to happen does not free me from *seeking* God in them when they do occur. If God is present in each place and moment, as the Ba'al Shem Tov teaches, God is present too in the events of history. It is our task to find these events meaningful, to find challenge within them as to how to better direct our lives in the face of them, which is to find God — or the Presence, or the divine spark — within them. If we ask where God is to be found in the Holocaust, we

usually think of the *shekhinah* compassionately identifying with the suffering, present also in the small acts of kindness, even in the ghettos and camps, that defied the horrors and kept a glimmer of humanity alive.

The return to Zion and the creation of a Jewish state in the aftermath of the Holocaust and at the very moment of the breakup of the colonial era in world history surely calls upon us to think about the meaning of those events, all the more so as we hear in them undeniable echoes of ancient prophecies. The coincidence of the birth of the Jewish state and the end of the colonial age tells us that a society created by Jews in what we believe to be a holy place needs to be built on the universal values of Judaism discussed above. Our faith and the legacy of our history will not permit a Jewish society to act as a colonial society, one in which a self-defined "superior" population imposes itself upon, and appropriates the resources, including the land, of a "native" human group, whom it then deprives of freedom. If it sounds to our ears as though Israel's founding might be too close for comfort to that description, it is *our* job, as Israel, to make sure that is not the whole story, to participate as best we can (from within or without) in the emergence of a noncolonialist Israel.

Any discussion of this subject has to be marked by compassion for all the sufferers and by awareness of the historical context. A third of our people were destroyed in a series of horrific events that came to define the term "genocide" for the entire human community. Those European Jews who were left after 1945 wanted more than anything else to leave that blood-stained continent and to go to the Land of Israel, to build a state or community of their own, free from Gentile domination. Who could oppose such a morally justified will? As Elie Wiesel used to say, Europe was glad to get rid of the survivors, so as not to have to look them in the eye and be reminded of its own guilt.

History put us in an untenable situation. How could anyone expect the Jewish refugees from Hitler, soon to be joined by a mass flight of Jews from Arab lands, to stop and consider that their new homeland was being built at someone else's expense? The myth that the Holy Land was "a land without a people," waiting to receive these "people without a land," fitted the needs of the moment too well. Unfortunately, it was not true, as the Jews already living in the land knew quite well. There has indeed been significant suffering on the other side as well. We Jews, of all people, need to be big and openhearted about acknowledging that.

For more than four decades now I have stood on the critical left flank of Israel's supporters, urging peace with the Palestinians, a negotiated return of territories, and a viable two-state solution to the problems of the Middle East. I am fully convinced that there is no long-term future for Israel without a two-state solution.[43] Above all, we need to recognize the full humanity and dignity of the Arabs with whom we are fated to share a land. I also firmly believe that this is the "message" we need to find in our current difficult situation. At a time of terrible interethnic conflicts throughout humanity, in an age when the nuclear threat means that we can no longer afford to take such hostilities lightly, the Jewish people, this "kingdom of priests and holy nation," reclaims and returns to its ancient homeland, becoming a party to the seemingly most intractable of all these conflicts. What is the message in this situation? We have the opportunity here to teach our truth — that of Ben Azzai's principle — in the most powerful way ever. We can do so by generosity, by seeing the humanity, including the pain, of the other, and by concluding that the only way to live in a Holy Land is to share it with its other inhabitants. If we cannot find it in our hearts to do that, even in the face of real obstacles and sometimes atrocious behavior by the other side, we and our tradition will have failed a vital test.

So far we are not doing too well. Arab intransigence and the horrors of the intifada years have weakened the vision of a humanitarian Zionism. We who believe in it, both in Israel and in the diaspora, have been too ready to allow it to fade. Most of all, we have reason to be concerned that Israel (and here too this name refers to all the Jewish people) not be overwhelmed by a Holocaust-dominated view of the world.[44] Ever conscious that we did not take the Nazi threat seriously enough, we now tend to put all our enemies in the same category as Hitler. We take seriously anyone who talks about destroying the Jews, pushing us into the sea, or wiping Israel off the map. How could we do otherwise? But we cannot allow this needed vigilance to paralyze us, to render us unable to trust. Sometimes one has to take risks for the sake of peace, for the possibility of coexistence, especially when the alternative, living forever within the bunker and behind barbed wire, is unacceptable. "The Arabs are not Hitler," we of the Left have insisted. Despite the worst of some of their preachers' rhetoric, most Palestinians are waiting for accommodation to reality and are as frightened as we are of the threatened apocalypse. A two-state solution to the Israel-Palestine conflict *must* be possible, and we (a "we" that includes Israel, the United States government, and world Jewry) need to be doing much more to make it happen. Israel will not be able long to survive as only a garrison state, both because garrison states do not have a good track record of survival and because such an existence is ultimately a betrayal of the best of Jewish values.

I write these words as a Jew who has chosen to live outside the Holy Land. I fully realize that their moral power would be infinitely greater had I chosen otherwise, and if my own life and that of my family were on the line each day, as are the lives of my fellow Jews in Israel. Some would say that my choice not to become an Israeli makes it illegitimate for me to express these views, which are vacuous when offered by one who lives abroad. But I cannot keep silent. All of us Jews, wherever we live, inherit the same name of Israel and the same tradition. We have the same prophets' words thundering in our ears. As our long history has shown, we also share a common fate. A threatened Israel threatens us all. I deeply hope not to live in an era in which there is no state of Israel. I thus find myself affirming Israel and challenging it, longing for it to be more the Israel of my dreams (which it has not been since 1967), while sympathizing with its sense of constant struggle for existence. I grow especially uncomfortable when I see Israel and its political leaders, for or against whom I have no chance to vote, speaking as the leadership of *my* Israel, the entire Jewish people, or seen as such by the world. When I see the so-called leaders (again, unelected) of my own diaspora Jewish community unwilling to criticize the state on any level, even when the good and holy name of Israel is clearly desecrated by its actions (using cluster bombs in Lebanon, uprooting olive trees in occupied Palestinian villages, demolishing homes without good reason, and so on), I come closest to despairing of the Jewish future.

There are other matters on which we diaspora Jews differ essentially, and sometimes even in loud argument, with the official Israeli point of view. Zionism has long viewed the figure of the wandering Jew as a tragedy of history, one to be overcome by the return to our ancient homeland and by the forging of a "new Jew" who was to emerge from that transformative process. Diaspora Jews are depicted by Israelis as physically unable to defend ourselves, unduly mercantile (and therefore trying to *buy* freedom rather than earn it honorably), living too much in the mind and too little in body and soil. From our point of view, there is a good deal of internalized anti-Semitism in this stereotype. The experience of building a new Jewish society, including that of fighting to defend it, was supposed to redeem us from these anomalies and bring about a new health and "normality" in the Jewish people.

This is not the place to debate the relative successes and failures of Zionism in creating a new Jew. Israel is clearly no longer a society based on the agrarian idealism that saw the new Jew formed by working the land. While secular Israeli values were largely shaped by a break with religion that was sharper and more clearly defined than the break that took place among Jews who migrated westward, in recent years it has become increasingly clear to Israelis and diaspora Jews that we are indeed a single people, sharing both a cultural legacy and a future. There are issues that divide us, to be sure. Diaspora Jews' tendency toward optimistic liberal universalism, so soon after the Holocaust, drives many Israelis crazy. They see our worldview as apologetic and naive, one that refuses to look at the precarious position of the Jew. Their blatantly higher regard for Jewish life and Jewish rights than for those of others, a kind of compensatory view seeking to make up for so many centuries of Jewish victimhood, often deeply offends what we diaspora liberals see as most sacred to our own Jewish values. This is especially true for us American Jews, who live in a society deeply scarred by the legacy of mistreating a minority. The analogy to America, however accurate or not, never leaves us, and we find ourselves quite horrified that Jews could create a society in which we are privileged over others.

A Diasporist Judaism

On one point the Zionist reading of contemporary Jewish history is surely right. With the state of Israel and a thriving Jewish society in its land, the involuntary exile of the Jews is at an end. Any one or community of us who chooses to do so may make the decision to live in Israel. Those of us — still a bit more than half of the Jewish people — who do not live there are voluntarily living as minorities abroad. We are *tefutsot*, "scattered" or diaspora Jews, but no longer *golah*, Jews in exile.[45] Why have we made this choice? What value do we find in living outside the land where so much of the Jewish future is clearly being shaped?

To answer this question we need to go back to Torah, where most of the narrative takes place outside the land. After receiving the Word, we set out on the road that leads away from Sinai. The rest of the story finds us in the wilderness, journeying in circles, trying to decide exactly what it is we heard and what sort of claims it makes upon us. It is no accident that the Torah, and with it each sacred year-cycle, ends just before Israel crosses into the Promised Land.[46] For us diaspora Jews, having lived this way for so many centuries, our wandering is not to be taken lightly. It is an essential part of the experience and legacy of Israel. While the oldest traditions (the rabbis following the prophets) viewed exile as a punishment for Israel's sins, in more recent centuries such diverse Jewish groups as Kabbalists and *hasidim*, on the one hand, and Reformers on the other, have offered positive evaluations of Israel's being dispersed throughout the world. Fallen sparks of holiness are scattered everywhere, taught the mystics. They lie waiting for Jews to discover them, uplift them, and restore them to their source. We are spread throughout the world in order to seek these, in order to look for God in the most unlikely places. The great spiritual adventure that the mystics find in Judaism precisely requires us to be everywhere in order to do our work of uplifting and transformation.[47] If a Jew finds himself or herself in an unexpected place, according to many a Hasidic tale, it is because there is something to be done there that only his or her particular soul can accomplish. A classic Hasidic text claims that it is easier to enter God's presence in the diaspora than in the Holy Land, just as it is easier to approach the king out at a country inn than in his heavily guarded palace.[48] The Reformers put it differently: they felt that we were scattered about the world in order better to fulfill our prophetic mission, to be a "light unto the nations" in teaching the values of justice and decency embodied in our prophetic heritage. Perhaps to the surprise of both mystics and Reformers, their messages are not that different from each other. The task of redemption calls upon us to live within the non-Jewish world, to stand as Abraham's descendents and be *'ivrim*, contrarians, in societies that are otherwise too monochromatic, to be an ongoing minority, struggling for survival, providing a certain leaven to otherwise uniform societies, and perhaps also showing the way to so many minorities seeking acceptance yet frightened of disappearing. The American Jewish experience has taught us that our presence as a moral voice, when we use it well, can add much to the broader society in which we live, even when we are only a small fraction of the population.

Let me try to explain this role of the Jew as contrarian by use of a perhaps surprising analogy. My framework here is the old six-day creation story.

Here it was, Friday afternoon. A little while before the sun was to set, God looked around at all He had made, including the animals on the sixth day, and said to His divine Self: "It's not quite enough! Heaven and earth are not quite finished. I need a partner, someone in My own image, someone I can love." So He made humans, for the sake of love. In order that they not suffer the same terrible loneliness He had known throughout eternity, He made them male and female, along with the incredibly ingenious and delicate mechanism of sexual attraction and love, where the same emotional toolkit would be used both to propagate the species and to express the most sublime of human feelings. Quite a feat!

But then God looked out over all these humans that were about to emerge and got worried. "Gee, they're pretty boring," He said. "All the same in too many ways. Something about them reminds Me of cattle, with all that breeding and all those generations. Will there be no one who bucks the system? No one to be different? Who will be the leaven in all this dough?" Then the thought came to the exalted divine Mind. "Know what I'll do? I'll count them off, and one in every ten I'll shape the other way round. I'll make them love the *same* sex instead of the other one! That will create dissonance, contrariness, oddity. Yes, some people will probably hate them. But think how many artists, poets, and philosophers they'll bring forth! They will save My humans from boredom, and someday they'll be blessed by all."

Just as God was feeling great about His new gay-friendly Self, however, a question arose. "What do you mean by 'bring forth'?" He asked. "Their reproductive mechanisms won't work, will they? How will they convey this cutting-edge, creative, dissonant culture from one generation to the next? How will they pass it on?"

Just then, Abraham happened to pass by. "Wait a minute!" He said . . . and the rest of this myth is history.[49]

What do I mean by this tale? I am claiming that we were somehow *meant* to be scattered through the world, to deny its easy truths, to raise unpopular questions. We created a contrarian religion, one filled with harsh rebellion against the reigning idolatry of its day. "Eyes have they, but they see not; ears have they, but they hear not" (Ps. 115:5–6) was a revolutionary broadside, not a little ditty to be sung on holidays. Our long centuries of living as a minority kept us in the role of contrarians throughout history. That experience was formative of the Jewish mentality. Even though we have become terribly regimented and conventional in our own set ways, something buried deep within us still remembers Israel's role as the great contrarians of history. We still long to smash idols. It was that contrary mind, after all, that got us to leave Egypt, that created the Torah, that brought God out of silence, and that broke the tablets.

Because of the Bible's great influence in shaping Western culture, the ancient history of Israel, from Abraham down through destruction and exile, is known throughout the world, teaching and inspiring millions who have never met a living Jew. But the second half of Jewish history, that of our wandering, persecution, and refusal to disappear, surely also has something to teach the world. If there are sparks of light to be raised from the later history of Israel, it is primarily our survival and uplifting of diaspora that we have to share with others. How and why did we survive so many centuries of oppression? Was it just our dogged stubbornness, a refusal to accept that we had been superseded by the more universalizing messages of Christianity and Islam, and finally by modernity? Was it the longing for renewal and return to our homeland, so much emphasized in our prayers, that kept us going? If so, we now have a chance to return to that homeland. Or was it a sense that all this dispersion and suffering itself had meaning, that we still had something important to give to the world through which we were scattered? That something must have to do with our ongoing role as contrarians, as questioners and challengers of our societies' grand assumptions and systems of values, as smashers of idols.

To be a committed diaspora Jew is to affirm that we have something of value to offer, a message that still needs to be heard. We have to ask ourselves what the world needs of us, what we can offer at this critical time in the history of human civilization. When put this way, it is clear that we need to put forth the loudest possible proclamation of our most essential truth: *Being is One, and each person is God's unique image.* There are plenty of idols still to be smashed in our world. The degradation of human lives has not lessened as we have "progressed" into the nuclear and cybernetic ages. Genocide, so-called ethnic cleansing, and other horrors characterize human life today. The use of religion as a weapon to divide humans from one another and to justify the most horrible — and clearly sacrilegious — acts of violence is especially disturbing. The new fundamentalisms — most violent in Islam but present in all the religions, including our own — express their fear and rage against modernity with the most horrible distortions of religion, using its great power to generate hate rather than love. Here "religion" itself has become the idol. Our witness is urgently needed. "Why was the human created singly? So that no man may say: 'My father was greater than yours.'" We need to be there, whether out there in the world or here in the American power center (today's "great city of Rome" of the Talmud), using our influence to proclaim that truth. Where is our voice today?

It is clear that a contemporary version of Ben Azzai's message will have to be expanded to recognize the holiness of earth, air, and water as well as that of human body and spirit, demanding that we care for the survival of other species alongside our devotion to humanity. *Mitzvah* in our day means taking responsibility not just for the ongoing advancement of evolution but for the survival of the planet itself. Human mastery over nature, the dream of science and technology since ancient times, has now reached heights unimagined by any prior generation. Combined with the rush toward worldwide industrialization, these very advances now threaten to destroy all that lives on earth. The two "commandments" that lie within the "Where are you?" addressed to every person — "Become aware" and "Share that awareness" — in our age are joined by a third: "Protect My earth! Save it from destruction!"

It was probably inevitable that the evolution of human mind and skill would bring existence to the point of being wholly subject to the conduct of this unique creature, the human being. Now as never before in our planet's history the fate of everything — all higher plant and animal life, at the very least — depends on actions taken or not taken by a single species. While this reality has grown to be increasingly true over centuries, fueled by human population growth and rapid technological advances, only in this new era, beginning in the late twentieth century, has it become apparent to us. This new consciousness dawned with the nuclear age, the sense that we were indeed capable of destroying everything. But it quickly turned to the much more participatory need to change human actions because of the greater threat of environmental self-destruction, the overwhelming urgency of our time.

Our age is also different in being a time when Jews, a tiny fraction of humanity, live in highly privileged and powerful circumstances, having some real influence regarding crucial decisions that face us all. This is true of Jewish leaders in the political sphere, in communications media, business, the academy, and lots of other areas. Because of the role of religion in American life, our society would be happy to learn that views which influential Jews hold on major issues are in part shaped by thoughtful study of their own traditions. This is a situation for which our prior history never trained us. Because of our great drive toward success and status in the postemancipation world and the special circumstances of life in America, Jews are now the most highly educated subgroup within our society. In many cases economic and political influence follows that level of educational achievement. By coincidence, providence, or whatever you choose to call it, we American Jews happen to play important roles in the United States, where some of the most difficult choices about our planet's future have to be taken. In Israel, Jews have attained independent statehood, which also places them in a position of responsibility for the future of the land and sets them in power over a significant non-Jewish minority.

How do we hear and preach God's word in this very different age? Through most of our history, oppressed Jews seem to have lived by a narrowly crafted version of the principle of Rabbi Akiva, loving and caring for "our own" while paying greater or lesser lip service to Ben Azzai's universal human values. Most later Jewish legal authorities suggest that we should treat Gentiles as well as we do Jews for the sake of "the ways of peace," which essentially means "in order to avoid anti-Semitism." We recognize the full humanity of Gentiles, that is, so that they will, one hopes, recognize ours. Much of this in-group thinking can be attributed, of course, to the long centuries of persecution Jews suffered, when those in power neither saw nor treated us as fully human. Our natural response was self-protection, a turning inward to our own moral "neighborhood," as it were, and living on a moral island.

In our day this self-isolation will no longer do. There is no threat of persecution that requires it. The time calls out for a Judaism appropriate to the new reality. The defensive medieval or *shtetl* reflexes no longer speak to the reality of our current situation. Naturally, the terrible experience of the Holocaust reawakened these reflexes, and all too much of Jewish public policy in recent decades has been determined by them. But these reactions are not the best that our tradition has to offer. They are not what the world needs of us in this hour.

In some vague and undirected ways we do see the Jewish witness to the need for change articulating itself. Bearers of Jewish names are prominent in all the Western movements for civil and human rights as well as for environmental protection. Some who carry those names are directly inspired by Jewish teaching; others, perhaps a majority, carry with them only a vague and highly secularized version of Jewish tribal memory, especially the memory of persecution. Cognizant of their own ancestors' sufferings, they seek to avoid such a fate for others. The fact that large majorities of American Jews, despite their rising economic fortunes, continue to support liberal and generous programs of social welfare also speaks to the ongoing subtle proclamation of our truth. The prominence of Jews in antiwar activities, in environmentalist groups, and in other causes that seek to benefit humanity and the planet, all point in the same direction. The memory of slavery and liberation from Egypt is carved deeply in our souls, more deeply than we can see.

We need a Judaism that will speak fully to the values of these Jews, among whom I count myself. Caring for the needy and raising the banner of human dignity are *mitzvot*, part of what we are most essentially obliged to do as Jews. So too are protection of the planet and concern for future generations. We do them not because they are au courant or represent the best of liberal politics; we do them because they are the very foundation of Torah, the teaching of Ben Azzai applied to the new circumstances of the twenty-first century. Such a positive and assertive diaspora Judaism must apply itself to universal human questions and to the contemporary human situation. Of course, its responses will be in the language and symbols of our own tradition, presented richly and without diminution. These will require "translation" both for Jews and for non-Jews who do not speak their language, but that is precisely what the theologian is here to do.

Kabbalah, Heschel, and the Commandments

Judaism remains a religion of *mitzvot*, powerful religious deeds with which we respond to the divine call. The most characteristic religious act of Judaism is "doing a *mitzvah*," a term that is sometimes extended beyond those things specifically commanded in the Torah. The tradition specifically values the Jews' sense of being commanded, insisting, contrary to our instinct, that "greater is the one who is commanded and does than the one who does without command."[50] But once again I ask how we today might hear the commanding voice. And what forms does it inhabit?

As a student of Kabbalah, I recognize that the mystical tradition has always placed great emphasis on the *mitzvot* and their power. Indeed, "the reasons for the commandments" was one of the first topics discussed by the early Kabbalists. In performing a *mitzvah*, they claimed, one is actually *giving* something to God, affecting the balance of energies in the cosmic realm. This is the most powerful and distinctive motif in my teacher Abraham Joshua Heschel's theology, encapsulated by the phrase "God in Search of Man."[51]

You will recall that my quest for a Jewish radical theology began with a question addressed to Heschel more than forty years ago. Heschel represented a unique strain within Jewish moral theology. Deeply shaped by the prophets (as well as by the experience of fleeing Nazi Europe), Heschel was allied with the most progressive American forces in opposing racism and unjust war. His closeness to Reinhold Niebuhr and Martin Luther King Jr. was well known and defined much of his public image. But that same prophetic influence made Heschel seem like something of a theological conservative. He spoke of a God who is personally concerned with and affected by human actions. He saw God as One who creates each human in the divine image so that we may fulfill the role of partnership with God, so that we may discover God's presence within the world and within our own souls and respond to it with heart and mind, but primarily by deed. The God who awaits this response is a God of pathos, the Source of human empathy.

Heschel learned about the secret and mysterious power of the *mitzvot* in the Hasidic world in which he was nurtured. The special love and devotion that Hasidic *rebbes* lavished upon the *mitzvot* is legendary; Heschel was surrounded by this in his childhood. He was not, however, a naive or literal believer. He understood the dangers of near-magical claims made for religious deeds, especially when treated in a mechanistic way. But he was also unwilling to abandon this dramatic sense of the cosmic importance of human deeds, which added so much to the value of human actions and the sense of divine/human partnership. He thus chose to undertake a very interesting shift in the way he read this part of the mystical legacy. When Hasidic *rebbes* spoke of the commandments as sublime secrets that affect the cosmic balance, they were usually referring to mystery-laden ritual acts: putting on *tefillin*, waving the *lulav*, sounding the *shofar*, performing ablutions in the *mikveh*, and so forth. Heschel agreed with his Hasidic forebears that God longs for us to do the *mitzvot*, that heaven itself is moved by our deeds. But he applied this first and foremost to the "commandments between person and person," that second half of the decalogue that refers to the way we treat our fellow humans. God indeed needs you to do the *mitzvot* — to feed the hungry, to care for the poor, to do justice, to sustain widows and orphans. These are the essence of *mitzvot*. It is primarily through these that you become God's partner in the world.[52]

I take this transformative insight to be central to the power of Heschel's teachings — the reason why his involvement in social issues was so deeply impressive. But what does a person like me do with this legacy? I do not have Heschel's ability to speak unself-consciously the personalist and pathos-laden religious language of the biblical prophet. For me the personal God is a bridge between soul and mystery, a personification of the unknown, a set of projected images that we need and use, rather than an ultimate reality. My awareness of projection (even if I do know that it can be read in both directions) makes it hard for me to slip comfortably into biblical language, as Heschel was able to do. His theology was indeed personalist, enriched by mystical overtones. Mine is mystical-panentheist, using personalist metaphors. The gulf between the two is not one I can ignore.

Yet I still affirm there is a God who seeks us out. The inner One, Y-H-W-H inseparable from existence itself, still wants to know where I am. It needs me (along with all the rest of you) as its embodiment (Dare I say "incarnation?"), called upon to do its work, to move the process of evolution ever forward, and, in our age as in none other, to help our planet to survive. I still hear the One ask me: "Where are you?" I respond to that question as a Jew, from within my people's covenant. This means *mitzvah*, an act in which I intend to be aware of God's presence, an act in which I still hope that the blessed holy One, mystery beyond all knowing, and *shekhinah*, the Presence that floods my heart, might be joined. In doing this, I retain a sense of partnership with the divine One, a conviction that the human deed makes a difference. I share the Kabbalistic faith that we humans (not just Jews, of course) are the other antipode that sends the charge back and reenergizes the One. Now more than ever.

Granted, the naive claim of God's essential humanity, including His providential concern for each widow and orphan, is a way of seeing that was lost to me at a young age, as I said at the very outset. A personalist religious language, when not unpacked or defined as symbol, leaves me behind. But that does not lead me to religious disengagement. The demanding voice — coming from a world far beyond words and language — is still very much alive. So is our need to respond.

The human ability to *give* needs some further elaboration here. A contemporary reading of Kabbalah will insist that each human being has something unique to offer, something needed by the world and even by God. Y-H-W-H, the Source and Giver of all life, is also the One who calls upon us to become givers, our own lives being the gift. To become a giver is to fulfill our Godlike existence, to realize the divine image, as Heschel taught, through the medium of our entire selves. The divine voice, however transverbally we may understand that phrase, still makes a demand of each of us, a unique demand of each unique person. Each of us indeed has something that only he or she can supply, a contribution urgently needed to sustain the divine economy or the balance of nature.

In Hasidism, this idea that each soul has a special gift to offer is often expressed by the raising of sparks, which I discussed earlier. But in Hasidic thought this is part of a wider view of *ha'ala'ah* or "uplifting." Everything in our lives can be raised to higher (or "deeper") levels, ultimately to be restored to its source in the One. This uplifting applies to our thoughts (all thoughts, even those that turn to sin or evil, are rooted in the single thought of God), our words (for at the silent root of language there is only the single word "Y-H-W-H"), and our deeds. Life is then a series of opportunities, chances to discover and to give to life that which we uniquely have to offer.

That is why the characteristic form of Jewish prayer is a *berakhah*, or blessing. To bless someone is to offer something of value, to convey a certain strength. When a child asks for a parent's blessing, what he or she seeks is some combination of approval, support, and love. The child is fortified by that blessing, is "given" something in the course of it. When a member of the clergy blesses troops going out to battle, the intent is that some divine protection is invoked; something of "power" is conveyed that will help to protect them. But in our prayers we repeatedly offer blessings *to God*. What can this possibly mean? Blessing is not just praise. We assert over and over again (a hundred times each day, the rabbis suggest)[53] that we have something to offer in the balance of the divine economy, something to *give*. God *seeks our blessing*, as it were, the strength of that which we alone have to offer, each of us uniquely. Of course, this act of giving to God really takes place deep within the heart, and the recitation of words is only its outer expression. The reality of our giving is ultimately vindicated only by our actions in the human world, where we are called upon to be engaged as givers as well.

Jewish Trinities, Male and Female

All of this language needs but little translation, I believe, to speak within the old/new evolutionary/Kabbalistic theological idiom I am putting forth here. We humans are participants in evolution, the ongoing process of divine self-manifestation, needed partners in that process. The greater the power we achieve over all the rest of existence, the more we are needed for this conscious partnership. The call to us is constant, echoing throughout our lives. As we stretch ourselves to become aware, to know the oneness of Being, and to live in response to that knowledge, we become givers to God. Torah is all that teaches us how to walk this path. *Mitzvah*, in its fullest sense, is the gift we have to offer.

"*God, Torah, and Israel are one*," the Kabbalists have long proclaimed. Translated into my own religious language, this means something like: "*The deep inner oneness of all being, manifest in silence, but flowing into sacred speech, is accessible to the seeking human heart, leading us to transformative action.*" The three are fully identified with one another. God *is* the silent inner Torah; Israel, rendering that silence into language, is the human heart struggling to uncover the hidden message (or "teaching," or "Torah") of existence, the fact that we are all one with God, the force of Being. As we discover this, we are called upon to give, to act in ways that strengthen that core of Being we call Y-H-W-H. "Israel add power and strength 'above.' "[54]

This is the essential teaching of a mystical Judaism for our day. Placed upon the grid of Kabbalistic symbolism, it would read something like this. Unspeakable Mystery (*'atiqa*) manifests itself in *tif 'eret*, "glory," the center of the Kabbalistic tree. *Tif 'eret* is "the blessed Holy One," the symbolic realm most identified with the personified God of Scripture. But *tif 'eret* is also the Written Torah, the verbalized form into which that God has "written Himself," as we have said. And *tif 'eret* is Israel, here in the form of *yisra'el sabba*, the elder Israel, the source of blessing to all who come in his wake. This is indeed a Jewish trinity, in that the three not only stand in relation to one another but are ultimately to be fully identified. "God," "Torah," and "Israel" are one.

Tif'eret is a "male" principle, which means that it is a font of energy, a source that radiates forth blessing. But each of these three dimensions of *tif'eret* also has a "female" counterpart, one that receives and takes in blessing. Parallel to God as "blessed Holy One" is *shekhinah*, the indwelling presence of God, the one that plays "Queen" to His "King" in the medieval landscape where Kabbalah was first articulated. Written Torah is linked to Oral Torah, the "female" side of the "male" Law; she is the act of endless reinterpretation, constantly reshaping the contours of received Torah, based on the ongoing input from each unique generation of her devotees. And Israel is also *kenesset yisra'el*, the Ingathering or Community of Israel, receiving into herself lost souls from the most remote corners of earth and the most pained human wanderings, making them realize they are part of the One. All of these (*shekhinah*, Oral Torah, *kenesset yisra'el*) are names of the tenth *sefirah*, positioned at the border of the divine realm; it is *she* who actually rules over the lower worlds. Once again, "God (indwelling *shekhinah*)," "Torah (oral tradition, interpretative freedom)," and "Israel (the embraced seeker)" are one.[55]

These categories of "male" and "female" are perhaps better understood as "giver" and "receiver." Each of us contains both *tif'eret yisra'el* and *kenesset yisra'el* within himself or herself. As psychologists have long understood, all of us contain elements of man and woman within our personalities. The Kabbalist and the Jungian are of one voice in telling us to accept and make creative use of our complex gender identity. Learning to be both givers and receivers of love, of energy, and of blessing is central to our growth and maturation as human beings. Our task is to take the energy of renewed life that we receive in each moment and offer it back in acts of giving, so that we humans, this broadly reconceived camp of Israel, do indeed "add power and strength 'above.'"

Learning to live with awe and wonder in the presence of Y-H-W-H,[56] hearing the voice from within the silence, understanding and responding to the call and the demand being made upon us — these are the essential way stations of the religious life. This is an entirely Hasidic, as well as an entirely contemporary, point of view. In the classical language of theology, I am offering a reconceptualization of both "Creation" and "revelation." I do so by affirming the mystical tradition's understanding that both of these are self-manifestations of the hidden God. Neither "world," the object of Creation, nor Torah, the object of revelation, is truly separate from its Source. Nor are we. This is the great truth we are here to discover and proclaim. This discovery, when allowed to spread throughout our lives, liberates and transforms us. It is a discovery of exultation and joy, a cause for celebration. It should uplift Yom Kippur as well as *Pesah*, the moment of inner stillness as well as the shout of freedom. But it brings us along onto the road of responsibility as well, now more than ever. When we set out on that journey, in deed as well as in word, we have begun the process of redemption, the third leg of the other Jewish theological tripod. Redemption is essentially a *human* task, that wrought by our living in active and engaged response to revelation.[57] "Salvation," with its more otherworldly focus, does not come into it. In contrast to classical Christian views (found in some Jewish sources as well), we humans are not sinners utterly dependent upon and waiting for salvation but rather are active and needed partners in this enterprise of existence and its ongoing evolution, to which God is utterly and irrevocably committed. "Messiah" will one day come to herald the completion of this ongoing redemptive journey, not to initiate it.[58]

Agenda for a Radical Judaism

The need for ongoing human participation in the quest for redemption is the context of the volume you have before you. Radical Judaism means a reframing of our contemporary perspective on the great questions, a leap forward that shows we are not afraid to be challenged by contemporary reality, while we remain devoted to hearing the greater challenge of God's voice calling out "Where are you?" anew in our age. This means a Judaism that takes seriously its own claims of ongoing Creation and revelation, even as it recognizes all the challenges to them. To "take them seriously" in our day cannot mean simply holding fast to them without question, dismissing the challenges of science and scholarship or seeking to avoid dealing with them. It means rather to rethink our most foundational concepts — God, Torah, and Israel and Creation, Revelation, and Redemption, to ask how they might work in the context of what we really believe in our age, and thus how they might speak to seekers in this century. Going back to the mountain and hearing the Word again, hearing it with clarity as the eternal voice speaks for our own day, will require a new sort of listening, one that has never yet existed, unique to this generation and to this moment.

I said above that the covenant is our own creation in response to Sinai. I affirm that we are still committed to that covenant, still bound by it. The moment of Sinai is an eternal one. Whenever we open our hearts to God as Jews, we find ourselves still standing at that mountain. Torah is just this moment being given; our heart is forever leaping forth to receive it. How could we not want to live in faith with such a moment? The covenant ties us forever to that event. Here we are, just two months out of Egypt, having been given the great gift of freedom by a power that we are just learning to name. Now we together confront the question "Who do we want to be?" What kind of nation will be fashioned from these liberated slaves? What is the right way to live in response to the great and transforming events that have happened in our lives? How do we respond in gratitude? Recognizing God's image, love of God and love of neighbor, and the ten commandments are the right starting places. But do they suffice?

We are still faced with those questions. To be a heterodox religious Jew, as I clearly am, is to believe that those questions remain eternally unresolved. Yes, the rabbis have been discussing them for centuries, and all those discussions are part of our heritage. That is *talmud*: an unending conversation about how to live. The prior rounds of this conversation are to be studied, loved, appreciated. But they do not bind or foreclose the discussion. To be a Jew is still to think about the right way to live, to be challenged to respond. How do we live a holy life after the Holocaust, with a third of our people dead and so many wounded by cynicism and despair? How do we stand before Sinai as a people that fully includes the voices of women equally with those of men? How do we lift our heads in God's presence in a time when Jews are seen by many, and with some justification, as oppressors rather than victims? Our response needs to change shape and grow in each generation as it is confronted with new and different challenges, but it still faces the same question. *Ayekah?* Where are you? How are you going to live? When we live badly, especially when we are selfish, mean, or uncaring, we are disgraced before our fellow Jews. "A Jew should know better" is something we all feel. What is "conduct un-befitting a member of the Jewish people?" We know it when we see it and we call it *ḥillul ha-shem*, a defaming of God's name, that name we all bear as part of the word "Israel." The echo of covenant is com-mingled with the memory of Egypt and the long history of persecu-tion in telling us when and how "a Jew should know better."

But where do we go from there? I am one of many Jews for whom the old halakhic rule book fails to work. I find it far too detailed, too restrictive. Its concerns with ritual minutiae and taboo overwhelm me and raise the specter of a civilization fallen victim to obsessive com-pulsion. I find its views of women, family, and sexuality quite hope-lessly outdated. Its legalism in dealing with human personal and inter-personal situations, whether those filled with joy or those fraught with pain and oppression, is sometimes exasperating to me. I find its privileging of Jews over others morally inadequate and inappropriate to our age. I need an "Israel" that has the courage not merely to tinker, not to stand crippled before lack of legal precedents within the system, but to go all the way back to the Source, the One higher and deeper than "the sources," to stand before the mountain again with only those ten words, and begin again to listen, to do, and to teach.

I believe with complete faith that new forms of Judaism will emerge in the state of Israel, America, and elsewhere, distilled from the multi-ple experiments in Jewish living that are currently taking place in the lives of diverse Jewish individuals, households, and small commu-nities. This is a process that will take several generations and cannot be rushed. Those who participate in this creative process are multiple and varied, including Jews by choice, refugees from ultra-Orthodoxy, and many whom they will meet in the middle. The new Judaism will not be created top-down by committees of rabbis or (God forbid) by presidents of major Jewish organizations. The *halakhah*, or pathway, of the future will be more flexible, more multistranded, than any we have known. It will only emerge from a new *aggadah*, a new articulation of Jewish faith that succeeds in capturing the hearts of generations of Jews. This narrative will take us back to the old tales, but with contemporary eyes and ears wide open. The voice calls forth each day. When we are ready, it will address us. My prayer is that this book constitutes a small step along that evolutionary path.

This is the moment for radical Judaism. We understand that all God can do is to call out to us, now as always. All we can do is respond — or not. The consequence of our failure will be monumental. God is indeed in need of humans; and we humans are in need of guidance, seeking out the hand of a divine Partner, one who "speaks" from deep within the heart, but also from deep within our tradition and its wisdom.

Such a time cries out for leadership, for covenant, and for *mitzvah*, all of them expanded and redefined for this hour. The most aware and progressive human voices have heard the urgency of the call. They know how late it is, how short is the time we have in which to act. For the past half century they have been combing through ancient traditions — Yogic, Tibetan, Native American, and many more — asking whether there is some forgotten piece of human wisdom, neglected in our rush toward modernity, that might offer us guidance and help us through the dangerous and frightening age in which we live. Might the covenant of Israel, this ancient priestly kingdom, read through the eye of the mystic sages, now opened wide as a source of learning for all, have something to say in this hour? Might that be the meaning of our unfulfilled messianic dreams? Will we be open enough, free enough, strong enough to allow that voice to speak?

NOTES

Introduction

1. All biblical translations are my own.

2. I am referring to Abraham Joshua Heschel (1907–1972), with whom I had the great privilege of studying as a rabbinical student in the mid-1960s. I have been reading him, teaching his writings, and engaging in conversation with him for half a century. Much of this book may be seen as a response to, and dialogue with, his work.

3. I am currently preparing a collection of Zeitlin's writings, including this essay, for publication in the *Classics of Western Spirituality* series of Paulist Press. On Zeitlin, including my claim of his influence on Heschel, see my essay "Three Warsaw Mystics" in *Kolot Rabbim: The Rivka Schatz-Uffenheimer Jubilee Volume* (Jerusalem: Jerusalem Studies in Jewish Thought, 1996), English section, pp. 1–58.

4. *The Language of Truth: The Torah Commentary of the Sefat Emet* (Philadelphia: Jewish Publication Society, 1998), pp. ixf.

5. Heschel actually referred to two specific Hasidic authors, the *Sefat Emet* (R. Judah Leib Alter of Ger, 1847–1905) and R. Zadok Ha-Kohen of Lublin (1823–1900).

Chapter 1. Y-H-W-H

1. In the background here are such works as Thomas Berry's *The Dream of the Earth* (San Francisco: Sierra Club, 1988); Berry and Brian Swimme's *The Universe Story* (San Francisco: Harper, 1992); and E. O. Wilson's *The Creation* (New York: Norton, 2006).

2. I have discussed this nontemporal sense of priority briefly in *Seek My Face: A Jewish Mystical Theology* (Woodstock, VT: Jewish Lights, 2003), pp. 55f. The point is that the One underlies the many then, now, and forever. This underlying is the true nature of its priority in the mystical context, one which is converted into temporality as mystical insight comes to be expressed in mythic narrative (since stories require a "before" and "after"). The contemporary Midrashist might see this hinted at in the syntactical awkwardness of *bereshit bara'*.

3. The relationship of "being" and "Being" in English is roughly comparable to that of *HaWaYaH* ("existence") and Y-H-W-H (its consonantal
equivalent, rearranged) in Hebrew.

4. This puts me in the camp, as Hillel Zeitlin would have said, of the Ba'al
Shem Tov's pantheism, as distinguished from Spinoza's. The distinction
between these was key to Zeitlin's return to Judaism and the starting point
of his neo-Hasidic philosophy. See his remarks in *Barukh Spinoza* (Warsaw: Tushiya, 1914), pp. 135ff., as well as in *Di Benkshaft nokh Sheynheyt*
(Warsaw: Velt-Bibliotek, 1910), pp. 34f.

5. I intentionally quote the verse around which Rabbi Shneur Zalman of
Liadi wove his essential mystical treatise *Sha'ar ha-Yihud veha-Emunah*
(the second part of *Tanya*), to indicate the strong Hasidic roots of the
theology I am articulating here.

6. Love and awe (*ahavah ve-yir'ah*, *dehilo u-rehimo*) are taken by the Jewish
ethical literature to be the twin pillars of religious emotion, ever to be
kept in balance with one another. For the Kabbalist they represent the
proper human embodiments of *hesed* and *din*, the right and left hands of
the cosmic Self. Classic treatments include Meir Ibn Gabbai's *'Avodat ha-
Qodesh* (Venice, 1567), 1:25–28, and (much expanded) Elijah Da Vidas,
Reshit Hokhmah (Venice, 1579). In this matter I find myself wholly within
the classical tradition.

7. In the idiom of Midrash, the hidden *aleph* of *'anokhi* lies behind the
dualizing *bet* of *bereshit*. See my discussion in "The Aleph-Bet of Creation: Jewish Mysticism for Beginners," *Tikkun* 7:4 (1992).

8. The reader may properly hear an echo of Martin Buber's words in *Eclipse
of God* (New York: Harper and Row, 1952), pp. 7ff. I too recognize the
difficulty in continuing to use this word, alongside the impossibility of
doing without it.

9. My discussion of this theological viewpoint, including its roots in an
understanding of the divine name, begins in my book *Seek My Face*.

10. Among the rabbinic phrases that leap to mind here are *ke-haden qumtsa'
di-levushey minney u-veyh* ("like the locust, whose garbing comes forth
from his own self" [Midrash Bereshit Rabbah 21:5]) and *hu meqomo shel
'olam ve-eyn ha-'olam meqomo* ("He is the 'place' of the world; the world is
not His place" [Bereshit Rabbah 68:10]).

11. The presence of the miraculous within the natural has a long history in
Jewish theological conversation. Some key prior participants in this con-
versation are Nahmanides, the MaHaRaL of Prague, and Levi Yitzhak of
Berdichev.

12. Jonathan Day, *God's Conflict with the Dragon and the Sea: Echoes of a Canaanite Myth in the Old Testament* (Cambridge: Cambridge University Press, 1985). For the presence and survival of this theme in later Judaism, see Michael Fishbane's "The Great Dragon Battle and Talmudic Redaction," in his *The Exegetical Imagination* (Cambridge, MA: Harvard University Press, 1998), pp. 41–55.

13. Parallel structures of thought in Kabbalah and astrophysics have been noted by several writers, including Daniel Matt, *God and the Big Bang* (Woodstock, VT: Jewish Lights, 1996); David Nelson, *Judaism, Physics, and God* (Woodstock, VT: Jewish Lights, 2005); and Howard Smith, *Let There Be Light: Modern Cosmology and Kabbalah* (Novato, CA: New World Library, 2006).

14. See Gen. 3:9. I have in mind also the Hasidic tale of Rabbi Shneur Zalman of Liadi's use of this verse in confronting his jailer in St. Petersburg. See especially Martin Buber's retelling of that tale in *The Way of Man* (Secaucus, NJ: Citadel Press, 1966), pp. 9ff.

15. This is the key theme in the voluminous writings of Rabbi Yehudah Ashlag (1886–1955), the leading Kabbalistic figure of the early twentieth century. This interesting author has much to teach, though his legacy has been distorted in various popular presentations.

16. Bereshit Rabbah 1:4; 8:7.

17. See Gen. 32:28 and commentaries and discussion in my chapter 4.

18. Key to my theological-moral position is R. Simeon ben Azzai's preference for Gen. 5:1–2 (creation of all humans in God's image) over R. Akiva's choice of Lev. 19:18 ("Love your neighbor as yourself") as the *kelal gadol*, the most basic rule of Torah. Talmud Yerushalmi (henceforth T. Y.) Nedarim 9:4 (41c). Everything else, in both *halakhah* and *aggadah*, needs to conform with this. When it does not, it needs to be reexamined. Yes, one may call this an "essentialist" approach to Jewish ethics, but it is one rooted in the rabbinic sources themselves. See the fuller discussion in chapter 4.

19. But I am interested in, and think we need to learn more about, the intelligence and communication skills of elephants, whales, primates, and others. We are told that King Solomon knew how to listen to and speak with animals. We will not reach his wisdom until we relearn this lost skill, among many others.

Chapter 2. Evolution Continues

1. Talmud Bavli (henceforth T. B.) Hagigah 15b.

2. On the whole process of the ongoing internalization of "spiritualization" of Judaism, see Ron Margolin, *Miqdash Adam* (Jerusalem: Magnes, 2005), pp. 57–122. This important study is soon to appear in English translation.

3. *On Dreams* 1:149; *On the Cherubim* 98–106; etc. On the question of Philo as mystic, see David Winston's brief remarks in my edited collection *Jewish Spirituality*, vol. 1 (New York: Crossroad, 1987), pp. 223ff., and more fully in Winston's "Was Philo a Mystic?" in Joseph Dan and Frank Talmage, *Studies in Jewish Mysticism* (Cambridge, MA: Harvard University Press, 1982), pp. 15–39.

4. Note that *tosafot*, Hagigah 14b, already question RaShI on this point.

5. North African Jewish intellectuals of the eleventh century were already writing under the influence of philosophy as absorbed and transmitted through Islam. See also the quotation from the Babylonian authority R. Hai Gaon, a century earlier, in the *'Arukh*, as quoted by B. M. Levin in *Otsar ha-Ge'onim* (Hagigah 14b), saying that "they did not ascend to heaven but were seeing and gazing within their own hearts, like one who perceives something quite clearly with his eyes."

6. Even the much more "tame" rabbinic sources sometimes reflect this. When God seeks to redeem Israel from Egypt, chaos rises in the form of the sea's resistance to splitting. See *Pirkey Rabbi Eliezer* 42 and the discussion by Rabbi David Luria in notes 26–28. In some late sources a monster called *Rahav shel Yam* is still to be found, rising out of the sea to side with the Egyptians and needing to be slain again. See *Midrash va-Yosha'* in Adolph Jellinek's *Bet ha-Midrash* 1:46f. That monster lives on in the imagination of medieval Kabbalists, the great serpent of sin, waiting to be aroused. Stirred to life by the waywardness of human passions, the cosmic powers that opposed the emergence of the universe are now dressed in the garb of moral "evil" and lead the wicked into rebellion against the rule of God. See Zohar 1:52a; 2:34a–b; etc. See also discussion by Isaiah Tishby in *Wisdom of the Zohar* (Oxford: Littman Library, 1989), pp. 464–474; 529–532.

7. This lies at the basis of Tishby's understanding of *tsimtsum* in Lurianic Kabbalah, a view that has more recently been subject to some questioning. See his *Torat ha-Ra' veha-Qelippah be-Torat ha-ARI* (Jerusalem: Schocken, 1952).

8. Some of these reflections on the figure of God in Biblical Israel are based

on thoughts expressed by my teacher Yochanan Muffs. See especially his recent book *The Personhood of God* (Woodstock, VT: Jewish Lights, 2005). I have learned much from Muffs, both in his classroom nearly a half century ago and again by reading and teaching his books.

9. The reacceptance of "myth" and its presence within Judaism characterize the thought of several leading scholars in our era. In particular I have in mind the writings of Michael Fishbane, Jon Levinson, and Yehuda Liebes.

10. *Pirkey Rabbi Eliezer* 19–20.

11. This claim is made by Franz Kafka in his *Parables and Paradoxes* (New York: Schocken Books, 1961), p. 29. On the parallel between Kafka and the Kabbalistic sources, see Nahum N. Glatzer, "Franz Kafka and the Tree of Knowledge," in his *Essays in Jewish Thought* (University, AL: University of Alabama Press, 1978), 184–191. The text to which Glatzer refers, "The Secret of the Tree of Knowledge," attributed to Rabbi Ezra of Gerona (Spain, mid-thirteenth century), has been translated in Gershom Scholem's *On the Mystical Shape of the Godhead* (New York: Schocken Books, 1991), pp. 65ff. We of the Western university know a great deal about that disjuncture, about the pursuit of knowledge unlinked from the love and unity of life, that which leads the tree quickly to reveal its potentially "evil" potency, even becoming, as the Zohar calls it, "the tree of death." Torah, the new Tree of Life, is intended precisely as an antidote to it. See chapter 3.

12. See sources quoted (around Gen. 4:26) in Louis Ginzburg, *Legends of the Jews* (Philadelphia: Jewish Publication Society, 1947), vol. 5, p. 151.

13. Hence the sages note on Gen. 6:9: *be-dorotaw*: Noah is considered righteous in *his* generation, but would not be thought so had he lived in the generation of Abraham or Moses. See especially Zohar 1:67b.

14. Thus the rabbis' reading (Bereshit Rabbah 12:9) of *be-hibare'am* in Gen. 2:4 as *be-Avraham* is not entirely unfaithful to the larger text.

15. Such a theologian, for example, is Rabbi Abraham Joshua Heschel of Apt (Opatow; 1748–1825, the ancestor of my teacher A. J. Heschel), who taught that God is envisioned by the prophet as seated on the throne (or the chariot of Ezekiel) because we have placed him there. That which "God asks of you" (Deut. 10:12) is that you depict God in human form (Adam = MaH = 45)! The "Adam" is *adam 'al ha-kise'*, the enthroned vision of God. See the passage quoted by Zvi Hirsch of Zydaczow, *'Ateret Zevi, aḥarey mot* (Lvov, 1871, 25a–b). There are earlier sources for this view as well, though not articulated quite so sharply.

16. I have discussed this Midrash in "The Children in Egypt and the Theophany at the Sea," *Judaism* 25 (1975): 446–466.

17. William Hallo, "Text, Statues, and the Cult of the Divine King," in *Congress Volume, Vetus Testamentum* supplement 40 (Leiden: E. J. Brill, 1988), pp. 59f.

18. Understand here, as throughout, that I see this statement fully translatable into my own post-Darwinian religious language: the One delights in being briefly manifest in this form as it delights in all others through which it reveals itself in the course of its ongoing evolutionary journey. ("Delight" in this context is a translation of *sha'ashu'a*, a term used in Kabbalistic sources to describe in quasi-erotic terms the pleasure God takes in each step of the ongoing process of self-manifestation.)

19. T. B. Berakhot 34b.

20. On the widespread and varied use of the royal metaphor in rabbinic literature, see David Stern, *Parables in Midrash: Narrative and Exegesis in Rabbinic Literature* (Cambridge, MA: Harvard University Press, 1991).

21. See *Tsava'at RiYVaSH* 18a, as quoted by Arthur Green and Barry W. Holtz in *Your Word Is Fire: The Hasidic Masters on Contemplative Prayer* (Ramsey, NJ: Paulist Press, 1977), p. 81.

22. See the rabbinic readings of Gen. 25:27.

23. See the treatment of this classical theme, as well as its later adaptations, in Alan Mintz, *Banished from Their Father's Table: Loss of Faith and Hebrew Autobiography* (Bloomington: Indiana University Press, 1989).

24. T. B. Baba Metsi'a 59b.

25. T. B. Shabbat 67a. The actual quote reads "sons of kings" or "royal children." I translate the phrase as it is later understood in the tradition. Cf. the statement by the Hasidic master R. Aaron of Karlin: "The greatest 'evil urge' is that the son of a king forget that he is a king's son."

26. This is perhaps given its boldest expression in the Kabbalists' hymn *Lekha Dodi*, by Shlomo Alkabetz of Safed, where God is uniquely addressed as "my Beloved." See my further discussion in "Some Aspects of Qabbalat Shabbat," in *Sabbath: Idea, History, Reality*, ed. Gerald J. Blidstein (Beersheva: Ben Gurion University, 2005), as well as the full-length treatment by Reuven Kimelman, *Lekha Dodi ve-Qabbalat Shabbat: ha-Mashma'ut ha-Mistit* (Jerusalem: Magnes, 2003).

27. Mishnah Yadayim 3:5. See my discussions of *Midrash Shir ha-Shirim* in "The Song of Songs in Early Jewish Mysticism," *Orim: A Jewish Journal at Yale* 2:2 (1987): 49–63, and "Shekhinah, the Virgin Mary, and the Song of Songs," *AJS Review* 46:1 (2003): 1–52.

28. The phrase originates with Daniel Boyarin in "The Song of Songs, Lock or Key: The Song of Songs as a Mashal," in his *Intertextuality and the*

Reading of Midrash (Bloomington: Indiana University Press, 1990), pp. 105–116. The notion of "washing over," however, has deeper Jewish roots. See R. Aaron of Karlin, *Bet Aharon* (Brody 1875) 144a, who reads the Zoharic phrase *bey ana raḥets* as "*In im kon ikh mikh ibervashn!*"

29. One important early Kabbalistic reading of the Song of Songs is available in English, translated by my late student Seth Brody. See Ezra ben Solomon of Gerona, *Commentary to the Song of Songs and Other Kabbalistic Commentaries* (Kalamazoo: Western Michigan University [Medieval Institute Publications], 1999).

30. For an introductory treatment, see my *Guide to the Zohar* (Stanford: Stanford University Press, 2004). This book was issued in conjunction with a new English translation of the Zohar with commentary by Daniel Matt. *Zohar: The Pritzker Edition* (Stanford: Stanford University Press, 2004–) will span twelve volumes and is scheduled for completion in 2015.

31. On this point see especially the discussion in my "Shekinah," supra, n. 27.

32. "Father" and "King" were especially one, we might add, if your thinking developed in turn-of-the-century Vienna, the capital ruled by Franz Josef, the most "fatherly" of all European monarchs.

33. Mekhilta shirta 3 (ed. Horowitz-Rabin, Jerusalem: Bamberger and Wahrman, 1960), p. 126.

34. Nowhere is this dual focus better seen than in the writings of Solomon Ibn Gabirol (c. 1020–c. 1057), author in Arabic of the highly abstract *Meqor Ḥayyim (Fons Vitae)* and of impassioned Hebrew verse frequently addressing God as Lover (often absent Lover) of Israel.

35. Simon Rawidowicz, "Saadya's Purification of the Idea of God," in *Saadya Studies*, ed. E. I. J. Rosenthal (Manchester, 1943), pp. 139–165.

36. But see José Faur's *Homo Mysticus: A Guide to Maimonides' Guide for the Perplexed* (Syracuse: Syracuse University Press, 1999).

37. Zohar 2:63a–b.

38. On the Kabbalistic side, see Tishby's detailed discussion, particularly regarding the latter strata of the Zohar, in his *Wisdom of the Zohar*, pp. 246–251.

39. See my brief outlining of the *sefirot* in *A Guide to the Zohar*, pp. 28–59, as well as the fuller treatment in Tishby, *Wisdom of the Zohar*, pp. 269–308.

40. *Pataḥ Eliyahu*, a passage from *Tiqquney Zohar* (Second Introduction), widely printed in prayer books. In Sephardic communities it serves as part of a daily early morning introduction to prayer; Hasidic Jews recite it on Friday afternoon, prior to receiving the Sabbath.

41. I discuss the history of this symbol in *Keter: The Crown of God in Early Jewish Mysticism* (Princeton: Princeton University Press, 1997).

42. For the origins of this phrase, incorporated by Alkabetz into his *Lekha Dodi* to refer to the *shekhinah*, see S. M. Stern, "The First in Thought Is the Last in Action: The History of a Saying Attributed to Aristotle," *Journal of Semitic Studies* 7 (1962): 234–252.

43. In addition to *A Guide to the Zohar* I have written an introduction to the *sefirot* addressed to the contemporary seeker in *Ehyeh: A Kabbalah for Tomorrow* (Woodstock, VT: Jewish Lights, 2003), pp. 39–60.

44. Zohar 1:3b.

45. On Luria and his system, see Lawrence Fine, *Physician of the Soul, Healer of the Cosmos: Isaac Luria and His Kabbalistic Fellowship* (Stanford: Stanford University Press, 2003).

46. I skip over the bizarre and fascinating developments in Jewish theology that took place within the Sabbatian messianic movement of the seventeenth and eighteenth centuries, both because this historical treatment has become rather long and because the movement had little lasting direct effect on later Judaism.

47. Hasidism, like the entirety of Jewish mysticism, tends to be quite exclusivist in its view of humanity. Jews are depicted as being essentially different from other humans, having greater spiritual capacities. This doctrine is technically not quite "racist," since conversion to Judaism is possible, and thus the higher states of soul are a spiritually rather than a physically borne legacy, but the result is much the same. Any contemporary "neo-" approach to either Kabbalah or Hasidism has to deal honestly with this uncomfortable part of the tradition, shift its application to include other humans, and deal with the legitimacy of other faiths, something that premodern Judaism was seldom able to do.

48. Hasidism mostly subscribed to the school of Kabbalistic thought that considered *keter*, the first of the ten *sefirot* in most systems, to be so beyond human ken as not to be counted. The decad then began with *hokhmah*, with a third *sefirah* of *da'at* added to complete the ten.

49. Primarily the writings of R. Dov Baer of Miedzyrzec and his circle. For discussion see Rivka Schatz-Uffenheimer, *Ha-Hasidut ke-Mistiqah* (Jerusalem: Magnes, 1968).

50. Hasidic homilies subtly combine the rabbinic understanding of *shekhinah* as indwelling presence with the Kabbalistic legacy of *shekhinah* as the divine consort. Taken together they come to mean that this world, led by the human soul, enters into mystical (or coital) union with the transcendent God.

51. The most thorough academic presentation of their ideas is to be found in

the writings of Rachel Elior, especially *The Paradoxical Ascent to God: The Kabbalistic Theosophy of Habad Hasidism* (Albany: State University of New York Press, 1993) and more briefly her "Habad: The Contemplative Ascent to God," in my collection *Jewish Spirituality*, vol. 1, 157–205. For a brief and somewhat more accessible guide to R. Aaron and his teachings, see Louis Jacobs's *Seeker of Unity* (New York: Basic Books, 1966).

52. For some key elements in this discussion, see Gershom Scholem, *Major Trends in Jewish Mysticism* (New York: Schocken, 1941), index s.vv. *Unio Mystica* and Union with God, and his "Devekuth or Communion with God," in *The Messianic Idea in Judaism and Other Essays* (New York: Schocken, 1971); Moshe Idel, *Kabbalah: New Perspectives* (New Haven: Yale University Press, 1988), pp. 59–73 and index s.v. union, and his *Hasidism: Between Ecstasy and Magic* (Albany: State University of New York Press, 1995), index s.v. union (*devequt*).

53. Moses Mendelssohn (1729–1786) was thought of as the ideal representative of early modern enlightened Judaism. He is to the Jewish Enlightenment much as Ba'al Shem Tov was to Hasidism: less the "founder" of the movement than the idealized figure whose life story was to stand as the beacon for future generations. For a full treatment of Mendelssohn see the masterful biography *Moses Mendelssohn* by my teacher Alexander Altmann (University, AL: University of Alabama Press, 1973).

54. Of course, the secularization of modern Jewry was a complex process, having important social and economic components. But I am claiming that it was partly due also to an internal religious and educational failure in which an increasingly educated (in the Western sense) population was shielded, for apologetic reasons, from much of the more interesting and potentially attractive theological literature that existed within its own tradition.

55. The writings of Jack Kornfeld and Joseph Goldstein, two leading Western teachers of the Vipassana Buddhist tradition, are particularly noteworthy in this regard.

56. See my essay "Hasidism: Discovery and Retreat," in *The Other Side of God: A Polarity in World Religions*, ed. Peter Berger (Garden City, NY: Anchor, 1981), pp. 104–130.

57. Missing from this discussion is the work of Mordecai M. Kaplan (1881–1983). Kaplan, an American thinker influenced by pragmatism, is sophisticated and rigorously honest in the raising of challenges to conventional theism, and the various alternatives he proposed through his long career have appealed to many. Unfortunately, he was completely alienated from

the mystical tradition and did not see the earlier roots it might have provided for a different approach to the question of God, which for Kaplan remained largely (though not wholly) within the realm of "the God-idea." His disciple Jack Cohen wrote a comparative study of Kaplan and R. Abraham Isaac Kook, *Morim Li-Zeman Navokh* (Tel Aviv: 'Eqed, 1993), which tried to bridge some of this distance.

58. The Zohar's definition of the sin of the Golden Calf (Zohar 1:3a) as worship of *eleh* ("these," as in "These are your gods, O Israel" [Ex. 32:4]), representing the *sefirot* that encompass divine personhood, detached from *mi*, the ultimate question that transcends them (*mi + eleh = elohim*, "God"), constitutes such a statement. The unspoken but clear implication is that worshipping the personal God alone, detached from the mystery beyond, is nothing but idolatry.

59. The BeShT's inverting interpretation of Lev. 20:17, where the term *ḥesed* is used to describe incest, is quoted several times in early Hasidic sources, especially by R. Menaḥem Naḥum of Chernobyl in *Me'or 'Eynayim*, *lekh* s.v. *ve-et ha-nefesh*; *mi-qets* s.v. *ke-divreykhem* (see my translation *Upright Practices and The Light of the Eyes* [Ramsey, NJ: Paulist Press, 1982], pp. 114f. and 267f.), *shemini* s.v. *va-yehi*; *shelaḥ* s.v. *be-masekhet*; *pinḥas* s.v. *va-yedabber*. The point is that there is only one love, the love of God, and that all other loves or erotic attractions, including those forbidden by the Torah, are fallen expressions of that love, capable of uplifting or redemption. This is early Hasidism at its most radical. It is the sort of *aggadah* that might well have been taken up—but alas was not—in some of the recent rabbinic discussions of homosexuality.

60. *Maggid Devaraw le-Ya'aqov* (Jerusalem, 1962) 17a.

61. Hence the interweaving of the letters of the two names (YAHDWNHY) found in Sephardic Jews' prayer books, influenced by Kabbalah.

62. A thorough treatment is to be found in Tishby, *Wisdom of the Zohar*, pp. 971–974.

63. *Otsar Mikhtavim u-Ma'amarim* (Jerusalem, 1986), pp. 75f. Quoted more fully in the introduction to my selection of teachings from the *Sefat Emet*, *The Language of Truth* (Philadelphia: Jewish Publication Society, 1998), pp. 36f. Behind it stand such earlier formulations as those found in Isaiah Horowitz's seventeenth-century classic *Shney Luḥot ha-Berit* (Two Tablets of the Covenant [Amsterdam, 1695]), Tractate *Shavu'ot* 189b, and the early Hasidic *Liqqutim Yeqarim* (Precious Selections [Lvov, 1868]) 12b.

Chapter 3. Torah

1. See my article "The Zaddik as *Axis Mundi* in Later Judaism," *Journal of the American Academy of Religion* 45:3 (1977): 327–347, as well as discussion by Moshe Idel, *Hasidism: Between Ecstasy and Magic* (Albany: State University of New York, 1995), pp. 189–207, and Ada Rapoport-Albert, "God and the Zaddik as the Two Focal Points of Hasidic Worship," *History of Religions* 18 (1979): 296–325.

2. This is my point of disagreement with such a work as Adin Steinsaltz's *The Thirteen-Petaled Rose* (New York: Basic Books, 1985), a marvelous modernizing of language that leaves the essential faith claims of classical Kabbalah unchallenged.

3. Here we see how very deep is the gap between my views and those of certain claimants to the mantle of Kabbalist in our day.

4. This sort of meditation on letters has ancient roots in Kabbalah and was much practiced in early Hasidism. Moshe Idel is the expert in this stream within Kabbalah, beginning with Abraham Abulafia in the thirteenth century, though based on even earlier roots evidenced in *Sefer Yezirah* (perhaps second or third century, in its earliest form) and *Otiyyot de-Rabbi Akiva* (eighth or ninth century). For the continuation of this tradition into Hasidism, see Idel, *Hasidism*, pp. 103ff. While it can easily be trivialized and hence mocked, it is a real part of the Kabbalistic legacy and was long considered one of its more esoteric tools.

5. Midrash Ekhah Rabbah 2:17.

6. Avot 1:1.

7. The broadening vision is based on the rabbis' claim *eyn ḥokhmah ela' Torah* (Midrash Tanḥuma va-yelekh 2). Literally: "There is no wisdom but Torah." The statement originally indicates that the term "wisdom," when appearing in Scripture, must refer to Torah. This statement and others following it ("There is nothing that is not hinted at in Torah" [Zohar 3:231a]) have been read both as calls for widening the scope of Torah and for limiting the definition of what "wisdom" one may legitimately pursue. Today it should best be used to broaden our notion of Torah. The "narrowing" means that Torah, "wider than the sea," concentrates itself so that it may all be present in the single letter or on the two tablets, just as *shekhinah*, which "fills the whole world" can also be concentrated between the two staves of the Ark.

8. T. B. Berakhot 11b. The daily study of Torah, a religious obligation, is to

be preceded by a blessing. See the daily prayer book, preceding *birkot ha-shahar* (the early morning blessings).

9. T. B. Sanhedrin 32a.

10. I do recognize the size of this "if." But it is essential. It needs to stand up against centuries of habit in which the progressive narrowing of legal options, due to increasing bodies of precedent, tended to influence and hence to narrow nonlegal aspects of the tradition as well, especially once the battle of Orthodoxy versus modernity was joined. This open-ended view of Torah and revelation is carried to an extreme in early Hasidism, where it is insisted that each generation has both a right and an *obligation* to reinterpret Torah according to its own needs and unique spirit. See the sources I quote in "Hasidism and Its Changing History," included in a special Hasidism issue of *Jewish History*, forthcoming. In the Hasidic discussion, this obligation to reinterpret was hardly used in the halakhic domain, where Hasidism remained quite conservative. But its strong voice within the sources is a major factor in the link I see between Hasidism and a contemporary radical renewal of Judaism.

11. T. B. Baba Batra 15a; Sifre Devarim 357; and see discussion by A. J. Heschel, *Heavenly Torah: Refracted through the Generations*, ed. Gordon Tucker and Leonard Levin (New York: Continuum, 2005). Here, as in much of this section, my thinking has been shaped by many years of reading and teaching Heschel's modern classic, now available in this English rendition.

12. T. B. Berakhot 31b; Gittin 60a.

13. See Heschel's discussion in *Torah min ha-Shamayim*, vol. 2, pp. 71ff., 360ff.

14. T. Y. Peah 2:6; Va-Yiqra Rabbah 22:1.

15. This is an essential theme of Hayyim Nahman Bialik's classic essay "Halakhah and Aggadah," still very worth reading. An English version may be found in Bialik's *Revealment and Concealment: Five Essays* (Jerusalem: Ibis, 2000).

16. Heschel, *Torah*, vol. 2, pp. 75ff. and sources quoted there.

17. Such poems belong to the category of *Azharot*, poetic renditions of the commandments, once recited on the festival of *Shavu'ot*. See *Encyclopedia Judaica* s.v. Azharot.

18. T. B. Makkot 24a . The verse quoted is Ex. 20:19, immediately following the text of the ten commandments. The view that Israel said this after the first two commandments were spoken, effectively interrupting God's revelation, is that of R. Joshua ben Levi. See the discussion in Mendel Kasher's *Torah Shelemah*, *Yitro* 452.

19. The latter phrase is of course my addition to the traditional formulation, but I see no alternative to it. If the prophet is truly a partner in the articulation of God's word and not merely a passive mouthpiece, the limitations of his own person and the times in which he lived must be reflected in the text as it emerged from his mouth or pen. Heschel is not quite willing to state this openly in either *The Prophets* or *Torah min ha-Shamayim*, but I believe it is clearly implied in his approach. I see full admission of it as vital to the self-understanding of a contemporary heterodox Judaism. Indeed, it might be the point of division between Heschel's attempt (thus far unsuccessful, as history has shown) to create an expanded notion of Jewish orthodoxy (the lowercase *o* is intentional) and my own clearly heterodox adaptation of his approach.

20. See Rosenzweig's letter to Martin Buber, June 3, 1925, published in the appendix to Rosenzweig's *On Jewish Learning* (New York: Schocken Books, 1955), pp. 117f., as well as the discussion by Rivka Horwitz in my collection *Jewish Spirituality*, vol. 2 (New York: Crossroad, 1987), pp. 360ff.

21. Quoted by his disciple R. Naftali of Ropszyce in his *Zera' Qodesh, Shavu'ot* (Jerusalem, 1971), vol. 2, fol. 40 b–c.

22. Scholem, "The Meaning of Torah in Jewish Mysticism," in his *On the Kabbalah and Its Symbolism* (New York: Schocken Books, 1974), p. 30. Scholem was much interested in the question I am discussing here, going back to early conversations with his friend Walter Benjamin.

23. T. B. 'Eruvin 13a.

24. *'Atiqa* (or *keter*) is identified with the divine name *ehyeh*, elements of the tetragrammaton headed by an *aleph*.

25. *Liqqutey MoHaRaN* 1:65, based on T. B. Menahot 29b.

26. This phrase is carried over into Hasidism from the language of medieval Jewish philosophy. Its best-known source is Judah Halevi's *Kuzari* 5:20.

27. This is the meaning I derive from R. Nahman's tale "The King and the Sage," or "The King's Portrait," with which I open my book *Seek My Face* (Woodstock VT: Jewish Lights, 2003) p. xiii.

28. Bereshit Rabbah 19:9.

29. Benjamin D. Sommer comes to a similar conclusion based on his reading of the same *aleph* passage in the *Zera' Qodesh*. See his "Revelation at Sinai in the Hebrew Bible and in Jewish Theology," *Journal of Religion* 79 (1999): 422–451. His view (and implicitly mine as well) is critiqued by Jerome Gellman in "Wellhausen and the Hasidim," *Modern Judaism* 26 (May 2006): 193–207. That there is an unspoken Orthodox/heterodox polemic behind this conversation should not be surprising.

30. To say it more fully, I reject the notion that commandment requires heteronomy. The argument of all the post-Kantian moralists who defend Judaism (from Hermann Cohen to Yeshayahu Leibowitz) assumes a somewhat simplistic and naive notion of the self and indeed of the distinction between "self" and "Other." I am claiming a notion of commandedness based on our recognition precisely that we are of the One, that we are part of something greater than our individual ego-selves. It is precisely that One, the universal Self, that speaks through us and within us; its "Where are you?" is the challenging call of our own truest root. It is thus transcendent and internal at once. To say it differently: mystical consciousness, developed out of the experience of inner life, allows for the possibility of a more nuanced view of selfhood than is found in most rationalist discussions of "self" and "other."

31. I have in mind here the rabbinic discussions of the distinction between Sabbath and festival holiness. The festival is hallowed by the words *meqaddesh yisra'el veha-zemanim* ("who sanctifies Israel and the seasons") because humans, through reporting the new moon, have participated in declaring which day is to be holy. So it is with the commandments as a whole. The divine voice calls on us to remember and to celebrate; the forms come about through us and evolve throughout our history.

32. The *mem* of place or location is joined to the Aramaic word *tsavta*, "together," rather than to the Hebrew stem *tsaveh*, "command."

33. I agree with Mordecai Kaplan that the notion of *'averah* ("transgression"), the counterpoint of *mitzvah*, should be removed from the ritual sphere. But I think this can be done without the reduction of *mitzvah* to the status of "folkway." A *mitzvah* not done is an opportunity not taken; this need not be understood as "sinful."

34. I am thus quite far from much that is said by and in the name of Emanuel Levinas, so widely revered by many thoughtful Jews in our time. Levinas would deny the value of mystical insight as a basis for moral living, since it refuses to see the ultimacy of "otherness." I firmly refuse to accept this premise. My neo-Hasidic ethos is based on the reality and truth of ultimate Oneness, a sense that we are all limbs of the same cosmic body (Adam Kadmon, or, to the Christian, Corpus Christi), our minds and hearts but free-willed outlets of the single universal Mind and Heart. I believe this forms a strong basis for ethical behavior, a system in which we recognize the distinctiveness of the other as we interact in this world, but also our underlying oneness as we ask the more ultimate question of who

we are. The writings of Hillel Zeitlin, which I am currently preparing for an English edition, will I hope provide an interesting counterweight to Levinas. This juxtaposition is, perhaps unsurprisingly, a continuation of the *hasid/mitnagged* debate, particularly that between Shneur Zalman of Liadi and Hayyim of Volozhyn, in the late eighteenth century.

35. The Hebrew *yehi*, of course, is nothing but a conjugating (the Anglophone Kabbalist might say "conjuring") of the divine name Y-H-W-H, drawing it forth into created existence.

36. See Hayyim Nahman Bialik, "Gilluy ve-Kissuy ba-Lashon," as well as the wonderful "Gemara" created around it at the Oranim Institute, edited by Eli Elon and Yariv Ben-Aharon, published as vol. 8 of the journal *Shedemot* (1997). This is the lead essay in Bialik's *Revealment and Concealment: Five Essays* (Jerusalem: Ibis, 2000).

37. Mishnah Avot 5:1 and T. B. Rosh Hashanah 32a.

38. I am aware of the possible degeneration of a neo-mystical Judaism, especially in a post-halakhic mode, into neopaganism, by which I mean an uncritical and irresponsible celebration of nature. I trust the reader will understand that the sense of human responsibility, both individual and collective, out of which I write, places this book at a considerable distance from such a move. Meanwhile, we could do well with a religious life that allows for a little more celebration of nature and its glory.

39. Psalms 104 and 148 would be good starting points for awareness of this consciousness. If you can't appreciate them in the Hebrew, read them in the unsurpassed early English translation of Sir Phillip Sidney and the Countess of Pembroke.

40. Among the sources for this link are Zohar 2:93b and the discussion by R. Moshe Cordovero in Pardes Rimonim 2:3. It is later taken up by various Hasidic authors, including the *Sefat Emet* in multiple places.

41. That Creation is a form of divine self-disclosure or revelation is taken for granted in Zohar. It is the implied meaning of the grand opening phrase of the Zohar on *bereshit: be-resh hurmenuta de-malka* (Zohar 1:15a), "As the King began to 'reveal' or 'authorize' Himself," referring to the self-manifestation of the hidden Godhead in the *sefirot*, preceding Creation.

42. T. B. Pesahim 61a.

43. Shemot Rabbah 41:7, playing on *harut* ("carved") and *herut* ("freedom").

44. Mishnah Avot 6:1 (*Perek Kinyan Torah*). That source mentions only a voice of warning, but later tradition weaves it into a web of sources that indicate an ongoing revelation. See sources and discussion in Scholem's

"Revelation and Traditions as Religious Categories in Judaism," in his *The Messianic Idea in Judaism and Other Essays* (New York: Schocken, 1971), pp. 282ff.

45. See Zohar 1:3a and note carefully its reading of Ex. 32:8 ("These are your gods, O Israel"), one that would dismiss much of Western religion as idolatry.

46. *Tzava'at RiYVaSH* (Brooklyn: Kehot, 1975) p. 24, #76.

47. The Hebrew term for Egypt, *mitzrayim*, is taken supraliterally by Midrashic and Hasidic readers to mean "straits," any inner "place" that narrows one's perspective.

48. Meir Simhah Kahan of Dvinsk, *Meshekh Hokhmah* (ed. Yehudah Kooperman, Jerusalem, n.d.), pp. 293ff. My thanks to my student and now colleague Sharon Cohen Anisfeld for pointing me to this source.

49. Mishnah Sanhedrin 4:5. This text and subject will be treated at greater length in chapter 4.

50. T. B. Nedarim 8a, Yoma 73b.

51. If you see me poised midpoint between Rosenzweig and Kaplan in that sentence, you've got me right.

52. See the comment by R. Nahman of Bratslav: "I *am* a 'know what to answer the heretic.'" *Hayyey MoHaRaN* II, 7:13. Cited in my *Tormented Master* (University, AL: University of Alabama Press, 1979), p. 317.

53. T. B. Shabbat 88b.

54. I am delighted to see that the new Reform prayer book *Mishkan Tefillah* has inserted the ten commandments alongside the morning shema'. This is a very worthwhile liturgical innovation, rectifying an ancient loss.

55. T. B. 'Eruvin 13a.

56. I am grateful to James Carroll for that formulation. He originally offered it with regard to anti-Jewish passages in the New Testament.

57. This is said quite openly in the mystical tradition, where Torah is understood to be the mysterious name of God: "He is His name and His name is He." R. Azriel of Gerona, *Perush ha-Aggadot* (Jerusalem: Meqitsey Nirdamim, 1945), p. 37.

58. The "seventy faces of Torah" are widely referred to in later Jewish literature as early rabbinic teaching, but their first mention is in Numbers Rabbah 13:15.

59. For one of many examples see *Degel Mahaneh Ephraim*, bereshit s.v. *zeh sefer toledot adam* #2 (Jerusalem, 1963), 6a.

60. See the discussion by Simon Rawidowicz in his "On Interpretation," *Proceedings of the American Academy for Jewish Research* 26 (1957): 83–126.

61. I refer to Bialik's famous essay "Halakhah and Aggadah." I discuss it in "Confessions of an Aggadic Jew" in the forthcoming Festschrift for Neil Gillman.

62. R. Shelomo of Radomsk, *Tif'eret Shelomo, Rosh Hashanah* (Jerusalem, 1992) 74b.

63. Zohar 2:99a.

64. T. B. Shabbat 105a.

65. *Sefat Emet, parashat ki tavo'. The Language of Truth*, pp. 327f. For earlier Hasidic treatment, see the BeShT as quoted in *Degel Mahaneh Ephraim, ha'azinu* s.v. *Ki lo' davar* (Jerusalem, 1963) 266a. See also R. Nahman of Bratslav, *Liqqutey MoHaRaN* I, 19:9, and his reading of *'osey devaro*. He also seems to understand that only we humans (speakers, *medabberim*) can bring God out of His silence and into speech.

Chapter 4. Israel

1. *Liqqutey MoHaRaN* II:63.

2. The classical triad of "God, Torah, and Israel" was already universalized by Franz Rosenzweig to refer instead to "mankind." While I am similarly a universalist, and this book, as has been made clear, aims to reach beyond Jewry, the place of "Israel" in a Judaic theology cannot be avoided. We need to struggle with both the glory and the demons of Jewish particularism.

3. Mishnah Sanhedrin 4:5

4. This is a paraphrasing of Heschel's oral teaching as I recall it, not a direct quotation from his writings.

5. See the important discussion by Yair Lorberbaum in *Tselem Elohim* (Jerusalem: Schocken, 2004), pp. 27ff., where he shows how the Maimonidean prism through which we are often trained to read early rabbinic sources in this case distorts their original meaning. Lorberbaum's book is soon to appear in English translation.

6. T. Jonathan to Gen. 5:3.

7. T. Y. Nedarim 9:5.

8. Perhaps I should say that he shares this place with Jesus of Nazareth, also martyred by the Romans, just a century earlier.

9. Mishnah Yadayim 3:5. It was Saul Lieberman who suggested that "the day when the Song of Songs was given to Israel" in that Mishnah most likely refers to Sinai. See also *Aggadat Shir ha-Shirim* (ed. Solomon Schechter [Cambridge, 1896]), line 22, a late Midrash in which Akiva is quoted as saying: "Had Torah not been given, it would have been possible to conduct the world by the Song of Songs." Quite a world!

10. T. B. Nedarim 50a.

11. T. B. Berakhot 54a.

12. I thus disagree with Loberbaum about the essential meaning of this debate. See his discussion in *Tselem*, pp. 131ff. I believe the discussion has implications regarding the commandment to propagate the species, and does take on a special poignancy because it involves the childless Ben Azzai—but that is not its essential meaning. The debate is rather about whether love suffices as a basis for the religious life.

13. See Alon Goshen-Gottstein's interesting explanation of why *tselem elohim* is so little used in halakhic discussion (he claims that its implications were well understood by the rabbis as being too universalistic for the halakhic universe they were seeking to create). "The Body as Image of God in Rabbinic Literature," *Harvard Theological Review* 87:2 (1994): 171–195. But see more recently Lorberbaum, *Tselem*, claiming that major areas of *halakhah* surrounding both reproduction/birth and death were shaped by this belief.

14. Midrash Va-Yiqra Rabbah 34:3.

15. Commentary to Deut. 21:23.

16. See Lorberbaum, *Tselem*, but also Mendel Kasher in *Torah Shelemah*, addenda to *Parashat Yitro*.

17. T. B. Berakhot 10a. Within the rabbinic materials, it seems fair to say that these soul-centered texts were probably the result of living in the Hellenistic milieu, while the notion of bodily form as *tselem* represented an older and more native tradition.

18. See the famous note by R. Abraham ben David of Posquieres, the earliest historical figure associated with Kabbalah, to Maimonides' *Mishneh Torah, Hilkhot Teshuvah* 3:7 and the discussion by Gershom Scholem in *Origins of the Kabbalah* (Philadelphia: Jewish Publication Society, 1987), pp. 211ff.

19. Quoted from the Zohar in *Tanya*, chapter 2, and frequently found in Hasidic writings. I have not found the original Zohar source and I suspect the text may have originated later.

20. Insofar as we know. The high regard our tradition places on uniquely human life necessarily devalues the lives of other species in comparison. While I am not ready to call for eliminating the claim for human uniqueness, it behooves us to be aware of this immodesty. The rabbis warned us long ago to remember, when we are overcome by pride, that even the mosquitoes were here before us (T. B. Sanhedrin 38a). They understood that precedence to be of one "day"; we understand it as some millions of years.

21. "Just as God fills all the world, so does the soul fill all the body." T. B. Berakhot 10a.

22. Hos. 11:9 and T. B. Ta'anit 11a–b.

23. See the comment of the *Sefat Emet* on "inscribe us for life," translated in my *Language of Truth: The Torah Commentary of the Sefat Emet* (Philadelphia: Jewish Publication Society, 1978), pp. 343f.

24. This is how I understand the Kabbalistic image of *kelipah*. The "cosmic" shells are projections of this psychological reality.

25. See the very rich treatment of Zoharic understandings of the *shema'* in Isaiah Tishby, *Wisdom of the Zohar* (Oxford: Littman Library, 1989), pp. 971ff.

26. The catchphrase "God, Torah, and Israel are one" is widely quoted in Hasidic sources in the name of the Zohar. Isaiah Tishby has shown in an article by that name (*Kiryat Sefer* 50 [1975]: 480–492) that in fact the full identification of the three is not found in any Zohar text and actually appears first only in the early eighteenth-century writings of the Italian Kabbalist and author Moses Hayyim Luzzatto.

27. It is interesting to note that in the Numbers passage, like most others, the second-person pronouns (pronominal suffixes, actually) are in the plural, while those in the first of the ten commandments (as we Jews understand it) are in the singular. It is *you*, as an individual, whom Y-H-W-H has brought forth from Egypt. But that individual sense of redemption itself serves to underscore one's sense of belonging to the newly liberated tribe.

28. Michael Wyschogrod's *The Body of Faith* (Minneapolis: Seabury Press, 1983) speaks touchingly of God's simply "falling in love" with Abraham, bearing all the irrational character of the ways we humans fall in love.

29. See my discussion of this in *Devotion and Commandment: The Faith of Abraham in the Hasidic Imagination*, Hebrew Union College, Efroymson Lectures of 1986 (Cincinnati: Hebrew Union College Press, 1989). See also *Avraham, Avi ha-Ma'aminim*, ed. Moshe Halamish et al. (Ramat Gan: Bar Ilan University Press, 2002).

30. Bereshit Rabbah 42:8.

31. Bereshit Rabbah 39:1.

32. The term "choose" is not used with regard to Abraham or the other patriarchs in Genesis. It does, however, appear in Neh. 9:7. The influence of this text on later Judaism is documented by its presence in the daily morning prayer service.

33. Bereshit Rabbah 39:14. See n. 56 below.

34. One way of understanding the *'aqedah* (binding of Isaac) story is as testi-

mony that Abraham would stand up and argue with God for the sake of others. How much greater, then, is his submission and humility in making no protest when God demands his own.

35. Bereshit Rabbah 67:4; 78:9.

36. T. B. Baba Metsi'a 84a.

37. From *avinu malkenu* in the High Holy Day and fast day liturgy.

38. The abstract noun *yahadut*, "Judaism," is postmedieval and is hardly used before modern times. *Yehudi* meaning "Jew" (as distinct from designating a southern-kingdom Judaean) begins in the book of Esther (2:5). But the "religion" of such a Jew was long to be called Torah or *halakhah*, not "Judaism." Conversion then meant linking one's communal association and personal fate to Israel, in accepting the essential faith claims and (according to Maimonides) certain basic practices of the tribe.

39. Note that this suggestion is quite distinct from the call in Israel for a way of "secular conversion." There the desire is for a way to join the Jewish people without any requirements of faith or religious practice. I am talking about an Israelite faith, accompanied by some sort of practice, for those who do not quite feel prepared join to join and link their fate to that of the Jewish people.

40. James Carroll's *Constantine's Sword* (Boston: Houghton-Mifflin, 2001) was a milestone in this ongoing process. The reader may want to see my brief response to Carroll in *Catholics, Jews, and the Prism of Conscience* (Waltham, MA: Brandeis University Press, 2001), pp. 27–41. I regret that the voice of this leading Catholic intellectual is not fully heeded in church circles.

41. Protest against the use of "Israel" as the name of the state began with the most prescient writings of Simon Rawidowicz. Much that concerned Rawidowicz in the early days of Israeli statehood (before his death in 1957) has in fact come to pass. See his *Bavel vi-Yerushalayim* (Waltham, MA: Ararat, 1957). For an English selection of Rawidowicz's writings in this area see his *State of Israel, Diaspora, and Jewish Continuity* (Hanover, NH: Brandeis University Press, 1986).

42. I do not, however, support Israel's "Law of Return" in its current form. I believe that the right to claim immediate Israeli citizenship as a Jew should now be limited to those who are persecuted or victimized for their Jewishness.

43. For this reason I have been utterly opposed to any irreversible settlement by Jews of the territories occupied in 1967 (the so-called "facts on the ground" approach). These lands should have been kept to create a Palestinian state when the Arab populace agreed to a full and lasting peace and

recognition of Israel as a Jewish state by its side. Settlement (alongside ongoing Palestinian intransigence and folly) has made the two-state solution much harder. The attitudes of parts of the settler population toward their Arab "neighbors" hardly need condemnation here; their actions speak for themselves. Any thought of a one-state solution evaporates when one looks at the history of nearby Lebanon. I fear that this is the tragedy which our messianists, their loud supporters, and our own timidity — with plenty of help from the other side — are bringing upon us.

44. Avram Burg's *The Holocaust Is Over: We Must Rise from Its Ashes* (London: St. Martin's Press, 2008), is an eye-opener in this regard.

45. I should make it clear that I agree that *all* Jews still live in *galut*, that is, in an unredeemed world, but this applies equally to Jews in the Holy Land and abroad. The distinction between *golah* (Jews in exile, outside the Land) and *galut* (the unredeemed state of existence, in a universal and almost metaphysical sense) is not a classical one, but the terms seem to have been used differently in recent times.

46. It was also no accident that Zionist educators, both in Israel and abroad, tried hard in the mid-twentieth century to move the textual emphasis from Torah narrative to that of the Early (historical) Prophets, Joshua, Judges, and Samuel. Those books tell of an Israel that crosses the Jordan, conquering and settling the land. But the shift, at least in diaspora Jewish education, was unsuccessful, unable to stand up to the weekly cycle of Torah readings in the synagogue and the long-standing centrality of the Torah text in the Jewish imagination.

47. Of course, as a religious nonimperialist, I do not believe that only Jews can "raise the sparks" that transform reality; all humans may engage in that work, however they describe it. But I believe that it is indeed important that some of us live outside a near-exclusively Jewish society precisely so that we can interact, as both teachers and learners, givers and receivers, with similarly dedicated people who represent different histories and spiritual languages, who will teach us and learn from us how to redeem sparks that might otherwise have gone unnoticed.

48. R. Dov Baer of Miedzyrzec, *Maggid Devaraw le-Ya'aqov*, ed. Rivka Schatz-Uffenheimer (Jerusalem: Magnes, 1976), #49, p. 70.

49. I am playing in the Midrashic tradition of exegeting Gen. 2:4 ("These are the generations of heaven and earth, when they were created"), where the consonants of *Be-HiBaRe'aM* ("when they were created") are identical with those of *be-AvRaHaM* ("through Abraham"). Abraham, contrarian but "straight," allowed for like "generations" to emerge.

50. T. B. Qiddushin 31a.

51. See my discussion in "Abraham Joshua Heschel: Re-casting Hasidism for Moderns" in *Modern Judaism* 29:1 (2009): 62–79.

52. As a traditionalist, of course, Heschel never denied the importance of ritual observance. His works were often used as a buttress to defend it. But if you look at the key thrust of his writings, it is clear that what God seeks of us in the first place are those *mitzvot* that demonstrate human decency, compassion for the oppressed and needy, and a response to the prophetic call for justice restored to God's world.

53. T. B. Menahot 43b.

54. Ekhah Rabbah 1:35; cf. R. Bahya to Deut. 33:26.

55. I am much attracted (in general) to the associative thinking of the *Tiqquney Zohar*, where it is clear that *Shekhinah = Torah = Kabbalah = Halakhah*, all of them differing aspects or iterations of the same single truth. See Ephraim Gottlieb's edition of the *Hebrew Writings of the Author of Tiqquney Zohar* (Jerusalem: Israel Academy of Sciences, 2006), the opening of the first passage, and Moshe Idel's comments in the introduction. I suggest that this reading of neo-Kabbalah should open new directions in contemporary Jewish feminist thought. Here *qudsha brikh hu* and *shekhinah* are equal partners, insofar as we all seek to be both givers and receivers.

56. In *God in Search of Man* (Philadelphia: Jewish Publication Society, 1955), p. 112, Heschel translates the *birah doleqet* of Bereshit Rabbah 39:1 as a "palace full of light" rather than a "burning tower." Is it the urgency of a world on fire or the beauty of a world full of light (or both?) that brings us to religious awareness?

57. The emphasis on human activity geared toward redemption is particularly strong in Lurianic Kabbalah. Scholem saw this as leading quite directly to the Sabbatian messianic outbreak of the seventeenth century (and, by implicatioin, also to Zionism). But this sense of human responsibility for redemption is also carried over into modern Judaism. While modern justice-driven liberal rabbis quote mostly from the prophets, their sense of the need for human deeds may historically be more directly rooted in the mind-set of later Kabbalah. Nothing epitomizes this more than the transition from *tiqqun* as a key term of the mystics to the revival of *tiqqun 'olam* as a way of expressing the Jewish obligation to "repair the world." On the modern usage see Gilbert Rosenthal, "Tikkun ha-Olam: The Metamorphosis of a Concept," *Journal of Religion* 85:2 (April 2005): 214–240.

58. My favorite messianic text is probably that of Rabbi Nahman's *Liqqutey MoHaRaN* II:61, translated in my *Tormented Master* (University, AL: University of Alabama Press, 1979), pp. 321f. Nahman's redeemer is a messiah of the mind, one whose consciousness is so expanded as to comprehend all of geohistory as but a moment.

GLOSSARY

Adam Kadmon. Primordial man; in Kabbalah, the depiction of the ten *sefirot* in anthropic form or, in Lurianic teaching, a pre-sefirotic emanation of divinity.

Adonay. "My Lord"; a circumlocution substituted for the tetragrammaton Y-H-W-H, pronunciation or writing of which is forbidden.

Aggadah. "Narrative, tale"; the narrative portions of the rabbinic corpus.

Ahavah. "Love"; religiously, the love of God, referring both to humans' love for God and God's love for the world.

'Akedah. The binding of Isaac, recounted in Genesis 22.

Akiva. Rabbi of the late first to early second century CE, martyred by the Romans c. 135.

Aleph. The first letter of the Hebrew alphabet. Not pronounced unless accompanied by a vowel sign.

Anokhi. "I am"; the opening word of the decalogue.

'Atiqa. "The elder"; the figure of God as an old man, based on the visions of Daniel. In Kabbalah, *'atiqa* is associated with the highest *sefirah*, preceding *hokhmah*, the first point of particular existence.

Ayin. "Nothing"; the designation of the highest of the ten *sefirot*, indicating that it underlies or precedes all forms of particular existence.

Ba'al Shem Tov. Israel ben Eliezer (1700–1760), the first central figure associated with Hasidism, around whose image the movement crystallized.

Ben Azzai. Simeon ben Azzai, sage of the early second century CE, a companion of Rabbi Akiva.

Berakhah. "Blessing"; the characteristic form of classical Jewish prayer, opening with the Hebrew phrase "Blessed are You Y-H-W-H our God, universal Ruler."

Bereshit. The opening word of the Hebrew Torah text, usually (but imprecisely) rendered as "In the beginning."

Bet. The second letter of the Hebrew alphabet, also used to indicate the number 2.

Da'at. "Knowledge." In Kabbalah, *da'at* serves as a third *sefirah* in those systems where *keter* is considered too recondite to be counted among the ten. In Hasidism, the term is used to refer to religious awareness or consciousness of God's presence.

Derash. "Homily"; the homiletical interpretation of Scripture characteristic of rabbinic tradition.

Devequt. "Attachment"; the joining of the soul to God as the ultimate goal of spiritual quest within Judaism.

Din. "Law." In Kabbalah, the term refers to the fifth *sefirah*, associated with the left and judging side of the divine self. It also is used (mostly in the plural *dinim*) to refer to negative or demonic forces that one seeks to overcome.

Eyn Sof. "Endless"; a designation in Kabbalah for the limitless and undefined reservoir out of which all existence comes, the utterly unknowable and mysterious side of the Godhead.

Ha'ala'ah. "Uplifting." The raising of sparks of holiness or of fallen souls, a key aspect of religious devotion as understood by later Kabbalah and Hasidism.

Halakhah. Literally: "walking." The path of conduct laid out by rabbinic Judaism; codified religious behavior.

Hanina ben Dosa. Second-century rabbinic teacher and miracle worker.

Haskalah. "Enlightenment." In modern times used to refer to the Jewish version of eighteenth-century European Enlightenment, featuring skepticism with regard to religious tradition.

Hesed. "Grace" or "love." The overflowing love of God for all creatures; the fourth of the ten *sefirot*, the right hand of the divine self. Often symbolized by Abraham.

Hokhmah. "Wisdom." In biblical sources, the ancient wisdom of God, existing prior to Creation. Identified with primordial Torah in rabbinic tradition. In Kabbalah, the second (in some systems first) of the ten *sefirot*, the "primal point" containing all further existence, the "father" of the sefirotic universe.

Kabbalah. Literally: "tradition," "that which has been received." Refers specifically to the esoteric doctrine of the *sefirot* promulgated by the Zohar and other teachings first written in Spain in the twelfth to thirteenth centuries and later works of that school. More broadly, designates the Jewish mystical tradition as a whole.

Kelipah. "Shell." In Kabbalah, the term refers to the "shells" or "husks" that surround the sparks of divine light and need to be broken through in order to redeem that light. In the popular imagination, *kelipot* are demonic forces.

Kenesset Yisra'el. "The Assembly of Israel." In rabbinic sources, the Jewish people depicted as the beloved earthly consort of God. In Kabbalah, a key term for the tenth *sefirah*, also called *shekhinah* or *malkhut*, the divine female who is wedded to (and exiled from) the blessed Holy One (*tif'eret*).

Keter, keter 'elyon. "Crown," "highest crown." The first of the ten *sefirot*, identified with the primal will of God to bring forth the universe.

Lulav. The palm branch used in the ritual of Sukkot, waved and shaken along with three other species.

Malkhut. "Kingdom." The tenth *sefirah*, the female hypostasis that receives the energy of the nine upper *sefirot* and channels it into the existence of the lower worlds, hence "bride" of God and "mother" of Creation.

Merkavah. "Chariot." The moving throne of God depicted in Ezekiel 1, forming the basis for a visionary and literary tradition of mystics who "descended" into a state of consciousness from which they reported on continuing journeys through the heavens and visions of the throne.

Midrash. Rabbinic interpretation of Scripture, often including fanciful rereadings of the text. The ongoing tradition of reinterpretation and the texts that record this tradition.

Mikveh. Ritual bath or bathhouse.

Mishkan. "Dwelling"; the tabernacle for God's presence, described in Exodus 25–40. Hence any dwelling place for the divine Presence in this world.

Mishnah. The second-century original codification of rabbinic teaching, focused chiefly on emerging *halakhah*.

Mitzvah. "Commandment"; one of the 613 commandments of the Torah, a derivative from them, or a rabbinic addition.

Nahman of Bratslav. (1772–1810), Hasidic master, mystic teacher, and storyteller.

Neshamah. "Soul" or "breath of life."

'Olam ha-Ba. "The world to come." In rabbinic sources, usually designates either the afterlife or the time following messianic redemption (the distinction between them is often vague). In Kabbalah, refers to the third *sefirah binah* and designates a world that is always a step higher or "ahead" of the world in which we live.

Pardes. The "garden" or "orchard" of mystical speculation.

Perud. "Separation." The sin of considering the *sefirot* as though they were fully separate from one another, hence raising the forbidden thought of multiplicity within the Godhead.

Peshat. The plain or obvious meaning of a Scriptural passage.

Qatnut. The "small" or "ordinary state of mind." Hasidic usage based on prior Kabbalistic terminology.

Sefirah, sefirot. The ten emanations of divinity that channel the energies of *eyn sof*, first into the configurations of the personified divine Self and then into the formation of the "lower" worlds and all that exists within them. Hence also the channels through which humans seek to "arise" in worship to return to their single divine Source.

Selihot. Penitential prayers, recited around the High Holy Days and on fast days.

Shefa'. "Bounty," or "influx." The flow of divine energy as blessing, coursing through the *sefirot* and into the world, constantly enlivening all existence.

Shekhinah. In rabbinic sources, a designation of God insofar as He dwells within the world. In Kabbalah, a designation for the tenth *sefirah*. Hasidic usage tends to conflate these two.

Shofar. The ram's horn blown on Rosh Hashanah.

Talmud. The great compendium of Jewish teaching, including both *halakhah* and *aggadah*, composed in the third to sixth centuries. Exists in both Babylonian and Jerusalem recensions.

Talmud Torah. "Study of Torah"; the ongoing participation of Jews in the study and expansion of the oral tradition.

Tefillin. Phylacteries, boxes containing key Torah passages, worn during weekday prayers.

Tif'eret. The sixth of the ten *sefirot*, depicted as the key "male" energy within the system, identified with "the blessed Holy One" of rabbinic tradition.

Tsaddik. "Righteous one." The "holy man" of Jewish popular religion throughout the ages. In Kabbalah, identified with the ninth *sefirah*, hence "potency" for energizing divine presence in the world. In Hasidism, the leader of a Hasidic community and object of communal veneration.

Tsimtsum. "Contraction." The self-contraction of God preceding Creation, required in order for a non-God or universe to exist. A key feature of Lurianic Kabbalah and Hasidic speculation, interpreted in various ways.

Yesh. "Existence." All that is, identified in Hasidic thought with the defined and finite universe that exists within *shekhinah*, distinguished from *ayin*, the world existing only potentially within *hokhmah*.

Yir'ah. The fear of God, awe before God's presence.

INDEX

Aaron of Karlin, 172n25, 173n28

Aaron of Staroselje, 68

Abel (biblical figure), 42, 43

Abraham (biblical patriarch), 44, 134, 135, 136, 152, 186n34

Abraham ben David of Posquieres, 184n18

Abulafia, Abraham, 177n4

Adam (biblical figure), 105, 106

Adler, Felix, 133

Akiva ben Joseph, 35, 37, 54, 77, 88, 114, 123, 155, 169n18, 183n9

Alkabetz, Shlomo, 172n26, 174n42

Altmann, Alexander, 175n53

Anisfeld, Sharon Cohen, 182n48

Ashlag, Yehudah, 169n15

Azriel of Gerona, 182n57

Ba'al Shem Tov (BeShT), 67, 68, 74, 75, 102, 145, 168n4, 175n53, 176n59, 183n65

Ben-Aharon, Yariv, 181n36

Ben Azzai, Simeon, 123, 143, 147, 154, 155, 156, 169n18, 184n12, 191

Benjamin, Walter, 179n22

Berry, Thomas, 167n1

BeShT (Ba'al Shem Tov), 67, 68, 74, 75, 102, 145, 168n4, 175n53, 176n59, 183n65

Bialik, Hayyim Nahman, 117, 178n15, 181n36, 183n61

Blidstein, Gerald J., 172n26

Boyarin, Daniel, 172–73n28

Brody, Seth, 173n29

Buber, Martin, 6, 10, 144, 168n8, 169n14, 179n20

Buddha, 95

Burg, Avram, 187n44

Cain (biblical figure), 42, 43, 136

Camus, Albert, 3

Carroll, James, 182n56, 186n40

Cohen, Hermann, 10, 180n30

Cohen, Jack, 176n57

Cordovero, Moses, 66, 181n40

Dan, Joseph, 170n3

Darwin, Charles, 9, 10

Da Vidas, Elijah, 168n6

Day, Jonathan, 169n12

Dov Baer, Maggid of Miedzyrzec, 68, 174n49, 187n48

Elior, Rachel, 175n51

Elon, Eli, 181n36

Esau (biblical figure), 137

Ezra ben Solomon of Gerona, 171n11, 173n29

Faur, José, 173n36

Fine, Lawrence, 174n45